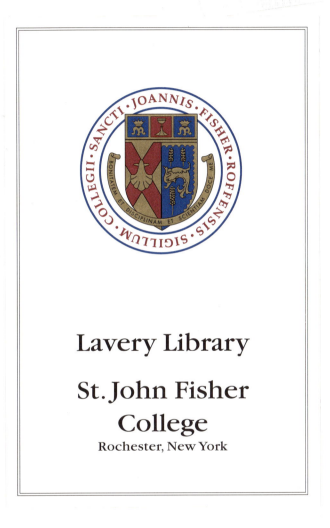

Lavery Library

St. John Fisher
College
Rochester, New York

CHOICE AND RELIGION

Choice and Religion

A Critique of Rational Choice Theory

STEVE BRUCE

OXFORD
UNIVERSITY PRESS

OXFORD
UNIVERSITY PRESS

Great Clarendon Street, Oxford OX2 6DP

Oxford University Press is a department of the University of Oxford.
If furthers the University's objective of excellence in research, scholarship,
and education by publishing worldwide in

Oxford New York

Athens Auckland Bangkok Bogotá Buenos Aires Calcutta
Cape Town Chennai Dar es Salaam Delhi Florence Hong Kong Istanbul
Karachi Kuala Lumpur Madrid Melbourne Mexico City Mumbai
Nairobi Paris São Paulo Singapore Taipei Tokyo Toronto Warsaw

and associated companies in Berlin Ibadan

Oxford is a registered trade mark of Oxford University Press
in the UK and certain other countries

Published in the United States
by Oxford University Press Inc., New York

British Library Cataloguing in Publication Data

Data available

Library of Congress Cataloging in Publication Data\

Data available

ISBN 0-19-829584-7

1 3 5 7 9 10 8 6 4 2

Typeset by Best-set Typesetter Ltd., Hong Kong
Printed in Great Britain
on acid-free paper by
Biddles Ltd
Guildford and King's Lynn

ACKNOWLEDGEMENTS

As always my greatest debt is to the late Roy Wallis, who taught me when I was an undergraduate, supervised my doctoral research, and gave me my first job. He also co-wrote the longer essay from which the first part of Chapter 2 is adapted. My interest in eastern Europe was first provoked by an invitation from Dr John Wolffe and Dr Anna Zelkina of the Open University to speak at a conference on religion in Europe. Prof. Eila Helander of the University of Helsinki very kindly invited me to speak at the 14th Nordic Conference on Sociology of Religion and I am grateful to the other participants for their comments on my lectures and for subsequent exchanges that inspired my interest in Lutheran state churches. Prof. Eileen Barker of the London School of Economics and Political Science invited me to address her graduate students. Prof. Penny Long Marler, of Samford University, Alabama, invited me to lecture to her students at Samford's London Study Centre. Dr Harald Hegstad of the Centre for Social Research, Oslo, invited me to address *Pluralisme og retradisjonalisering: en nettverkskonferanse* in Granavolden, Norway, in December 1998. Another stimulus was provided by the University of Leicester which asked me to examine Alasdair Crockett's doctoral thesis.

A number of Nordic colleagues assisted with the data in the first part of Chapter 4 and I would like to thank them while absolving them of any responsibility for my mistakes: Prof. Pal Repstad of Agder College, Kristiansand, and the University of Oslo, Prof. Ole Riis and Lene Kühle of Aarhus University, Dr Kimmo Kaariainen of the Research Institute of the Evangelical Lutheran Church of Finland, Prof. Göran Gustafsson and Prof. Thorleif Pettersson of Lund University, Prof. Per Tangaard of the Norwegian Lutheran Church, and Dr Susan Sundback of Åbo Akademi. Data from the World Values Survey (WVS) was made available by the ICPSR and the ESRC Data Archive at the University of Essex. Paula Surridge of the University of Aberdeen helped extract data from those sets.

Finally I would like to thank Hilary Walford, who, as ever, diligently copy-edited the text and saved me from my prose.

CONTENTS

LIST OF FIGURES AND TABLES

Figures

Tables

ABBREVIATIONS

BBC   British Broadcasting Corporation
BSA   British Social Attitudes
EKD   Evangelishche Kirche in Deutschland
ESRC   Economic and Social Research Council
FRG   Federal Republic of Germany
GDR   German Democratic Republic
ICPSR International Consortium for Political Science Research
NCR   New Christian Right
RAMP Religion and Moral Pluralism
SCM   Student Christian Movement
TM   Transcendental Meditation
URC   United Reformed Church
WVS   World Values Survey

Introduction

A brief account of why this book was written might also explain its tone. If there are occasional hints of exasperation, it is because the whole project was born out of frustration with the malign influence of a small clique of US sociologists of religion. I know that my country is markedly less religious now than it was in my childhood or the childhood of my father and grandfather. Scottish towns are decorated with redundant and converted churches; within five miles of me there are six churches that have been converted into private houses. There are no new churches. I know enough of the history of my country to have no doubt that most Scots of the seventeenth century attended the religious rituals of the church, prayed, read their Bibles, tried to follow the social teachings of the clergy, gave money to the church, and celebrated the significant events of their lives, their community, and the agricultural year in church to a far greater extent than do my contemporaries. In early 1998 two things brought the extent of secularization home to me. First, I read that, for the first time in its 150-year history, the Free Church of Scotland had no students training for the ministry. Secondly, I was invited by a group of leading Scottish Methodists to a meeting in Stirling to discuss the Church's future. Fewer than thirty people, most of them elderly, met in a church badly in need of renovation and looked at membership figures that showed, quite unambiguously, that Scottish Methodism would disappear within my lifetime.

Furthermore, it is obvious that the gaps left by the decline of the Christian denominations and sects are not being filled by new religions. It is now thirty years since the Scientologists opened their 'Come in for a free personality' test shop on the Bridges in Edinburgh and they have still failed to recruit a larger following than a junior league football side. The Moonies would have trouble fielding a football team. One Episcopalian church in Inverurie was taken with the Toronto Blessing and through it lost more members than it gained.

Of course there were irreligious people in previous eras just as there are religious people today. What matters is the balance and I have no doubt that Britain is vastly more secular now than it ever has been before.

I am not alone in this view. It is held by almost everyone who has given the matter a moment's thought: people old enough to compare now with some 'then', scholars of every discipline, politicians, and church leaders. In fact, it is held by everyone except a handful of US sociologists who are committed to a particular theory of human behaviour that is incompatible with the historical record. Hence history must be revised.

The easiest response to Rodney Stark and his colleagues would be to ignore them. Unfortunately, they write and publish a great deal in a system where the capacity of academic journals far exceeds the supply of worthwhile papers. So long as others in the profession ignore them, they can make such assertions as 'all but one of the published tests of our theory support it' and gloss over the more obvious point that most historians and social scientists interested in religious change do not think their ideas are worth taking seriously. The result is that quite serious errors of fact (never mind of interpretation) are published in journals, repeatedly reasserted by the same small group of authors, and thus come to acquire sufficient 'facticity' that younger US scholars, who know little of religion in Britain or Europe, may take them as reliable.

The peer review system, in which papers for publication are vetted by three or four experts, is intended to prevent the simply mistaken being published in serious journals, but it often fails. Reviewers may not know enough about the subject in question. I recently reviewed a very plausible paper about religion and politics in the former GDR that could easily have been riddled with errors, for all I knew. The process may also fail because the editor refuses to take seriously the reservations of the referees. When asked to comment on one paper by Stark and his colleagues, in addition to expressing my doubts about parts of the argument, I identified a number of errors of fact. The editor explained that he wanted to publish the paper because 'we have a problem getting papers from established people in the discipline' and it duly appeared with none of the errors corrected.

That experience persuaded me that the best response was to produce a detailed critique of the rational choice approach to religion. This book is, I hope, the stake through the vampire's chest.

A word of advice to the reader is in order. Those familiar with my work will find little new in Chapter 1. I have now summarized my explanation of secularization so often that it is difficult to add variety without making the case less rather than more clear. The reader who is not a professional sociologist of religion and who does not want to become embroiled in unnecessary detail can skip the first section of Chapter 2 without losing the thread. Finally, I apologize for the statistical detail. If their previous responses to criticism are any guide, Stark and his colleagues will not be in the least moved by the wealth of data that refutes their case, but I have felt obliged to present an inordinate amount of empirical material in order to persuade those who have not yet taken a side in the great debate.

1

Choice: Origins and Consequences

THIS book is concerned with a largely novel situation in human life: the possibility of choosing a religion. There have been some societies, though not many, that have allowed religious minorities to follow their Gods in peace, but never before have so many people been free to choose or had such a range to choose from. To put it another way, it used to be possible to guess people's religion from their nationality, region, and class. An eighteenth-century Swede was a Lutheran. A nineteenth-century citizen of Cork of native Irish stock was a Roman Catholic; if descended from English settlers, an Episcopalian Protestant. Such regularities are now rare.

This first chapter will explain how we have come to this place by explaining the origins of two closely related phenomena: religious liberty and religious diversity. I will begin with some quotations that exemplify the start and finish of the process of social mutation that has brought us to the consumerist culture of the late twentieth century. All concern truth and our attitudes to those with whom we differ over it. The fourth-century bishop Augustine of Hippo made his view of tolerance clear when he wrote: 'There is an unjust persecution which the ungodly operate against the Church of Christ; and a just persecution which the Churches of Christ make use of towards the ungodly. . . . The Church persecutes out of love, the ungodly out of cruelty.'[1] Such confidence and such a clear divide between those on the side of the angels and the rest are sadly common. One might almost call it the human default position, certainly for cultures that worship a single creator God. Even in Hinduism, where we might suppose that the multiplicity of shapes that can be inhabited by the cosmic consciousness would blunt the tendency of one group to be horrible to another, we find aggressive nationalist movements.

As he dissented from the orthodoxy of his time, we might have expected the Protestant Reformer Martin Luther to take a more charitable view of diversity, but he heavily constrained his idea of freedom of conscience. It cannot, he argued, 'be absolute freedom because no one can be free from the obligations of truth'.[2]

My third quotation comes from the *Basis of Faith*, written for the British Student Christian Movement (SCM) in 1910 by Tissington Tatlow, a young

Church of Ireland evangelical. Tatlow and others had been working to extend the movement's support beyond its original evangelical Protestant base. Although the SCM recruited well in the universities, Tatlow found access to the Church of England's theological colleges blocked by clergy suspicious of the movement's evangelical and 'low-church' origins. Tatlow had to find some form of words that would encompass a broader range of Christians without offending the existing supporters. His formulation was so successful that it was adopted by the 1910 World Missionary Conference in Edinburgh and became the credo on which the entire ecumenical movement was to develop.

The Student Christian Movement is interdenominational in that while it unites persons of different religious denominations in a single organization for certain definite aims and activities, it recognises their allegiance to any of the various Christian Bodies into which the Body of Christ is divided. It believes that loyalty to their own denomination is the first duty of Christian students and welcomes them into the fellowship of the Movement as those whose privilege it is to bring into it, as their contribution, all that they as members of their own religious body have discovered or will discover of Christian truth.[3]

The statement sensibly avoided determining which bodies were Christian and thus allowed the gradual expansion of what would be acceptable. It also contained the first hint of relativism. At the heart of Tatlow's draft was the discovery of the silver lining of fundamental unity inside the dark cloud of apparent contradiction. Where previously, in what was known as 'undenominational' work, cooperation required that differences be tactfully overlooked, now they were to be celebrated while the law of non-contradiction was suspended. Where the Bishop of Hippo would, out of love, of course, persecute those who differed from him, the bishops of the major Christian churches that formed the ecumenical movement at the start of the twentieth century would eventually endorse everything from high Catholicism through the evangelicalism of the Salvation Army to the pantheism of American native religion.

The fourth quotation comes from Sir George Trevelyan, doyen of British New Age spirituality, who concluded one account of his beliefs with the words: 'This is what things look like to me. If it doesn't seem like that to you, you don't have to accept what I say. Only accept what rings true to your own Inner Self.'[4]

A Vocabulary

So that we have a coherent set of terms with which to discuss changes in religion, I want to introduce a typology developed by Roy Wallis from the work of Ernst Troeltsch, Roland Robertson, Bryan Wilson, and Benton Johnson (see Fig. 1.1).[5]

Religious organizations and cultures differ greatly in the demands they make of their members. Indeed they differ fundamentally in the way they think about such notions as membership. Some claim to themselves absolute power to describe the nature of the afterlife, to tell us how to obtain salvation, and to determine how we should live in this world. In the West we may find strange the Islamic notion of the Sharʿia, but the Christian Church in the Middle Ages tried to regulate the economy and small conservative sects still tell their members how to dress, and how, and what, and with whom they should eat. In addition to differing in reach, religious organizations differ greatly in the extent to which they demand conformity. For obvious reasons, the largest organizations, those that dominate entire societies, combine high self-regard and considerable toleration of laxity. This follows inevitably from the need to encompass different abilities to live the religious life. If everyone followed the highest calling of the medieval Christian Church or modern Burmese Buddhism and became a monk, the economy would cease to function. One solution is to allow a social division of labour. Some people become monks; most till the fields and feed the monks. Such specialization can be built into the life course. The elderly, who have completed the normal domestic tasks of raising a family, may retreat from the world and devote themselves to spiritual matters. The major religious traditions can also handle the problem of varying degrees of attention to spiritual teachings by having a system that allows sins to be periodically wiped away by some spiritual exercise. The Catholic tradition's practice of confession, repentance, and penance evolved to deal with human frailty. However, there is a difference between tolerating laxity and tolerating challenges to authority. As it had little choice, the medieval Christian Church accepted that most people would not maintain its high standards. What it did not accept was any attack on its claim to be God's sole representative on earth. As well as tolerating a wide variety in the quality of the religious life of the common people, a religion that seeks to accommodate and dominate an entire society must also be on comfortable terms with that society's temporal powers. It cannot for long offer a radical challenge to the political or economic order.

Contrast that with the 'sect'. Periodically religions emerge that demand full compliance, that insist on dominating every aspect of mundane life, and that seek to reshape radically political and economic relationships.

We can readily think of many examples of a very different sort of religion, that not only tolerates diversity but positively revels in it. It makes few claims on its members, does not try to command every aspect of social life, and sees itself as only marginally better than its competitors.

Sociologists have often tried to impose some simple ordering framework on the vast array of human religious experience and there is considerable consensus about what sorts of features tend to cluster. That is, we suppose that there is a 'sociologic' informing the combination of characteristics. For example, it is not an accident that highly demanding religions either recruit relatively few people or are short lived. Radical fervour in religion, as in politics, is too rich a dish to be eaten by most people as a staple diet. The attraction of the Wallis model for grouping and labelling religions is that it highlights the most important features of any religion in a very economical manner by reducing the salient issues to just two: the first is concerned with access to power within the group; the second with the relationship between the group and the wider society. Wallis first asks how the group sees the core of its ideology. Does it believe that it and only it has the ear of God or does it see itself as one among a variety of enlightened groups? In Wallis's terms, is it uniquely or pluralistically legitimate? The second question concerns how successful the group has been in recruiting from, or selling itself to, the wider society. Is it seen as respectable or deviant? The church and the sect types have in common the belief that they and only they have access to the divine truth. The medieval Christian Church or the Roman Catholic Church in most places until very recently believed that it and it alone was correct; every other religious organization was, at best, 'our separated brethren', at worst heretics. Protestant sects such as the Exclusive Brethren also take the view that they and they alone have the Way. But there is considerable difference in the popularity, acceptability, and prestige of these bodies. In France or Britain the Catholic Church is respectable; the Exclusive Brethren are deviant.

External conception

		Respectable	Deviant
Internal conception	Uniquely legitimate	CHURCH	SECT
	Pluralistically legitimate	DENOMINATION	CULT

Fig. 1.1. A typology of ideological organizations

Source: Roy Wallis, *The Road to Total Freedom: A Sociological Analysis of Scientology* (London: Heinemann, 1976), 13.

If we look at the bottom half of Fig. 1.1, we can see that what unites the denomination and the cult is that they do not claim a unique possession of the truth. Denominations think they have something valuable to offer but they recognize many other organizations as being every bit as valid. They think of themselves in the terms of Tatlow's description of the SCM. Similarly, most purveyors of cultic wisdom and esoterica do not claim the monogamous commitment of their followers (and if they did, they would not get it). Indeed, the relationship between purveyor and consumer is so loose that terms such as member, adherent, and follower are usually inappropriate in the cultic milieu. Cults see themselves as simply one of many guides on the single but very broad road to enlightenment. Again what separates them is the top line: the extent to which they have succeeded in establishing themselves in their society. The Methodists are a respectable part of our social and cultural landscape; cults are not. Or at least they are not yet.

It is important to stress that, unlike the popular usage of 'cult' to mean any religion we do not like, there is no moral judgement implied in any of these terms. My points are, first, that religious organizations manifestly differ in their structure, rigour, longevity, attitudes to the rest of society, and attitudes to other religions, and, secondly, that the enormous range of descriptive detail can usefully be simplified into four types, defined by the organizations' self-understandings and by societal responses to them.

There are two reasons for introducing these terms. First, they will be used throughout this book as a shorthand. Secondly, I believe that we can use them to describe the major changes in the religious climate of the Western world. The basic proposition that runs through this study is that, without much damage to the historical record, the mutations of religion in modern industrial societies can be described as follows. The church type dominated the pre-modern world. The early modern world was characterized by the church and a range of competing sects. Religion in the modern industrial world is primarily of the denominational type, with a residue of sectarianism in particular social and geographical locations. And, at the end of the twentieth century, the cultic type is becoming more popular as the denomination and the sect decline.

Historians of religion expert in any of the settings I discuss may object to such a crass gloss, but I believe that we can recognize that the details of any particular society will show considerable deviation from this model and that the model captures an important truth that justifies its simplifications.

This is not just a story of change. It is also a tale of decline. The road from religion embodied in the great European cathedrals to religion as personal preference and individual choice is a road from more to less religion. From the Middles Ages to the end of the twentieth century religion in Europe (and its offshoot settler societies) has declined in power, prestige, and popularity. That is, this is an account of the secularization of the West. I will present no evidence for that claim at this preliminary stage. Because I want to address competing explanations of the changes that have occurred, detailed evidence will be presented in the context of describing specific countries and responding to particular arguments.

Secularization

The path to liberty of religion is part of the much wider process of secularization, which I will explain in the rest of this chapter. As a matter of preliminary ground-clearing, I want to stress here that the secularization approach, as I understand it, does not claim universal application. In showing how features of the modernization of the West undermined the plausibility and reach of religion, I am explaining the past of a particular sort of society. My sociology rests on history and geography. There is no implication that societies of the 'second' or 'third' worlds must follow the patterns of development found in the old world. I will put it this bluntly because it is so often misunderstood: secularization is not inevitable. The patterns described here will be repeated anywhere else only if new circumstances match the old. Of course, the power and prestige of the West give its characteristics a degree of pre-eminence as a model for others to emulate (or react against), but, rather than seeing our past as a template that others must follow, I am struck by the unlikelihood of the changes I will explain.[6]

As will become clear from the number of times I refer forward and backward, there is a degree of artifice in the ordering of the parts of the explanation. It is very rarely the case that one thing causes another. More often there is mutual causation: one set of changes feeds back to reinforce its causes. None the less the story cannot be told all at once. It must be told in sequence.

Differentiation

Modernization entails social differentiation, by which I mean the fragmentation of social life as specialized roles and institutions are created to handle specific features or functions previously embodied in or carried out by one role or institution. If that sounds cumbersome, an example will make the point. The family was once a unit of production as well as the social institution through which society was reproduced. The fashion of some middle-class professionals to work at home notwithstanding, most economic activity is now conducted in distinct settings that have their own values. We leave home to go to work. At work we are supposed to treat customers alike, paying attention only to the matter in hand. We are not supposed to vary our prices according to the race or religion of the purchaser. At home we are supposed to behave in a discriminatory manner: to treat my wife and children like all other women and children is to miss the point. The public sphere is instrumental, pragmatic, and rational; the private sphere is expressive, indulgent, and emotional.

In addition to the indirect effects described shortly, increased specialization has the direct effect of 'secularizing' many social functions that in the Middle Ages either were the exclusive preserve of the Christian Church or were dominated by the clergy. Education, health care, welfare, and social control were once all in the domain of religious institutions; now we have specialist institutions for each. The shift of control was gradual and proceeded at various speeds in different settings, but religious professionals were replaced as specialist professionals were trained and new bodies of knowledge or skill were generated. Where religious institutions retain what we would now regard as secular functions, those functions are performed by lay professionals trained and accredited by secular bodies, and are exercised within an essential secular value frame. For example, the Church of England provides various forms of residential social care, but its social workers are tested in secular expertise, not piety, and they are answerable to state- rather than church-determined standards. Spiritual values may inspire the Church's involvement in social work, but there is very little in the expression of that inspiration that distinguishes it from secular provision.

As the functions of society become increasingly differentiated, so the people also become divided and separated from each other. Structural differentiation was accompanied by social differentiation. The economic growth implicit in modernization led to the emergence of an ever-greater range of occupation and life situation. The emergence of social classes was usually accompanied by increasing class conflict; it is certainly accompanied by class avoidance. We can see it in physical distance. In feudal societies, masters and servants lived cheek by jowl. The master might ride while the servant walked, but they travelled together. The straw given to the master might be clean, but master and servant often slept in the same room. In medieval Edinburgh all manner of people occupied the same tenements and threw their excrement into the same street. When the Georgian 'new town' was constructed, the classes separated out into their own areas.

The physical proximity of different classes in feudal society was possible because everyone knew their place. 'Stations' were so firmly fixed that the gentry did not need to fear that allowing the lower orders to occupy the same space would give them ideas 'above their station'.

The plausibility of a single moral universe in which all people have a place depends on the social structure being fixed. With the proliferation of new social roles and increasing social mobility, traditional integrated organic or communal conceptions of the moral and supernatural order began to fragment. When the community broke into competing social groups, the religiously sanctified vision of that group, united under its God, also broke up.

As classes and social fragments became more distinctive, so they generated metaphysical and salvational systems along lines more suited to their interests. People came to see the supernatural world as they saw the material world. Thus feudal agricultural societies tended to have a hierarchically structured religion where the great pyramid of Pope, bishops, priests, and laity reflected the social pyramid of king, nobles, gentry, and peasants. Independent small farmers or the rising business class preferred a more democratic religion; hence their attraction to such early Protestant sects as the Presbyterians, Baptists, and Quakers.

However, modernization was not simply a matter of the religious culture responding to changes in the social, economic, and political structures. Religious innovation itself was a cause of differentiation and influenced its shape. David Martin neatly summarized a major unintended consequence of the Reformation when he wrote that 'The logic of Protestantism is clearly in favour of the voluntary principle, to a degree that eventually makes it sociologically unrealistic'.[7] Belief systems differ greatly in their propensity to fragment. Much of the variation can be explained by the assumptions about the availability of authoritative knowledge that lie at the heart of the beliefs. To simplify the possibilities in two polar types, some religions claim a unique grasp of the truth while others allow that there are many ways to salvation.[8] The Catholic Church claims that Christ's authority was passed to Peter, the first Bishop of Rome, and was then institutionalized in the office of Pope. The Church claims ultimate control of the means to salvation and the right finally to arbitrate all disputes about God's will. So long as that central assertion is not disputed, the Catholic Church is relatively immune to fission and schism. As the beliefs that one needs to abandon in order to depart from Rome go right to the heart of what one believed when one was a Catholic, such departures are difficult and are associated with extreme social upheavals, such as the French Revolution. Thus in Catholic countries the fragmentation of the religious culture that follows from structural and social differentiation tends to take the form of a sharp divide between those who remain within the religious tradition and those who openly oppose it. So Italy and Spain have conservative Catholics traditions and powerful Communist parties.

In contrast, the religion created by the Protestant Reformation was extremely vulnerable to fragmentation because it removed the institution of the church as a source of authority between God and man. It is important to note that, though Catholic apologists use this as a stick with which to beat Protestants, it is a sociological, not a theological observation. If, by reading the Scriptures, we are all able to discern God's will, then how do we settle disputes between the various discernings that are produced? Being theists who believed in one God, one Holy Spirit which dwelt in all of God's creation, and one Bible, the Reformers could hope that the righteous would readily agree, but history proved that hope false. Tradition, habit, respect for learning, or admiration for personal piety all restrained the schismatic tendencies, but they could not prevent them. The consequence of the Reformation was not one Christian church purified and strengthened but, because it coincided with social differentiation, a large number of competing perspectives and institutions. In Protestant countries, social differentiation took the form not of a radical divide between clerical and secular elements but of a series of schisms from the dominant traditions. Rising social classes were able to express their new aspirations and ambitions by reworking the familiar religion into shapes that accorded with their self-image.

Societalization

Societalization is the term given by Bryan Wilson to the way in which 'life is increasingly enmeshed and organized, not locally but societally (that society being most evidently, but not uniquely, the nation state)'.[9] If differentiation can be seen as a blow to small-scale communities from below, societalization was the corresponding attack from above. Close-knit, integrated, communities gradually lost power and presence to large-scale industrial and commercial enterprises, to modern states coordinated through massive, impersonal bureaucracies, and to cities.

Religion, Wilson argues, has its source in and draws strength from the community. As the society rather than the community has increasingly become the locus of the individual's life, so religion has been shorn of its functions. The church of the Middle Ages baptized, christened, and confirmed children, married young adults, and buried the dead. Its calendar of services mapped onto the temporal order of the seasons. It celebrated and legitimated local life. In turn it drew considerable plausibility from being frequently reaffirmed through the participation of the local community in its activities. In 1898 almost the entire population of my local village celebrated the successful end of the harvest by bringing tokens of their produce into the church. In 1998 a very small number of people in my village (only one of them a farmer) celebrated the Harvest Festival by bringing to the church vegetables and tinned goods (many of foreign provenance) bought in the local branch of a national supermarket chain. In the first case the church provided a religious interpretation of an event of vital significance to the entire community. In the second, a small self-selecting group of Christians engaged in an act of dubious symbolic value. Instead of celebrating the harvest, the service thanked God for all his creation. In listing things for which we should be grateful, one hymn mentioned 'jet planes refuelling in the sky'! By broadening the symbolism, the service solved the problem of irrelevance but at the cost of losing direct connection with the lives of those involved. When the total, all-embracing community of like-situated people working and playing together gives way to the dormitory town or suburb, there is little held in common left to celebrate. The contemporary societal system relies less on the inculcation of a shared moral order and more on the use of efficient technical means of eliciting and monitoring appropriate behaviour. Where we once tried to control behaviour with the all-seeing internal eye of the Godly conscience, we now try to control it with the all-seeing eye of the closed-circuit television camera.

The consequence of differentiation and societalization is that the plausibility of any single overarching moral and religious system has declined, to be displaced by competing conceptions that, while they may have had much to say to privatized, individual experience, could have little connection to the performance of social roles or the operation of social systems. Religion retained subjective plausibility for some people, but lost its objective taken-for-grantedness. It was no longer a matter of necessity. Rather, as indicated by US government forms that ask you to state 'the religion of your preference', it became a matter of choice, a leisure activity.

Again it is worth stressing the interaction of social and cultural forces. The fragmentation of the religious tradition that resulted from the Reformation hastened the development of the religiously neutral state. The development of a successful economy required a high degree of integration: effective communication, a shared legal code to enforce contracts, a climate of trust, and so on. And this required an integrated national culture.[10] Where there was religious consensus, a national 'high culture' could be provided through the dominant religious tradition. The clergy could continue to be the schoolteachers, historians, propagandists, public administrators, and military strategists. Where there was little consensus, the growth of the state tended to be secular. In Ireland and the Scandinavian countries, a national education system was created through the Catholic and Lutheran churches respectively. In Britain and the USA it was largely created by the state directly. However, even where a dominant church retained formal ownership of areas of activity, those still came to be informed primarily by secular values. Church schools may 'top and tail' their product with their distinctive religious traditions, but the mathematics, chemistry, and economics lessons are the same in Ireland's church schools as in England's state schools.

Rationalization

While differentiation and societalization are essentially changes in the structure of societies, a third significant process—rationalization—largely involves changes in the way people think and consequentially in the way they act. Again, social and cultural forces interact. Social changes may rationalize culture, but they do so by amplifying existing rationalizing tendencies that have religious origins. Peter Berger has plausibly argued that the rationality of the West has Jewish and Christian roots. The religion of the Old Testament differed from that of surrounding cultures in a number of important respects. The religions of Egypt and Mesopotamia were profoundly cosmological. The human world was embedded in a cosmic order that embraced the entire universe, without any sharp distinction between the human and the non-human, the empirical and the supra-empirical. Such continuity between people and the Gods was sharply broken by the religion of the Jews. As Berger puts it: 'The Old Testament posits a God who stands outside the cosmos, which is his creation but which he confronts and does not permeate.'[11] The God of Ancient Israel was a radically transcendent God. He made consistent ethical demands upon his followers and he was so remote as to be beyond magical manipulation. We could learn his laws and obey them, but we could not bribe, cajole, or trick him into doing our will. There was a thoroughly demythologized universe between humankind and God.

In the myths of ancient Rome and Greece, a horde of gods or spirits, often behaving in an arbitrary fashion and at cross purposes, made the relationship of supernatural to natural worlds unpredictable. First Judaism and then Christianity were rationalizing forces. By having only one God, they simplified the supernatural and allowed the worship of God to become systematized. Pleasing God became less a matter of trying to anticipate the whims of an erratic despot and more a matter of correct ethical behaviour. Judaism was also a rationalizing force in that, by elevating him, it removed God from the world. He created it and he would end it, but, between start and finish, the world could be seen as having its own structure and logic. This conception of God and the universe was carried over into Christianity.

As the Christian Church evolved, the cosmos was remythologized with angels and semi-divine saints. The Virgin Mary was elevated as a mediator and co-redeemer with Jesus. The belief that God could be manipulated through ritual, confession, and penance undermined the tendency to regulate behaviour with a standardized and rational ethical code. No matter how awful one's life, redemption could be bought by funding the Church. However, this trend was reversed as the Protestant Reformation demythologized the world, eliminated the ritual and sacramental manipulation of God, and restored the process of ethical rationalization.

Formalizing what was pleasing to God made it possible for morality and ethics to become detached from the supernatural. The codes could be followed for their own sake and could even attract alternative justifications. For example, 'Do unto others as you would be done by' could be given an entirely utilitarian justification in a way that 'Placate this God or suffer' could not. In that sense, the rationalizing tendency of Christianity turned against its progenitor.

A similar point can be made from the way in which people thought about various aspects of the social and material world. Science is not easy for cultures that believe that the world is pervaded by unpredictable supernatural spirits and divinities. Systematic exploration of regularities in the behaviour of matter requires the assumption that matter is indeed regular. It is hard to discover the laws of physics if one supposes that volume may be measured by the displacement of water one day but not the next. Such a culture may produce the odd Archimedes, but it retards the development of a community of scholars directing sustained effort to the study of the material world. In that simple sense, the Judaeo-Christian tradition, by simplifying a supernatural menagerie to one God and supposing him distant from the material world, made way for modern science.

The less that God was directly implicated in the day-to-day operations of the universe, the freer people were to explore that universe and elaborate theories of its operations that paid only lip service to the creator. Many early scientists wanted to demonstrate the wonders of God's creation and thus to prove the existence of God, but the development of a healthy tradition of rationalistic scrutiny in time subverted what it had been intended to protect. By freeing the way for empirical enquiry, and for pragmatic and instrumental treatment of this world, the Judaeo-Christian tradition created its own problems.

A related sense of *rationalization* involves the pursuit of technically efficient means of securing this-worldly ends. One of its most potent forms is the development of technology. Technically efficient machinery and procedures reduced uncertainty and thereby reduced reliance upon faith. The domain over which religion offered the most compelling explanations and the most predictable outcomes shrank. Innovating farmers intent on improvement found that crop rotations did more to clean the soil of weeds and parasites than did prayer. This did not prevent pious farmers using prayer as a supplement and some may even have elaborated the theory that break crops clean the ground only if accompanied by religious rituals, but experience would soon have refuted that claim. The growth of technical rationality gradually displaced supernatural influence and moral considerations from ever wider areas of public life, replacing them by considerations of objective performance and practical expedience.

The Reformation played a particular role in demystifying the world. Just as the medieval Church retarded and temporarily reversed the ethical rationalization inherent in Judaism and early Christianity, so the development of science was retarded by the Church's imposition of orthodoxy on all fields of thought. The Church claimed to speak in an unchanging and authoritative fashion not only on matters of behaviour but also on the behaviour of matter. The Reformation, by breaking the power of the Church (albeit in many places replacing it with the power of a church), made way for a variety of thought and for the questioning of tradition that is so vital to natural science. There is also a positive connection, argued for by Robert Merton. He ably demonstrates that a strong desire to demonstrate the glory of God by displaying the majesty of his creation, the rational and systematic attitude of the Protestant ethic, and the Puritan's desire to control the corrupt world all combined to produce in seventeenth-century England a great interest in natural science.[12]

I have deliberately placed science and technology after structural and social differentiation in my explanation of secularization because I want to make clear the relatively small part played by science in displacing religion. Often the two are seen as competing systems of explanation and it is supposed that the latter was pushed out by the former. Of course, many of the beliefs of the early Christians have been shown to be wrong. The earth is round and not flat. The earth moves round the sun, not vice versa. The earth and human life are vastly older than the ages traditionally taken from biblical accounts. While scientists recognize that there are still huge gaps in our knowledge, there is a consensus that an evolutionary model along the lines of Darwinism offers a better explanation of the origins of species than does the account of divine creation in seven days given in the Old Testament book of Genesis.

For all that, I do not actually think that science has directly contributed much to secularization. The arguments between Darwin and Huxley and leading churchmen may have gripped middle-class Victorians, but they hardly penetrated to ordinary people. Anyway, to insist that one set of beliefs lost popularity because another proved it wrong is to miss the difference between truth and plausibility. There are all sorts of ways in which we can insulate

our beliefs from apparently contradicting evidence. We can avoid hearing
the troublesome evidence or we can dismiss it by blackening the character of
those who bring the bad news. For example, many American fundamentalists
accuse evolutionists of being sexually promiscuous and left wing. But such
strategies require social support. The isolate who stands against the consensus is a lunatic and will be treated as such. To maintain a shared belief
system one needs a social strategy that organizes shared defences against the
cognitive threats. Where such resources are available, new ideas, no matter
that they might be better supported by the evidence, can readily be ignored
or rejected.

Although it is not possible to draw a single line between the two classes of
ideas, it is useful to distinguish between specific propositions (for example,
species evolved by natural selection) and more subtle assumptions about the
nature of the world. My point is that, with the right social support and in
the right social context, the threat to one's beliefs from specific counter-
propositions can be neutralized. It is far less easy to avoid being influenced
by widespread and powerful but subtle assumptions about the nature of
the world. As Martin says, with the growth of science and technology, 'the
general sense of human power is increased, the play of contingency is
restricted, and the overwhelming sense of divine limits which afflicted previous generations is much diminished'.[13]

Although Peter Berger is widely associated with the secularization
approach, one particular strand of his thought has been neglected.[14] In an
exploration of the social psychological effects of certain styles of modern
work, Berger, Berger and Kellner argue that, quite irrespective of the extent to
which we are aware of it, modern technology brings with it a 'technological
consciousness', a certain style of thought, that is difficult to reconcile with
a sense of the sacred. An example is 'componentiality'. The application of
modern machines to production involves the assumption that the most
complex entities can be broken down into their components, which are
infinitely replaceable. Any 1990 Volkswagen Golf radiator will fit any 1990
Golf. The relationship between the engine and one radiator is expected to be
exactly the same as that between the engine and any other matching radiator.
There is nothing sacred about any particular bond. Another fundamental
assumption is 'reproducibility'. Technological production takes it for granted
that any creative complex of actions can be subdivided into simple acts that
can be repeated infinitely and always with the same consequence. While there
is no obvious clash between these assumptions and the teachings of most religions, there are serious incompatibilities of approach. There is little space for
the eruption of the divine.

Science and technology have given us a notion of cause and effect that makes us look first for the natural causal explanation of an event. When an aeroplane crashes with the loss of many lives, we ask not what moral purpose the event had but what was its natural cause. And, in so far as we keep finding those causes (a loose engine nut or a terrorist bomb), we are subtly discouraged from seeking the moral significance.

In modern worlds, religion is most often and extensively used for the dark recessive areas of human life over which control has not been established by technology: unhappiness, extreme stress, and the like. When we have tried every cure for cancer, we pray. When we have revised for our examinations, we pray. We do not pray instead of studying and even committed believers suppose that a research programme is more likely than a mass prayer meeting to produce a cure for Aids. Our notion of the scope of divine then is much smaller than that of pre-industrial man. This is not to trivialize the events and problems that still cause many of us to turn to God. The unexpected death of a loved one or the injustice of some act of suffering may be enormously important to us. In that sense the 'gaps' in our rational control and intellectual understanding of our world may loom very large. But they do so in an individualized manner. They are personal, not social problems.

To summarize, I am suggesting that the effect of science and technology on the plausibility of religious belief is often misunderstood. The clash of ideas between science and religion is less significant than the more subtle impact of naturalistic ways of thinking about the world. Science and technology have not made us atheists. Rather the fundamental assumptions that underlie them, which we can summarily describe as 'rationality'—the material world as an amoral series of invariant relationships of cause and effect, the componentiality of objects, the reproducibility of actions, the expectation of constant change in our exploitation of the material world, the insistence on innovation—make us less likely than our forebears to entertain the notion of the divine.

Egalitarianism and Cultural Diversity

The link between modernization and inequality is paradoxical. We need not explore the many differences between modern and traditional sources of power to note that, at the same time as creating classes shaped by what Marx called the forces of production, industrialization brought a basic egalitarianism. As with all the previously mentioned social changes, it is important to recognize the contribution that religious innovation made here. Although the Protestant Reformers were far from being democrats, one major unintended consequence of their religious revolution was a profound change in the relative importance of the community and the individual. By denying the special status of the priesthood and by removing the possibility that religious merit could be transferred from one person to another (by, for example, saying Masses for the souls of the dead), Luther and Calvin reasserted what was implicit in early Christianity: that we are all severally (rather than jointly) equal in the eyes of God. For the Reformers, that equality lay in our sinfulness and in our obligations, but the idea could not indefinitely be confined. Equality in the eyes of God laid the foundations for equality in the eyes of man and before the law. Equal obligations eventually became equal rights.

Though the details of his case need not concern us here, Gellner has plausibly argued that egalitarianism was a requirement for industrialization; a society sharply divided between high and low cultures could not develop a modern economy.[15] The spread of a shared national culture required the replacement of a fixed hierarchy of stations and estates by more flexible class divisions. Economic development brought change and the expectation of further change. And it brought occupational mobility. People no longer did the job they had always done because their family had always done that job. As it became more common for people to better themselves, it also become more common for them to think better of themselves. However badly paid, the industrial worker did not see himself as a serf.

The medieval serf occupied just one role in a single all-embracing hierarchy and that role shaped his entire life. A tin-miner in Cornwall in 1800 might have been sore oppressed at work, but in the late evening and on Sunday he could change his clothes and his persona to become a Methodist lay preacher. As such he was a man of prestige and standing. The possibility of such alternation marks a crucial change. Once occupation became freed from an entire all-embracing hierarchy and became task specific, it was possible for people to occupy different positions in different hierarchies. In turn, that made it possible to distinguish between the role and the person who played it. Roles could still be ranked and accorded very different degrees of respect, power, or status, but the people behind the roles could be seen as in some sense equal. To put it the other way round, so long as people were seen in terms of just one identity in one hierarchy, the powerful resisted egalitarianism because treating alike a peasant and his feudal superior threatened to turn the entire world upside down. But, once an occupational position could be judged apart from the person who filled it, it became possible to maintain a necessary order in the factory,—for example, while operating a different system of judgements outside the work context. The mine-owner could rule his workforce but sit alongside (or even under) his foreman in the local church. Of course, power and status are often transferable. Being a force in one sphere increases the chances of influence in another. The mine-owner could expect to dominate

the congregation but he would do so only if his wealth was matched by manifest piety. If it was not, his fellow churchgoers could respond to any attempt
to impose his will by defecting to a neighbouring congregation.

To recap, the fragmentation of the all-embracing feudal order with its
organic communities allowed the radical individualism inherent in the Protestant Reformation to emerge in three closely related ideas: that everyone was
much-of-a-muchness, that the individual was (at least in theory) autonomous,
and that in future societies would have to deal with individuals and not communities. The practical consequences of these ideas were slow to be worked out
and many changes came only with considerable struggle and blood-letting. The
old élites were not keen to give up their powers, but gradually the principles of
egalitarianism and individual autonomy gave birth to the universal right to own
property, to be free from the arbitrary exercise of power, and to select one's
political leaders. Many rising groups on achieving liberty for themselves were
less than keen to allow others behind them to benefit. None the less, the modernization of the economy allowed the gradual expansion of the notion of
rights and of the scope of those rights.

Modernization brought with it increased cultural diversity in three different ways. First, populations moved and brought their language, religion, and
social mores with them into a new setting. Secondly, the expansion of the
increasingly expansive nation state meant that new groups were brought into
the state. But, as I have already suggested, even without such changes in the
population that had to be encompassed by the state, modernization created
cultural pluralism through the creation of classes and class fragments with
increasingly diverse interests. Especially in Protestant societies, where such
class formation was accompanied by the generation of competing sects, the
result was a paradox. At the same time as the nation state was attempting to
create a unified national culture out of thousands of small communities, it
was having to come to terms with increasing religious diversity.

As this has been misunderstood surprisingly often, I will risk losing the
reader because of repetition and stress that diversity need only force secularization in the context of a culture that accepts a basic egalitarianism and a
polity that is more or less democratic. A society in which almost everyone
shares a particular religion can give that faith pride of place in its operations.
An authoritarian hierarchical society can ignore or suppress religious minorities (and even religious majorities): dissenters need not be tolerated, they can
be massacred or exiled to the Gulag Archipelago. But a society that was becoming increasingly egalitarian and democratic and more culturally diverse had
to place social harmony before the endorsement of religious orthodoxy. The
result was an increasingly neutral state. Religious establishments were abandoned altogether (as in the case of the constitution of the USA) or were

neutered (the British case). As already noted, this reduces the social power and scope of organized religion. While freedom from embarrassing entanglements with secular power may have allowed churches to become more clearly 'spiritual', the removal of the churches from the centre of public life reduced their contact with, and relevance for, the general population.[16]

The separation of church and state was one consequence of diversity. Another, equally important for understanding secularization, was the break between community and religious world view. In sixteenth-century England, every significant event in the life cycle of the individual and the community was celebrated in church and given a religious gloss. Birth, marriage, and death, and the passage of the agricultural seasons, because they were managed by the church, all reaffirmed the essentially Christian world view of the people. The church's techniques were used to bless the sick, sweeten the soil, and increase animal productivity. Every significant act of testimony, every contract, and every promise was reinforced by oaths sworn on the Bible and before God. But beyond the special events that saw the majority of the people in the parish troop into the church, a huge amount of credibility was given to the religious world view simply through everyday social interaction. People commented on the weather by saying 'God be praised' and on parting wished each other 'God Speed' or 'Goodbye' (which we often forget is an abbreviation for 'God be with you').

The consequences of increasing diversity for the place of religion in the life of the state or even the local community are fairly obvious. Equally important but less often considered are the social–psychological consequences of increasing diversity: it calls into question the certainty that believers accord their religion.

Ideas are at their most convincing when they are universally shared. Then they are not beliefs at all; they are just an accurate account of how things are. The elaboration of alternatives provides a profound challenge. Of course, believers need not fall on their swords just because they discover that others disagree with them. Where clashes of ideologies occur in the context of social conflict (of which more below), or when alternatives are associated with people who can be plausibly described as a lower order and thus need not be seriously entertained, the cognitive challenge can be dismissed. One may even elaborate a coherent theory that both explains why there are a variety of religions and reasserts the superiority of one's own. This is exactly what the evolutionary-minded Presbyterian missionaries did in the nineteenth century. They argued that God in his wisdom had revealed himself in different ways to different cultures. The animism of African tribes was suitable for their stage of social development, as was the ritualistic Catholicism of the southern Europeans. As these people evolved, they would move up to the most fulsome understanding of God, which was Scottish Presbyterianism!

But while such explanations of diversity can immunize some believers against doubt, they work only for so long as they are widely shared. They are thus undermined by the same condition they were designed to treat. And that condition is most virulent when religious diversity is internally produced through fragmentation within one society.

When the oracle speaks with a single clear voice, it is easy to believe it is the voice of God. When it speaks with twenty different voices, it is tempting to look behind the screen. As Berger puts it in explaining the title of *The Heretical Imperative*, the position of the modern believer is quite unlike that of the Christian of the Middle Ages in that, while we may still believe, we cannot avoid the knowledge that many people (including many people like us) believe other things.[17]

In a final observation about the impact of pluralism, I would like to trace one causal connection back to the power of science and technology. Pluralism is implicated in the primacy of scientific explanations in that it weakens the plausibility of alternatives. The rational basis of science and the social structures of training, examination, and dissemination of results that protect that base mean that there are fewer disagreements among scientists than there are among the clergy. Despite the disillusionment with the authority of the secular professions commonly voiced in the last quarter of the twentieth century, they still command the sort of respect enjoyed by the medieval Church. If the pathologists say that forty-seven elderly people in Lanarkshire died of bacterium E. Coli., almost all of us will agree with the conclusion. We may then wish to add a divine or supernatural additional explanation of why these people ate that contaminated meat, but, because we do not share a religious culture, we will not be able to agree on whether it is even appropriate to search for such religious significance, let alone what the significance might be. Concentrating our explanations of life events on the material world brings more agreement than searching for religious messages. That the religious culture is badly fragmented weakens the ability of religious explanations to complement, let alone compete with, naturalistic ones.

Five Basic Patterns

The above account proceeds at a very high level of abstraction. Before we can go much further, we need to become more concrete. As I will argue later, one of the fundamental weaknesses of the rational choice approach to religious behaviour is that it attempts to explain too much with just one principle. To avoid that mistake, I need to add to the 'deep structure' of secularization introduced above some important variations in how religion changes in particular societies by noting vital differences in theology, church structure, church–state relations, and the role of religion in ethnic conflict. Following the work of David Martin, I want to suggest that we can understand the central features of the settings that concern us if we consider five basic trajectories from the Reformation onwards.[18]

1. In some countries (mostly those that industrialized late) Catholicism remained dominant. Revolutionary France is the prime example. A monolithic organic or communal ideology was supported by national élites that resisted the rising forces of liberalism and socialism. During the ensuing confrontation, liberalism created strong opposing organic secularist ideologies with an anti-church bent. The society split into clerical and anticlerical blocks. In this category fall the cases of Catholic west and south European states. France, Italy, Spain, and Portugal remained strongholds of Catholicism *and* in the twentieth century produced the strongest Communist parties in western Europe.

2. Where Protestantism became dominant, liberalism and socialism were themselves able to draw upon dissenting strands within the Protestant faith. Social fragments could develop deviant interpretations of the dominant religious tradition to legitimate their concerns and criticize the social position, political power, and mores of superior groups. Religion itself did not become a central focus of conflict. The battles concerned only the particular privileges of its various forms. In most cases, religious minorities called a halt to their attacks on the state church once it had been sufficiently weakened to allow them to thrive. Once the guts had been pulled and it became clear that to weaken further the main church would invite secularists to press for the weakening of all churches, dissenters backed off. In this category fall the north European countries of Britain and Scandinavia.

3. Between these two types lie the dual societies, divided between large blocs of Catholics and Protestants. Here 'pillarization' occurred as each confession created a wide range of distinctive institutions to serve the social and political needs of its people. While religious attachments remained relatively high until well into the twentieth century, Catholics and Protestants had increasingly to collaborate to retain a Christian character to the society in the face of liberal and secularist forces. To take the example of Holland, in 1980 the Dutch Catholic party merged with the two Protestant parties to form a single Christian Alliance.

Such collaboration, however, could take place only where, as in Holland and Switzerland, Catholics and Protestants had come to agree on the issue of national sovereignty—often in the course of securing freedom from imperialistic domination. Where national sovereignty remained unresolved, however, religion was likely to be the basis of divergent national aspirations, and thus to remain a symbolic focus of dispute. The obvious case is Northern Ireland.

4. There are Catholic states in which class formation and social differentiation have not issued in widespread sharp antagonism towards the church, because the church has provided a central focus of cultural identity in the face of an imperialistic neighbour that tried to impose an alien set of cultural values and identities upon a reluctant populace. Religious adherence remained strong as an expression of protest and of rejection of alien values and domination, and as an expression of cultural and social integrity. The obvious cases here are Poland and the Irish Republic. To a lesser extent the national Lutheran churches of Scandinavia play a similar role.

5. Finally there are the migrant societies that exemplify the toleration solution to religious diversity. Where, as in the USA, the society was formed from a wide range of migrant religio-ethnic groups, religious dissent was universal. No one religious expression was uniquely identified with the social élite. Religious freedom became a central value of the nation. In any particular area one religio-ethnic group might be so dominant that it resembled the exporting home country, but the overarching social, political, and economic institutions were secular. Often there was considerable initial conflict as the first waves of settlers tried to maintain and defend their social and economic status, and the status of their religion, against the culture of later groups. But the logic of numbers and the threat of social disorder put paid to such attempts at domination. Religious adherence in general became part of national identity, but religious expressions themselves adapted to the secular values of the society.[19] All the Protestant-dominated immigrant-based societies (the USA, Canada, Australia, and New Zealand) display this pattern to a greater or lesser extent.

Retarding Tendencies

These specific historical and cultural patterns suggest a simple principle: differentiation, societalization, rationalization, and cultural diversity generate secularization except where religion finds or retains work to do other than relating individuals to the supernatural. This principle helps explain not only some of the patterns outlined above, but also some of those to be found within particular societies. We might say that religion diminishes in social significance, becomes increasingly privatized, and loses personal salience except in two broad contexts, those of cultural transition and cultural defence.

Cultural Transition

Where social identity is threatened in the course of major cultural transitions, religion may provide resources for negotiating such transitions or asserting a new claim to a sense of worth. Will Herberg made this point the centre for his explanation of what he termed the American paradox.[20] On the one hand, Americans are fond of churches; on the other, much American religion does not seem especially religious. The answer lies in the social functions of religion for migrants to the USA: religious institutions provided resources for the assimilation of immigrants into American society. Ethnic religious groups provided a mechanism for easing the transition between homeland and the new identity in America. The church offered a supportive group that spoke the same language, shared the same assumptions and values, but that also had experience of, and contacts within, the new social and cultural milieu.

A similar pattern was evident among Irish migrants to nineteenth-century Britain. They congregated where others had gone before. They established a religious community and its appropriate institutions and roles as soon as they could, and within that community they reasserted their cultural integrity and their sense of self-worth. They often fell away from observance before families and cultural institutions had been established, but they often became more observant—perhaps even more observant than they had been at home—when these were in place.

There is another important manifestation of the tendency for religion to retain significance, even temporarily to grow in significance, where it comes to play a role in cultural transition, and that is in the course of modernization itself. Modernization disrupts communities, traditional employment patterns, and status hierarchies. By extending the range of communication, it makes the social peripheries and hinterlands more aware of the manners and mores, lifestyles and values, of the centre and metropolis, and vice versa. Those at the centre of the society, the carriers of modernization, are motivated to missionize the rest, seeking to assimilate them, by educating them and socializing them in 'respectable' beliefs and practices. They are moved to improve and elevate the masses in the rural areas and those who move to the fringes of the cities and there pose the threat of an undisciplined or radical rabble on the doorstep. Sectors of the social periphery in turn are motivated to embrace the models of respectable performance offered to them, especially when they are already in the process of upward mobility and self-improvement.

Industrialization and urbanization therefore tended to give rise to movements of revival and reform, drawing the lapsed and heterodox into the orbit of orthodoxy.[21] The new converts and their overenthusiastic religion often offended the dominant religious organizations. They solved the awkwardness of their position by seceding (or being expelled) and forming new sects. Methodism in late-eighteenth- and nineteenth-century Britain is a prominent example. Religious dissent by the formerly deferential middling and lower orders marked a withdrawal from the old system of dependency on parson and squire, an assertion of their autonomy, and the acceptance of religious values and practices that endorsed their recently acquired socio-economic and democratic aspirations. Evangelicalism gave a spiritual legitimation to the desire for improvement within these strata, while inculcating the values and habits of thrift, conscientious hard work, self-discipline, sobriety, and the deferral of gratification that would assist them to the realize those values.

Although industrialization and urbanization tend, then, in the long term to undermine traditional community and thereby to subvert the basis on which religion can most readily flourish, in the short term they can be associated with an increase in attachment to religious bodies. To summarize, modernization can create a new role for religion as a socializing agent in times of rapid social change.

Cultural Defence

The second great role for religion is as guarantor of group identity. Where culture, identity, and sense of worth are challenged by a source promoting either an alien religion or a rampant secularism and that source is negatively valued, secularization will be inhibited. Religion can provide resources for the defence of a national, local, ethnic, or status-group culture. Again, Poland and the Irish Republic are prime examples, but Northern Ireland can also be included, as, in more attenuated form, can other 'dual' societies, or the peripheries of secularizing societies, resistant to the alien encroachment of the centre.

In Britain, for example, we see this in the greater attachment to their religious institutions shown by the Welsh and still more the Scots for the first three-quarters of the twentieth century. The national cultures and identities became associated with presbytery and chapel against the attempted cultural domination of English Anglicanism or metropolitan secularity. Whatever other virtues being temperant chapel-goers might have had for the Welsh, it had the added advantage of making them different and better than the encroaching English.

In the USA, the greater attachment of southern and mid-western states to traditional Protestant religious forms is in part explained by the desire of native-born Anglo-Saxon Protestants to mark themselves off from later waves of immigrants. Influxes of Catholics and Jews and the attempts of a secularist establishment in the north and east to impose unwanted social and cultural patterns throughout the republic provoked cultural defences from the peripheries. The more peripheral and culturally distinct the region, the more likely religion is to provide a focus of resistance, the more so yet when language no longer provides a viable basis for the assertion of cultural difference.

It is worth going back over the basic elements of the secularization thesis and noting how ethnic conflict can inhibit their development. Consider first structural differentiation. The account given above assumes that there are no specific obstacles to the increasing autonomy of social functions, but clearly hostility between religio-ethnic groups can prevent or retard the process. For example, where its people have been unable to dominate the national culture, the Catholic Church has insisted in maintaining its own schooling system. Though the minority cannot entirely evade the state's social control systems, it may still prefer pre-emptively to exercise its own church-based controls on the behaviour of members.

In the classic model of functional differentiation, the first sphere to become freed of cultural encumbrances is the economy. Yet, even in what we regard as the pre-eminent site for rational choice, ethnic identification may be a major constraint on the maximizing behaviour that is the fundamental principle of economic rationality. In Northern Ireland attempts to impose rationality on the world of work (through various Fair Employment Acts) have largely failed to prevent the exercise of religio-ethnic preferences in hiring policies (especially in small firms that do not depend on the state for contracts and thus cannot be easily controlled). People exhibit their ethnic identity in personal consumption, which is beyond state regulation. The Northern Ireland small-business sector is irrational in that small towns often support one Protestant and one Catholic enterprise where the market can profitably sustain only one. Especially at times of heightened tension, Protestants and Catholics boycott each others' businesses and travel considerable distances to engage in commerce with their own sort.

Consider next what Wilson called 'societalization'. A beleaguered minority may try to prevent the erosion of the community. Deviants who attempt to order their lives in the societal rather than the community mode may be regarded as disloyal and treacherous and punished accordingly. For example, in the ethnic conflicts in Bosnia and Northern Ireland, those who marry across the divide have been frequent targets for vigilantes keen to clarify and maintain their boundaries.

Finally, ethnic conflict mutes the cognitive consequences of pluralism because the prevalence of invidious stereotypes allows a much more thorough compartmentalizing and stigmatizing of alternative cultures. The gradual shift to relativism as a way of accommodating those with whom we differ depends on us taking those people seriously. Where religious differences are strongly embedded in ethnic identities, the cognitive threat of the ideas of the others is relatively weak. Thus Scottish Protestants in the nineteenth century deployed caricatures of the social vices of the immigrant Irish Catholics as a way of avoiding having to consider them as Christian.

Conclusion

I would now like to recap the above account using the language introduced at the start of the chapter. Modernization made the church form of religion impossible. The communal organic religion of the church type requires either cultural homogeneity or an élite sufficiently powerful to disregard diversity. Societies expanded to encompass ever larger numbers of religious, ethnic, and linguistic groups, and improved communication brought increased knowledge of that diversity. Even without such colonization, industralization itself produced internal diversity. In the religious sphere, the consequence was usually the proliferation of sects (though, in the Lutheran context, many revivalist movements were contained within the church). After a period of trying to enforce conformity the state gave up and a climate of religious toleration developed.

By and large the Protestant sects were not advocates of toleration; they wished to purify the religious establishment so that the imposition of religious orthodoxy would be justified by it being the correct religion. It was only after failing to achieve power, either through becoming the majority religion or effecting a minority *coup*, that many of them discovered the principle of toleration and evolved into denominations.

Thus far, in what must be a massively simplified view of the history of religion in the West, we have seen the church form faced with competition from a proliferation of sects and then both churches and sects tending to become denominations. The decline of mainstream Christian traditions and increasing liberalism reduced the stigma that was attached to religious innovation at the same time as increased affluence, travel, and faster global communication were making available a wide variety of new religious ideas. First with the new religious movements of the 1960s and 1970s and then with the New Age religion of the 1980s, we have seen a flowering of alternative religions; some reworkings for the Western mind of traditional Eastern religions, others spiritualized versions of lay psychotherapies. No better example of the increasing toleration of innovations is our attitude to witches. In the eighteenth century they were regarded as agents of Satan deserving only of death. In Britain in the early twentieth century Alistair Crowley and his small coterie were regarded with morbid fascination, but there were few serious attempts to curtail his activities. At the end of that century, the Aberdeenshire *Press and Journal* could with a straight face report that a 'white witch' intended to prosecute a Church of Scotland minister for criticizing his pagan activities.[22]

In the terms used by Wallis, some of the new religions of the 1960s and 1970s are sects; others cults. In the main it has been the more sectarian new religions (such as Scientology, the Unification Church, or Krishna Consciousness) that have attracted the greatest amount of attention and opprobrium. This is no surprise: the more sectarian movements typically demanded the greatest changes in the lives of their adherents and were thus most likely to be thought to possess the malign powers of 'brainwashing'. However, it was the more cultic (hence least radical and demanding) movements that proved most popular. But 'popular' here is a relative notion. Although I will argue that the cultic new religious movements and New Age spirituality are, in evolutionary terms, most fitted to the individualist and consumerist ethos of our modern world, they have not attracted anything like the support that has been lost to the mainstream denominations and the sects. Hence in talking about changes in the dominant forms of religion I am also talking about the decline in the popularity, power, and presence of religion, something that will be amply illustrated in subsequent chapters.

It is not an accident that most modern societies are largely secular. Industrialization brought with it a series of social changes—the fragmentation of the lifeworld, the decline of community, the rise of bureaucracy, technological consciousness—that together made religion less arresting and less plausible than it had been in pre-modern societies. That is the conclusion of the vast majority of social scientists, historians, and church leaders in the Western world. If there is any originality in my account of these changes, it is only in the stress I give to diversity. Where others have begun their explanation for the decline of religion with the increasingly neutral state, I have drawn attention to the cause of that neutrality. Although the idea that citizens should not have their rights constrained by religious affiliation had become sufficiently well established as part of liberal and democratic discourse by the middle of the nineteenth century that it became part of democratic reform, even where there was little or no need for it, it has its origins in practical necessities. The cultural diversity created by, among other things, structural and social differentiation pushed religious identity (and with it all but the blandest religious ideas) out of the public arena and into the private sphere.

Again it is largely a matter of emphasis, but I have also stressed the impact of diversity on the way in which people who wish to remain religious can hold their religious beliefs. The removal of support at the level of social structure has a corresponding effect on the social psychology of belief. The dogmatic certainties of the church and sect are replaced by the weak affirmations of the denomination and the cult.

That the above account of secularization might be termed the orthodox view does not mean that it goes unchallenged. The next chapter will introduce a radical alternative.

2

Rational Choice Theory

ALTHOUGH the secularization case made in the previous chapter is widely accepted by historians and social scientists, a number of small and specific criticisms have been made. The relative weight of various causes has been much debated, as has the extent to which we can generalize from the past of the Western industrial world to other societies. There has also long been one general reason for rejecting the whole approach. Despite the strong evidence of declining interest in religion, some scholars, usually philosophers and theologians, have argued that enduring secularization is impossible because there is something about the human condition that persistently leads us to ask spiritual questions. If nothing else, our mortality leads us to hope that there is more to life than meets the eye and causes us to search for a 'meaning' to life.

However, it is only in the last quarter of the twentieth century that such views have been articulated in a fully elaborated social-scientific theory and it is that to which I turn in this chapter. In the first half I will consider the rewards and compensators theory developed by Rodney Stark and William S. Bainbridge. In the second I will consider the rational choice model that Stark later embraced. Although both theories have been extensively advertised by Stark's prolific published output, both have been equally widely ignored, most pointedly by the people who know a lot about the countries that Stark uses to illustrate his theories. Given the weaknesses I will identify in his work, such neglect may seem fully justified and the reader may wonder why I bother to devote so much effort to detailed criticism of a fundamentally misguided approach. Masochism apart, there are two reasons. First, Stark and his colleagues often inadvertently raise important questions about the nature and role of religion and these deserve to be addressed. Secondly, their mistakes allow me to refine the views presented in the previous chapter.

Rewards and Compensators

The Stark–Bainbridge theory begins with the premiss that people seek to gain rewards, which are things that they are prepared to expend costs to secure. Some rewards that people seek are scarce or unavailable. When highly desired rewards seem not to be available directly, people accept *compensators* instead. Since this term is crucial, we should be clear about its meaning. In one place, Stark says: 'Compensators are a form of I.O.U. They promise that in return for value surrendered now, the desired reward will be obtained eventually.'[1] Bainbridge and Stark say compensators are 'sets of beliefs and prescriptions for action that substitute for the immediate achievement of the desired reward. Compensators postulate the attainment of the desired reward in the distant future or in some other unverifiable context. Compensators are treated by humans as if they were rewards.'[2] Compensators are 'postulations of reward according to explanations that are not readily susceptible to unambiguous evaluation' and 'intangible substitutes for a desired reward'.[3]

Compensators may be specific, such as a cure for warts, or general, such as the meaning to life. Some desired rewards are 'of such a magnitude and scarcity that only by assuming the existence of an active supernatural can credible compensators be created'.[4] Hence, as long as people seek such rewards, secular systems of belief will be unable to compete with religious ones in the production of credible compensators.

Two things supposedly follow from this. First, if a religious organization shifts away from supernaturalism, it weakens itself because it reduces its ability to provide strong compensators. This, according to Stark and Bainbridge, is why liberal Protestantism has been in decline. Defectors from liberal churches do not embrace secular humanism but they 'may'—a curiously cautious note this—'eventually be drawn to a more traditional faith'.[5] Even if they are not so drawn, their children will be. So secularization is a self-limiting process, and, where major religious denominations succumb, they will be replaced by new faiths of a more supernaturalistic kind offering more credible compensators.

Secondly, organizations that address themselves to the 'biggest and most persistent human desires' will tend to 'shift from naturalistic to supernaturalistic premises'.[6] The failure of rewards to materialize will increase the demand for compensators and for the introduction of the supernatural as their credible source:

in pursuit of goals of immense value which cannot be obtained through direct means, humans will tend to create and exchange compensators . . . Not only do naturalistic organisations lack the resources for great compensators which are present in religions, but when they get too close to the matters with which only religion can deal, they tend to become religious too.[7]

The cases of Synanon, The Process, and, Scientology are analysed in these terms, and elsewhere, Transcendental Meditation.[8]

I will now look closely at three areas of weakness in this model: the conceptualization of rewards and compensators, the underlying approach to explanation, and the interpretation of the evidence presented for the theory.

Defining Terms

The notion of compensator is a slippery one. It is contrasted with that of reward, which is anything someone is prepared to expend costs to obtain, but it does not seems entirely comparable in scope. A compensator is not only something that people are prepared to expend costs to obtain (and thus a type of reward); it is also the *promise* of a future reward and an *explanation* of how such a reward may be secured. A compensator is a form of reward not only because people are prepared to expend costs to obtain it, but also because, according to Stark and Bainbridge, 'explanations are rewards of some level of generality'.[9] But if compensators are also rewards, then the claim that, when rewards are not immediately available, people will instead accept compensators becomes circular. It certainly undermines any force in the claim that people treat compensators as rewards, or that they may mistake the former for the latter.

Part of the difficulty of having a concept like *compensator*, with its three elements of reward, promise of future reward, and explanation of how to achieve future reward, is that the force of the argument advanced may derive from slipping between one meaning and another. That being unable to secure scarce rewards now we are likely to accept mere promises for the future (compensators) seems somehow a more original and telling point than that, being unable to secure our desired rewards now, we will accept explanations of how we can secure them some time in the future after following appropriate procedures. When we recast the proposition in this form, we see that the notion of compensation is redundant and misleading. Explanations are not substitutes for rewards that should be compared with *explanations* of how to obtain scarce and distant rewards, nor can they be compared with them. Whether rewards are plentiful and immediately present, or scarce and distant, they will have explanations as to how they may be obtained. It is *explanations* of how to secure proximal rewards, not rewards on the one hand and explanations on the other. A description of how to achieve something can hardly be a substitute for something difficult of attainment. A university prospectus and a set of degree regulations are not a substitute for a degree. The reward is not abandoned as impossible to secure and the explanation accepted *instead*; rather, armed with our explanation of how to achieve it, we actively seek the reward in a new location.

It may be, of course, that, if one reward is not available or difficult to obtain, we may aspire to some other reward instead. If I cannot be respected by my colleagues, perhaps I can be loved by my spouse. If I cannot obtain happiness in this life, then I might look for it elsewhere. In that sense, one reward may substitute for another or provide some compensation. I may be prepared to accept the promise of a reward in a future life for what I cannot have now, but the promise does not substitute for the tangible this-worldly reward. It may make present misery easier to endure while I wait to secure that reward in the future, but it is only the future *reward* itself that can substitute for what I cannot have here and now.

Stark and Bainbridge's idea of rewards causes as many problems as their notion of compensators. Rewards seem to be acceptable to Stark and Bainbridge under that label only if they are tangible, concrete, and immediate. Anything else somehow becomes merely symbolic, unreal, and thus a substitute for some present gratification. But such a view is not sustainable. Interest on a bank deposit may not be immediate but it is none the less tangible, when, in the future, it arrives. Some rewards are not sought immediately. Unusually old age may be highly desirable and even scarce, but I do not want it yet. Rather it is a desired future increment to what I might otherwise expect, and the advice of brokers on investments, of doctors on smoking, are thus not compensators, substitutes for future reward, but only sound guidance on how to secure it.

Moreover, being intangible does not render a reward spurious. There may or may not be good evidence for life after death, but people who have an abundance in this world may still seek it as simply another valuable asset worth securing if it is going, and thus not as a substitute for anything at all.

Stark and Bainbridge have implicitly assumed too simple a model of reward. They radically divide the concrete and immediate from the distant and intangible. Rewards comprise only the former, and the latter are thus something that people will accept only if the concrete and immediate gratifications cannot be secured. They fail to see that rewards may fall anywhere within the range defined by their poles of the immediate and the distant. What Stark and Bainbridge see as firmly opposed and sharply distinct are, at best, distinguished only as a matter of degree. If we desire wealth, we desire it not only today but tomorrow and next year. Similarly, the desire for immortality is a desire not only to live forever, but to live today and tomorrow as well. Their conceptualization of human desires is a highly materialistic one. They assume that the promises of religion cannot be desired for their own sake, but only as substitutes for something else. For Stark and Bainbridge religion is inherently faulty and can be desired only as compensation for an unavailable something that is better because it is this-worldly and immediate. In short, while most social scientists try to remain neutral about the truth claims of religion, Stark and Bainbridge build their theory on the premisses that are substantively atheistic.

Explanatory Models

A related problem derives from the rather outmoded conception of explanation and proof that Stark and Bainbridge employ. Their distinction between rewards and compensators rests on the assumption that the former are real and thus, by implication, that the explanations advanced as to how to secure them are verifiable. Compensators, on the other hand, entail 'empirically unsubstantiated faith' or 'explanations that are not readily susceptible to unambiguous evaluation'; they are 'unverifiable', or, in the case *of specific* compensators, 'when evaluated are found wanting'.[10] They assert, perhaps a little disingenuously, that 'surely there is nothing controversial about distinguishing between statements that can be tested and those that must be taken on faith'.[11] But this claim is far from uncontroversial. Once again, difficulties arise from the multiplicity of definitions employed, but the general claim being advanced is that we can distinguish without difficulty between the *empirical* claims of naturalistic belief systems and the *metaphysical* claims of religious and magical beliefs. However, each side of this dichotomy turns out to be far less clear-cut than Stark and Bainbridge suppose.

One mistake derives from their assumption that they need not consider the explanations leading to the attainment of tangible, this-worldly rewards. The rewards appear, and thus are verifiable (or they do not appear and are therefore false). But verifiability is a property not of rewards, but rather of the explanations as to how they are to be achieved. And, of itself, the appearance of the reward (or not) tells us nothing about whether or not the explanations regarding such rewards are true. If I am told that by betting on Prince Danube in the 4.30 I will double my money because the favourite has been doped, actually doubling my money tells me nothing with certainty about why I won.[12]

On the other side of the dichotomy, however, things are similarly more complex than Stark and Bainbridge presume. Although some of the claims of religion and magic may be metaphysical and thus untestable, many are not. Stark and Bainbridge are forced to recognize this in the case of magic. The shaman's 'specific compensator' of a cure for warts is clearly not untestable, so they dismiss it as obviously false.[13] But can the claim be so readily dismissed without testing? Before being subjected to appropriate empirical scrutiny, the shaman's claim is every bit as valid as the doctor's promise that, if certain medical procedures are followed, the warts will disappear. And the doctor's claim may be equally false, yet it is not advanced as an example of a compensator.

Some claims advanced by science and medicine, like those of religion and magic, cannot readily be tested. But that does not make the promise of a method for interplanetary travel or a cure for schizophrenia any the less testable in principle, or otherwise *logically* (rather than practically) distinct from the promise of an electrically powered car or a cure for goitre. We cannot become slaves to the knowledge of the day in our decisions as to how to explain the beliefs of social actors. We cannot explain someone's beliefs one way today when scientific expertise is inadequate to test it effectively, and another way tomorrow when a new testing mechanism is invented. The explanation of the belief is the explanation of the belief, and cannot vary according to the prevailing consensus about it, or the sophistication of experimental practice (although, clearly, *having* new experimental evidence may itself be *another* reason for, and hence explanation of, belief). If tomorrow we secure good experimental evidence for auras or telepathic signals, that will not change one iota why people believe in those things *today*, nor, therefore, should it change our explanations for today's beliefs.

The claims of religion and magic typically involve many assertions no less readily testable than the claims made at the frontiers of science. If Transcendental Meditators do begin flying around major metropoli under their own steam, that will be powerful support for the explanations offered by Maharishi Mahesh Yogi.

The important difference between scientific and religious beliefs is not that one type is false and the other true, or that one is readily and the other only with great difficulty subjected to empirical evaluation. Most people do not hold their beliefs on the basis of scientific tests anyway, but on the basis of experiential evidence, or on authority, or because they have never had any reason to doubt the views into which they were raised. The difference lies in the way that the beliefs are treated. In the case of science, the institution is typically structured in such a manner as to encourage testing and even disconfirmation, while, in the case of religion, the institution will tend systematically to protect the claims it advances from falsification (cases of dogmatic resistance to innovation in science and critical churchmen notwithstanding). But that is to say no more than that, in their professional capacity, church leaders are not scientists and vice versa, and tells us nothing about different *modes* of explanation—rather than merely different *substantive* explanations—required to account for them holding their respective beliefs.

The underlying assumption held by Stark and Bainbridge, that different modes of explanation are required for true and for false beliefs (or those that are and those that are not readily susceptible of empirical evaluation, verifiable, and so on), has long been common in sociology. Beliefs that we regard as true are taken to need no further explanation in order to understand why they are held. Beliefs that we regard as false, however, are explained in a quite different manner. If you believe what is evidently false or clearly resistant to proof, we need to provide a causal story saying how this could happen. That story usually identifies some factor extraneous to the rational deliberations of the actors concerned that is held to account for this deviation from good sense. Such explanatory dualism will not do. The fact that something is true does not explain why the belief is held. People have historically been at least as prone to believe what is false as what is true. Hence, we need to know, even of true beliefs, why they are held at this particular time and by these particular people. Belief in what is true needs as much explanatory background as belief in what is false.

I will start by distinguishing beliefs that accord with people's usual criteria for judgement from ones that do not. In the first case, we explain why beliefs are held by referring to the criteria, norms, and standards that provide actors with good reasons for entertaining those ideas. This does not rule out social explanations of why some people find some notions plausible: because these good reasons can never be logically complete, there is always room for showing that the conclusions thus derived also served certain interests that the actors hold dear. Given that logic and their formal procedures could never be complete guides, actors may always have added reason for accepting one interpretation rather than another.

In the case of beliefs that appear not to fit with the actors' appropriate criteria, we must adopt a different strategy. First, we must consider the possibility that we have simply misunderstood. If not that, then we may argue that the extraneous reasons had a peculiarly compelling force, which led the actors to believe something regardless of where reason pointed in this particular case. You think you are protesting about trade-union rights because they offend against your principles of civil liberty, but, from such evidence as your unwillingness to object to near-identical infringements of individual freedoms by major corporations, I conclude that in this case you are coming to conclusions that do not accord with your criteria for making such judgements. I therefore conclude that your beliefs are not reasoned but are instead a product of right-wing media manipulation. Although such a style of explanation is common currency in the social sciences, it is very rarely justified.

The usual mistake of social scientists is to argue that, because the actors' beliefs do not accord with what we regard as appropriate criteria, they must be explained by reference to pathology, social structure, or some similar compelling sociological or psychological factor such as inability to tolerate the frustration of desire. All such accounts are guilty of ethnocentrism: of believing that everyone should think in the same terms as we do and that rationality means using our intellectual criteria. This is only marginally less arrogant than believing that all people should believe *substantively* as we do, and that, if they do not, their beliefs require some mode of explanation that differs from the explanation for our own rational and true beliefs.

The Stark–Bainbridge approach has much in common with the sociological study of moral protest movements. Sociologists have found it hard to comprehend how campaigns oriented to the pursuit of symbolic goals could not have some ulterior, concrete, material motive in the desire for the improvement or maintenance of the social position of the moral crusaders.[14] Committed to uncovering hidden motives beneath public rhetoric, sociologists have widely rejected the possibility that symbolic goals and values could *really* be what actors sought in such enterprises, and imputed to them motives derived from an analysis of the presumed latent functions of such beliefs and actions.

In all such cases sociologists adopt an ontological position; they take sides. They assert that certain things exist or do not exist, either on the authority of scientists or on the basis of their own supposedly superior insight into the nature of reality. But such claims cannot be warranted sociologically. Whether the world is as currently asserted by scientists, whether there is life after death, and the like, are not matters on which sociologists possess any superior knowledge. Hence their intuitions on such matters cannot be employed as the basis for sociological arguments about why people act as they do.

To the believer, salvation is as real as his wage packet and undoubtedly of greater value. To the millenarian, the coming of the Messiah is as tangible as the social organization of which he is a member and may be of far greater importance. To the moral crusader, the importance of keeping pornography off the streets is of greater moment than retaining his social position. That Stark and Bainbridge cannot see how anyone would turn to transcendental concerns unless thwarted in their pursuit of material rewards does not entail that the actors involved think or feel as they do. This is not to say, of course, that no one ever adopts supernatural goals in compensation for their failure to secure this-worldly material rewards. Such a response is undoubtedly quite frequent. Having a friend in Jesus is a great solace for the lonely, just as the promise of post-millennial power is a welcome hope for those who suffer deprivation and stigma in the pre-millennial world. But to say that religion may on occasion provide compensation for failure to secure present tangible reward is not to advance a theory of religion, only a theory *about*

what religion is or does for some people at some times. I see the factors leading
people to accept religious beliefs and goals as many and various. Stark and
Bainbridge have elevated one of these to the status of complete explanation.

The Evidence

In this section I will examine the evidence adduced by Stark and Bainbridge
to support three specific propositions derived from their theory. First, they
assert that 'for religious organizations to move markedly in the direction of
non-supernaturalism is to pursue the path to ruin'. Secondly, they claim that
secularization is self-limiting, and that even where 'major religious organizations may turn towards secularism and crumble . . . new faiths will arise offering a stronger version of the supernatural. These new faiths will prosper as
the old ones fade.' Thirdly, they believe that 'naturalistic meaning systems are
at a relative disadvantage in dealing with the biggest and most pervasive
human desires . . . and thus there will be a tendency for organisations that
attempt to grapple with such problems to shift from naturalistic to supernaturalistic premises'.[15] Before I explore the detail of such cases, however, it
must be said that I agree with these claims. The fact that I do so while dis-
agreeing with the theory they allegedly support suggests that a problem may
exist in the interpretation of what they mean and why they occur. I believe
that Stark and Bainbridge misinterpret the evidence, which can perfectly well
be explained without the extravagant and conceptually flawed theoretical
superstructure upon which their account depends.

   In support of their theory, Stark and Bainbridge make much of the decline
of the liberal Protestant churches. But they pursue some rather tortuous reasoning to bring this fact into compatibility with their theory. The admitted
facts are that conservative churches have generally fared better than liberal
ones in the second half of the twentieth century. Nowhere is this more evident
than in Protestant Europe. Stark and Bainbridge claim that this is a result of
conservative churches offering bigger and better compensators. However, as
they are forced to admit, there is little evidence that those who leave liberal
churches do so in order to join conservative alternatives. They, therefore, claim
that it is not the defectors who are recruited to conservative supernaturalism,
but their children. Apart from one or two striking cases of prominent agnostics and atheists whose children have been so recruited, the evidence for such
a claim is scant indeed. In the main, conservative churches recruit from their
own families rather than from the families of agnostics and liberals. Indeed,
the relative rarity of people moving great ideological distances in their religious choices is one of the key predictions of the rational choice theory to
which Stark later became attached.[16]

Stark and Bainbridge marshal a diverse range of evidence in support of their view that naturalistic systems of belief cannot, in the long run, compete with supernaturalistic ones and thus that secularization is limited by the emergence of new religions offering more credible compensators. This evidence generally takes the form of correlations between the emergence of new faiths and low membership of traditional churches. This is very weak evidence indeed. That new faiths may arise when old ones decay is not at issue. This is only to be expected in terms of *availability* for recruitment. Where old faiths are strong, there is no market at all, or only a very limited one, for new faiths. Where many are unchurched, *some* will doubtless be available for recruitment to new faiths. What is important is the ratio of those so recruited relative to the total lost by the old faiths. The scale of the decline in the major denominations and that of the growth of the new religious movements are simply not comparable. The Protestant churches in Britain lost over half a million members between 1970 and 1975 alone. The conservative churches that were growing gained about 14,000 new members, which makes no impression on the overall decline. Moreover, in the face of such decline, the suggestion that the new religious movements are making an impact upon any substantial number of the unchurched, with only 588 resident British Moonies in 1980, is hardly compelling.[17] The scale of the problem can be illustrated with the example of Canada. Between 1961 and 1991 the proportion of Canadians who ticked the 'no-religion' box in the census rose from 1 to 12.4 per cent. Many of those who claimed a religion show little or no commitment to it: for example, the United Church of Canada's own membership figures amount to less than 30 per cent of those who claimed in the census to belong to it. So we can safely take the figure for 'no-religion' people, over 3 million, as a gross underestimate of the real size of the unchurched. At least 3 million and more likely 10 million Canadians are available to join new religious movements and the most generous estimates would put the total membership of such innovations in the low tens of thousands. Reginald Bibby, who has spent thirty years surveying Canadian religion, concluded that, far from taking up the slack left by the decline in the mainstream churches, 'the new religions typically fare worse than the old ones'.[18]

The third type of evidence presented concerns the evolution of a number of organizations in the broad Human Potential movement. Stark and Bainbridge show that a number of groups and organizations that sought to meet the demand for 'the biggest and most persistent human desires' gradually became more religious. Examples would be the evolution of L. Ron Hubbard's Dianetics into the Church of Scientology and changes in a group known as The Process.[19] The issue, however, is why the change. To support the Stark–Bainbridge theory, the transition must have been because those involved saw that the movement had failed to provide the rewards originally promised, and therefore were attracted by the supernaturalistic compensators offered in substitution. But there is no evidence for this, largely because Stark and Bainbridge eschew biographical data. An analysis of the biographies of followers of Dianetics shows that many did in fact believe Dianetics had failed to provide what it had promised, and they therefore quit the movement for other things.[20] Those who remained through the transition to Scientology either believed they had received substantial naturalistic rewards, or had been looking for something spiritual all along, and saw what Dianetics could offer as a step towards that ultimate goal. Similarly, Roy Wallis's interviews with former members of The Process showed that those who persisted through its various transformations into a religion believed that it had in fact been producing the goods and that the benefits produced opened up a new range of goals to pursue *in addition* to the earlier goals, and they therefore remained with it.

There is every reason to suppose that the case of Transcendental Meditation (or TM) is analogous, except that TM always had a spiritual core that appealed to some of the more religiously inclined followers. It is likely that it was those already attracted by the spiritual promises of cosmic consciousness and the like, rather than those who experienced the movement as having failed to provide naturalistic rewards, who remained attached when it developed more explicitly supernaturalistic beliefs and practices.[21]

I have already advanced an alternative explanation for the emergence of new faiths where church attendance is low: all that is at issue here is a question of *availability*. This, in turn, is a consequence of separation from traditional systems of belief, and is clearly related to such factors as geographical and social mobility. The evidence does not support any suggestion that these new faiths are replacing the old ones, or taking up much of the constituency of the unchurched. Stark and Bainbridge may claim that new religions appear as more or less random mutations, and that the one best adapted to the circumstances and that will grow into a vast new faith has not yet appeared or not yet taken off. But *in the long run* it will. Such a claim is, of course, prophecy, not prediction. It is mere pious hope, has no empirical standing, and cannot be used to strengthen a formulation quite unable to stand without it.

What alternative theory would I advance for the other evidence adduced by Stark and Bainbridge? First, I would reject their preference for a single 'theory of everything'. There seems no compelling reason to expect that the particular phenomena that they group together should have a single cause. However, the decline of liberal Protestantism and the changes in the Human Potential movement do have one thing in common: in their different ways, both are in part consequences of a diffuse belief system. I will say more about this in Chapter 7 and will present my alternative explanation here in only summary form.

Some movements are committed to a conception of the individual that sees him or her as the final arbiter of the good and the true. The authority to rule on the legitimacy of any set of beliefs (and attendant practices) lies only with each person. There is no external or higher power. As a result, the beliefs of the movement are *diffuse.* People synthesize various selections to suit their own tastes. New ideas are simply added to the sum total of legitimate ideas; there is no possibility of producing a neat, coherent set of dogmas. With no controls over ideological development, change is not only likely but inevitable.

In the Human Potential movement, for example, there has been a vast proliferation of ideas and practices since its emergence. Although typically each new practice is launched as a total solution, in the course of time each becomes merely an additional tool, a component in a composite of techniques and ideas available to the practitioner, and synthesized into the personal corpus of beliefs and practices of the client. Over the course of time too, the movement has developed a more spiritual cast, with many practitioners becoming followers of spiritual gurus such as Bhagwan Shree Rajneesh, the emergence of transpersonal psychologies such as Psychosynthesis, and a growing interest in spiritual ideas and related practices among followers and practitioners.

Stark explains these developments by the failure of earlier naturalistic beliefs to produce the rewards sought. I would argue that failure of a sort was indeed one—but only one—factor leading people in a more spiritual direction. Many early leaders in the Human Potential movement had envisaged it as a total way of life, but, with the passing of the early phase of enthusiasm along with the counter-culture of the 1960s, it became clear that most participants were involved only on a part-time and less-than-fully committed basis. The movement began to grow more commercial as many enthusiasts—now leaders and practitioners—sought to make a living where they had not been able to found a way of life. Those who were disinclined to opt back into the commercial conventional world from which they had sought to distance themselves in the counter-culture were often attracted to more spiritually inclined movements such as Rajneeshism or Arica that contained an extensive round of personal growth activities within the framework of a spiritual ideology and a community of the like-minded. In this sense, greater spirituality was a result of the failure of the movement to provide the rewards sought in terms of a way of life by some participants, but it did not provide a *substitute* for that reward, it actually produced it. In Arica and the Rajneesh movement, these seekers found the expressive way of life that they desired. Moreover, spirituality grew as a consequence of other factors quite contrary to the Stark–Bainbridge proposals. For example, many people who came into the Human Potential movement found it produced considerable effects upon them. The very success of its methods gave rise to new questions, awakened new interests, and thus provoked further search, again leading in a more spiritual direction as followers and practitioners sought to find a general explanation and plan behind the effects of diverse particular practices and remedies. The very diffuseness of the movement ideology itself encouraged a spiritual drift for many who found that the rewards they sought had been produced. Just as Hindu philosophy can explain and justify the worship of thousands of different gods and spirits, so a religious ideology can bring together and make sense of a smorgasbord of secular therapies. In brief, I am suggesting that increasing the spiritual elements in the Human Potential movement offers viable solutions to problems caused, not by the failure of the movement to produce the goods, but by the diffuseness of the movement's ideology.

The story of liberal Protestantism is similar. Once the belief in the Bible as the unchanging inspired Word of God, speaking to every person in every culture in the same way, was abandoned, epistemological individualism became possible. Who would define the truth? If our perceptions of the Christian message change when our culture and society change, if there is always 'new light', then who decides what is really light and what is darkness in disguise? Allowing the faith to change is not a serious problem in the Catholic and Orthodox traditions, where there is a permanent body to arbitrate, but, coupled with the inherent democracy of the Protestant 'priesthood of all believers', the outcome is diffuseness and eclecticism. To put it bluntly, almost the only thing that unites liberal Protestants is their not being Catholics or conservative Protestants. Liberal Protestantism cannot be defined by any set of dogmas. It has no doctrinal statements. For that reason it cannot decide who is saved and who is not saved. There are no membership tests. It is this failure to be able to specify who is not saved that explains the universalist tendency in liberal Protestantism. Given an incipient universalism (which is manifest in some radical theologians) there is little point in evangelizing. It is thus hardly surprising that liberal Protestantism has declined.

Stark and Bainbridge offer an explanation of the parlous state of liberal Protestantism that hangs on the supposed failure of the product to satisfy the consumer. Their evidence here is weak because they are working from single-shot survey data. They do not have longitudinal surveys or biographies of liberal Protestants that show dissatisfaction with rationalistic beliefs to be the cause of liberals defecting to conservative Protestant churches. All the available evidence points to the conclusion that socialization rather than conversion is the key to conservative Protestant success and liberal failure. Conservative Protestantism, with its epistemologically authoritarian beliefs, can serve as the basis for doctrinal statements, membership tests, and patterns for training new members into conformity. The sons and daughters of liberal Protestants were raised, not in alternative institutions, but in those of the secular world. Most of them went their own ways, not because they were dissatisfied with their liberal religion, but because going one's own way is the logic of liberal Protestantism.

What of a case like Scientology? Wallis has argued that the transition to a more supernaturalistic mode of belief and practice was indeed a response to failure to some extent and for a limited range of people, perhaps limited to the leader, Ron Hubbard himself.[22] Hubbard saw that certain things had been achieved by Dianetics, but that the movement's epistemological individualism had jeopardized and nearly destroyed it. The introduction of Scientology was, therefore, a strategic response to the precariousness of Dianetics. By arrogating authority, a step legitimated by the introduction of a transcendental system of belief, Hubbard could monopolize control and separate his movement from competitors and conventional institutions. The more religious form in this case was as much a response to problems of polity as to a failure to attain naturalistic goals. But, while failure in this sense may explain the behaviour of the leader, it tells us nothing about why members followed him, and we would argue that the Stark–Bainbridge account entirely misconceives what transpired for those followers.

To summarize my alternative explanations of the trends identified by Stark and Bainbridge, I have argued that the key is the precariousness caused by diffuseness. The changes were thus quite incidental to the movements being religious or, alternatively, not sufficiently religious.

In concluding this section, I want to draw attention to a general feature of Stark and Bainbridge's work that is also significant for evaluating Stark's later rational choice approach. Many of the problems stem from the relationship between theory and method. In pursuit of a universal theory of religion, Stark and Bainbridge fail to appreciate the importance of cultural context. We can see this in their use of 'reward'. What counts as a reward for any group of actors will depend on their culture, and, if that culture is supernaturalist, then religious values and goals will loom as large as material rewards and goals. Moreover, the religious aspirations, just like the material ones, will be acquired by socialization, not by reaction to the failure of this-worldly ambitions. At best, therefore, because it rests on the supposed dissatisfaction of religiously mobile individuals, the Stark–Bainbridge thesis would have relevance only for the convert and not for the mass of religious believers born and socialized into the faith of their fathers.

Stark and Bainbridge might claim that it is only because religion does possess the characteristic that they impute to it, the power to provide general compensators, that those socialized into it remain committed. However, as they claim that religion is the only credible source of some general compensators, and that no naturalistic belief system can compete with these in the long run, it is not at all clear why anyone should abandon their religious beliefs, any more than it is clear how long is the long run.

Stark and Bainbridge propose that supernatural beliefs are invented as substitutes for what believers cannot secure now in this world. They fail to see that, if not torn out of cultural context, the sequence can plausibly be reversed. Since most people are born into a social world in which religious beliefs already exist, belief in another world with supernatural characteristics opens up the possibility of wanting things there *as well as*, rather than *instead of*, here. The choice of the former theory over the latter would seem to depend on the prior arbitrary relegation of religious beliefs to an ontologically inferior status.

The discussion of particular cases, such as the changes in cults that led them in a more religious direction, and the two-generation account of the decline of liberal Protestantism in favour of conservative Protestantism exhibit the common problem of being unable to distinguish groups and individuals. Stark and Bainbridge observe certain changes taking place at the group level (for example, that recruitment declines, possibly creating dissatisfaction among those who had hoped for certain this-worldly benefits from rising recruitment; the movement then increases its supernatural promises) and assume that the same people are involved in each case. They suppose that it is those who were dissatisfied who embraced supernaturalism, but this relationship is nowhere demonstrated. Throughout, they operate at the level of aggregate data, providing no serious support of their claims at the level of individual biography. In brief, I believe that some of the main problems with the Stark–Bainbridge theory come from an excessive distance from their subject matter. They make inferences about the motivation of groups of actors on the basis of aggregate data. Knowing little about the meanings that the actors attached to their circumstances, Stark and Bainbridge commit the familiar error of supposing that the actors probably feel the same way that they would if they were in that position. Fundamentally, the method of research does not allow Stark and Bainbridge to understand the people whose behaviour they are explaining.

Supply-Side Theories of Religious Change

If we suppose, as Stark and Bainbridge do, that the demand, desire, or need for religion is more or less stable, then the manifest variations in the pace and intensity of religious activity, commitment, and interest must be explained by variation in supply.

At this point Stark's interest in denying secularization meets an important trend in US intellectual life: the imperialism of economists. Despite their inability to predict or manage the economy, economists have been attempting to encompass ever larger fields of human activity. Recent extensions of economics into sociology have largely been inspired by the work of Gary Becker, who argues that

the economic approach is a comprehensive one that is applicable to all human behavior, be it behavior involving money prices or imputed shadow prices, repeated or infrequent decisions, large or minor decisions, emotional or mechanical ends . . . Support for the economic approach is provided by the extensive literature developed in the last twenty years that uses [it] . . . to analyze an almost endlessly varied set of problems, including the evolution of language, church attendance, capital punishment, the legal system, the extinction of animals and the incidence of suicide.[23]

Before considering some applications of rational choice to religion, it is useful to clarify what Becker means by 'the economic approach' so that the extent to which any of the following arguments truly rests on a distinctive approach can be assessed. For Becker, the economic approach to human behaviour rests on the assumption that people engage in maximizing behaviour. From that base, economists have produced a number of theorems that Becker lists, giving in each case 'non-economic' examples. A rise in prices reduces quantity demanded, and this is as true for the demand for children as it is for eggs. If the cultural expectations change so that parents are expected to spend more time and effort raising their children, then they will have fewer of them. A rise in price increases the quantity supplied and this applies as much to the participation of women in the labour market as to the amount of beef reaching the shops. Competitive markets satisfy consumer preferences more effectively than monopolistic markets, be it the market for aluminium or the market for ideas. A tax on the output of a market reduces that output, be it an excise tax on gasoline that reduces the use of gasoline, punishment of criminals (which is a 'tax' on crime) that reduces the amount of crime, or a tax on wages that reduces the labour supplied to the market sector.[24]

With the economic approach clear, we can consider some details of applications to religious behaviour. But first a common confusion should be removed. The economic explanation of religious behaviour that concerns me and the authors discussed is a general theory of action built on the concepts above. It should not be confused with the observation that many individuals in religious organizations (as elsewhere) are bothered about money and act in this or that way because of their financial concerns. It is quite possible for people to deal with money in irrational ways. The extent to which financial concerns are implicated in the behaviour of religious organizations has no necessary bearing on the value of Becker's extension of economic explanations, which is concerned with the logic of action and not its focus.

The rational choice theorists believe that the popularity of religion in the USA is a consequence of there being a free market in religion. Roger Finke argues that the overall consequence of the changes in the structure of religion in colonial America is this: 'Deregulating the market increases the level of religious mobilization'.[25] Much of his account is borrowed from the observations of Alexis de Toqueville, a Frenchman who travelled in America in the 1830s.[26] In his native France there was one church and religion was not popular. In America he found innumerable sects and a vibrant religious culture. He concluded that in each society the first characteristic explained the second. In France, monopoly caused indifference. In America, competition caused commitment. The basic contrast between old and new worlds was enthusiastically embraced by American social scientists keen to see their country as dynamic and modern and became part of the taken-for-granted self-image. In the late 1980s Finke, Stark, and other critics of the secularization approach dusted it off and updated the language with borrowings from Becker's imperialist economics.

The supply-side claim that religious belief and behaviour are determined by the structure of the religious market or environment intertwines at least four analytically separable variables: pluralism, market share, competition, and regulation. Although they have much in common, there are important differences in the implied models of action and in what would count as good tests.[27]

The *pluralism* proposition is that, the greater the number of religions on offer, the greater the variety and hence the greater the chance that any particular person will find something to his or her tastes.[28] Closely related to this, but not the same, is the claim that the officials of religious organizations with a very large *market share* will fail to respond to the religious needs of their actual or potential followers.[29] Monopolists get lazy. This is treated as if it was simply the inverse of *competition*, though it is clearly not. Some cases of small market share result from competition; the small Pentecostal sect in a world of Protestant sects would be an example. But others are found in the very different circumstance of near monopoly: Protestant churches in France, for example. We should expect a great deal of difference in the religious lives of people in such very different settings.

Competition is the motor that drives the supply-side model. Religious organizations, irrespective of market share, will work hard to attract and keep supporters if they have to compete. But competition is itself a consequence of the legal and political framework for the religious environment, so the supply-side model begins with *regulation*.[30] In most European countries, a single church was supported by the state (and reciprocated). Whether in Catholic, Lutheran, or Anglican models, the state church used state power to restrict competition and to subsidize itself.

In explaining why new sects succeeded in the USA. Finke describes deregulation as reducing 'start-up costs'. Although not initially addressed within the context of a comparison between the USA and Britain, it is clearly the vital point because there were as many seeds of dissent in eighteenth-century Britain as there were in early America (indeed the American sects were mostly imports from Britain). The major difference between the settings is the popularity of those dissenting movements. If one is determined to avoid the obvious explanation of why they did better in the USA than in Britain—that there was greater demand in the former—then low start-up costs offers a possible explanation. Because the USA had a free market in religion, new 'firms' were not put at a competitive disadvantage. Finke is, in effect, drawing on the general economic principle that the cheaper the product the more people will buy to explain a particular pattern of religious choice, but can we accept the applicability of the general proposition to this particular case?

The early Christian Church had very high start-up costs; Christians were persecuted and some were used as lion feed. The early English Quakers were persecuted but thrived. Of course it is anyone's guess how well English nonconformity would have done if the state had not tried to protect the Anglican Church, but we do know that the state's attempts to increase the cost of dissent by confining legal, political, social, and economic rights to adherents of the established church failed. Dissenters were jailed, had their property confiscated and their meeting houses closed, and were barred from public office, but dissent flourished. At this point of the argument it is enough to note that there appears to be no universal connection between costs and appeal.

The supply-siders assert that low start-up costs produce increased innovation. If it is easy to start new religions, more people will do it. The proliferation of religions in turn means that there will be some type of religion to suit everyone. The free market allows greater variety and greater variety ensures greater consumption.

A third plank of the free-market model concerns the ideological associations of religion. De Toqueville noted that 'the division of American Christianity into innumerable sects prevented any denomination from developing an alliance with the state and thereby protected the integrity of the faith'.[31] As I argued in the first chapter, when societies modernized, the ties of feudalism were relaxed and groups of people began to develop and articulate their own interests. Where they found the church on the side of the old order, they were likely to extend their political dissent into religious dissent. A state church firmly allied to the ruling class could not accommodate that; political dissent became hostility not just to the church but to religion in general. While this observation may hold for France, the example de Toqueville had in mind, its extension by Finke to Britain is implausible. While we can find many examples of Scottish and English congregations being alienated from their respective parish churches by their minister's toadying to the local gentry, we can also find many examples of them responding by forming their own religious organizations. Where Finke makes his mistake is in neglecting inherent features of churches in favour of market situation. The crucial difference between France and Britain was that in the latter the established churches were Protestant. Catholicism rests on a vision of the faith that places the Church at its centre. To defy the Catholic Church is to cease to be a Catholic. For all the mundane power enjoyed by the Church of England, it did not have the same theological defence. One could quite easily criticize a Protestant church and still remain a Protestant.[32]

A moderate version of this argument has always been part of the secularization approach. David Martin made the point that, unlike some other national churches, the Church of England failed to remain a 'popular' church.[33] However, given that dissent was always possible, and only periodically costly, the idea that unhappiness with the national provider of religious offices explains why England became secular is stretching the point too far. It would explain only why the disgruntled did not make their own provision if they were already rather uninterested in so doing. That is, it might make a difference at the margins but it cannot take the weight that the supply-side approach requires.

It is worth adding here that the possibly delegitimating links between a state church and an oppressive social order make a case only for *some* diversity being beneficial for religion. It does not follow that diversity will have a continuing positive association with religious vitality. As I will suggest below in considering the religious life of Aberdeen, we may conclude that a degree of fragmentation of the dominant culture is sometimes an advantage while still concluding that continued and ever-greater competition has debilitating effects, as described in Chapter 1.

Even if a monopoly church does not alienate a large part of its people by being too cosy with the upper classes, it will, according to the supply-siders, suffer from a wide variety of inefficiencies. These have been identified by Laurence Iannaccone, who has been crucial to the development of the rational choice approach. Stark has always been interested in a type of sociology that borrows economic metaphors, but Iannaccone, a free-market economist who studied with Gary Becker, does not use the language of economics metaphorically. Of state churches, Iannaccone says: 'One might expect state churches to cost more per practising member and to produce members with lower than average levels of religious knowledge and belief. One of the sources of higher costs is likely to be higher than normal wages for the state church's clergy and higher than normal required levels of seminary training.'[34] As with so many of the supply-side generalizations, this is only partly true. Again, what are largely features of the beliefs and history of particular religious traditions are mistaken for features of their market situation. Taking the points in reverse order, the length (and hence cost) of clerical training will have more to do with religious and class questions than with legal status. The importance given to the organization as the carrier of truth means that the Catholic Church has very long training periods (at least for its core clergy; the ordinary priest may require less knowledge). In some countries the Church has run boarding schools to start priestly training in the pre-teen years. In addition to wishing to instil a great deal of knowledge in its functionaries, it also wishes to ensure loyalty, especially from its geographic outposts. Hence the practice of drawing the brightest young ordinands from the provinces into Spain or Rome.

Whether a religion stresses knowledge of texts over experience is also germane. Scottish Presbyterians are typical of those brands of Protestantism that require detailed knowledge of scripture and insist that their clergy be trained in the biblical languages of Greek and Hebrew. Note that this is the case for the Presbyterian Church of Ireland (which is a dissenting church) and for the Presbyterian Church of Scotland (which is a state-established church). Likewise 'high' Islam requires lengthy training in Arabic, the Koran, the Law, and the Traditions. However, the Pentecostal variety of Protestantism and popular Islam place greater emphasis on the piety and spiritual experiences of the clergy and hence typically call for less formal training.

The nature and extent of clerical training also has much to do with the social class from which the clergy is drawn. At the extremes of high and low class, there is little training. When it was common for the younger sons of the nobility and the gentry to take holy orders in the Church of England, little formal instruction was given because little was thought necessary. The education of a gentlemen was considered sufficient. In the eighteenth century the sole test for admission to holy orders was a series of questions asked by the Bishop's chaplain, questions that any civilized and well-read Christian could have answered. It was only when the middle classes began to replace the lesser gentry that the Church of England established formal training programmes.

Likewise there seems to be no simple connection between establishment and overall wage levels. Prior to the reforms of the mid-nineteenth century,

English bishops lived like princes but many vicars and curates were extremely ill-paid. Furthermore, we find state-church regimes varying considerably in the mechanisms for determining the levels of taxation to be used to pay for religious offices. The established Church of Scotland in the eighteenth century was often in a parlous condition because it was funded by a tax on the property of 'heritors', who themselves made decisions about clerical salaries, church building, school building, and poor relief. Those heritors who had little sympathy for the Kirk and little sense of their own social and religious obligations kept assessments down and the cost of religious provision very low.

This raises a further query about the supposed deleterious effects of state funding. Later I will consider the assertion that public funding discourages the clergy from serving their parishioners well. Another possibility is a variant on the delegitimating case made above: as civil servants, the state clergy enjoy a standard of living conspicuously higher than most of their parishioners, who generalize their resentment into a dislike for religion. Again, that seems possible, but the case would have to be taken church by church. Certainly most clergy of the Church of Scotland were not much better off than their people.

A final complication: not all state-established churches are funded by the state. In Britain, the Church of Scotland and the Church of England retained their legal status but had their funding base significantly altered. Their rights to land taxes were commuted into capital sums and for most of the twentieth century they have been on the same financial footing as the dissenting denominations—reliant on a combination of contemporary donations and the income from invested capital.

Iannaccone's claim about average levels of religious knowledge is probably untestable. First, it is impossible to separate what people learnt in church from what they gained elsewhere. Secondly, there is the historically specific obstacle to comparison: religious monopolies tend to be characteristic of pre-modern societies, where illiteracy meant that levels of knowledge about everything (and not just religion) were low. However, we do know one thing that should make us cautious of accepting Iannaccone's claim. As Gallup has discovered, present-day Americans—the beneficiaries of a religious free market—are often woefully ignorant of the basic tenets of their faith. In contrast, Finns, subject to compulsory religious education, have proved themselves reasonably well informed about things they do not much believe. In a study in the early 1960s, 94 per cent could recite accurately the Lord's Prayer.[35]

Iannaccone may inadvertently have hit upon an important observation and then missed the point. It is certainly the case that levels of religious knowledge seem to have some connection with one particular kind of competition:

bitter conflict. In a world of consensus, especially where the religion gives high place to ritual rather than to belief, a great deal of knowledge is not required. A few simple phrases and actions will suffice for salvation. But in settings of considerable ethnic conflict (for example, in Liverpool or Belfast or Glasgow in the nineteenth century), one group of believers may feel obliged to learn more about why they are superior. Hence the popularity of Anti-Popery evening classes, in which students conned such publications as the *Hand-Book for the Study and Discussion of Popery with Special Reference to its Political Relations*.[36] However, this seems some way from the general claim and does not seem to fit well the modern US situation, where a plethora of organizations compete for members within a largely tolerant culture and by advertising peripheral virtues (such as the friendliness of the services) rather than by directly criticizing others for heresy.

To return to the general claim that monopolies are inefficient, the example of the Catholic Church offers an obvious problem. One would have thought that the Catholic Church, far more often a monopoly than any Protestant competitor, was a model of efficiency. By insisting on celibate clergy, it can maintain its staff with living expenses and pocket money. There are no families to provide for and (a considerable burden from the mid-twentieth century onwards) no expensive pension schemes to maintain. Catholic efficiency can be seen very clearly if we compare the ratio of church attenders to clergymen for various religious organizations. In Australia in 1996, whereas the Baptists, Presbyterians, and Churches of Christ had 74 attenders per cleric and the Anglicans 76, the Catholic Church had 349.[37] The work rate of Catholic clergy poses a problem for the general supply-side assumption that a direct link between earnings and popularity has a positive effect on the motives of the clergy. In times and places there have been rich priests, but by-and-large Catholic priests are, by the standards of the wider society, extremely poorly paid, if one can describe their method of remuneration as 'pay'. Yet this has not prevented them working extremely hard to serve the perceived needs of their people.

The Protestant requirement for democratic participation in services and accountability meant a national structure of local congregations. Thus, in the growing cities, Protestant national churches and the dissenting organizations tried to recreate the rural parish structure. In contrast, the Catholic Church often built one large central church and repeated its Masses as often as was necessary to accommodate the Catholics of the area. Thus, while Protestant organizations invariably offered more seats than they had participants, in large towns and cities the Catholic Church often had more participants than it had seats. It is hard to think of this as inefficiency. Again the point missed by the rational choice theorists is that the differences between the Catholic

Church and Protestant sects and denominations owe far more to theology and ecclesiology than to market situation.

Iannaccone talks much of the inefficiencies of monopolies but overlooks the manifest inefficiencies of competition. The most obvious is unnecessary duplication. As Robin Gill has persuasively argued, denominational rivalry in nineteenth-century Britain caused massive overprovision of places.[38] I will give just three illustrations of the 'efficiencies' created by competition. In Middleton-in-Teesdale in the north of England, in addition to the parish church there were two identical Methodist chapels a few hundred yards apart. The first had never been full, but a dispute in the congregation had led to half the families leaving and building an identical structure next to the building they had left. In south Edinburgh there is a crossroads known as 'Holy Corner' because five Protestant church buildings confront each other. None was ever remotely close to being full. The third example is the entire church, manse, and school building programme of the Free Church of Scotland in the second half of the nineteenth century. Instead of establishing themselves in areas of poor provision and thus completing the patchy national structure of the Kirk they had left, the Free Churchers targeted the same affluent middle-class section of the population or built close to the Kirk (and preferably both). The result was eighty years of expensive and pointless overprovision and, after the re-union of 1929, the closure of hundreds of church buildings.

The elaboration of the supply-side arguments is accompanied by the presentation of elaborate statistical data that are claimed to 'test' the predictions of the model, but, of course, the supply-siders select those indices of religious behaviour that best fit the propositions. The evidence will be considered in detail in the next two chapters. Here I will note that the general claim that religious participation increases with the freedom of the religious marketplace and the extent of diversity is confounded by the case of Roman Catholic cultures. Iannaccone admits that 'Protestant attendance rates are strongly related to market structure but Catholic attendance rates are largely independent of it'.[39] He tries to explain this anomaly by distinguishing between state-supported churches (the example is the Lutheran Churches of Scandinavia) and non-state monopolies (the Catholic case).

This is an important distinction and will be dealt with at length in Chapter 4, but it increases rather than reduces the damage done to the proposition by the Catholic case. Given that the final point of the supply-side model is to explain the religious behaviour of ordinary people, it would seem that those elements of the story that relate to the virtues of competition (low costs, wide choice, hungry clergy) are more germane than the sometimes formal features of state regulation. Of course, the two are intimately connected, but the only supposedly deleterious consequences of legal establishment that are not also encompassed in stories about competition are the taint of association with the state and the demotivating aspects of state funding. The first, of course, assumes that the regime is unpopular! The examples already given are the Catholic Church in France and the Church of England in the early nineteenth century. We might add the Catholic Church in most Latin American countries this century. We see something very different in the Scandinavian countries, where the state churches have become popularly associated with national identity and, in the second half of the twentieth century, with social democracy. The remarkable thing about the Scandinavian churches is how few people exercise their right not to pay church taxes. The Norwegians and the Swedes do not claim any great interest in religion and they are not great churchgoers, but they like their church enough to pay for it. Yet, although the Scandinavian countries have state churches, they also have greater diversity than Poland. That one of the major world religions thrives in circumstances where there is almost no market in religious ideas (though there are secularist attacks on the Catholic Church in France, Spain, Portugal, and Italy) calls into question the value of the model.

If, as rational choice theorists claim, free markets are associated with greater religious vitality because they better satisfy consumer demands, then it should be the case that, as a religious market becomes freer and as competition increases, so should the consumption of religious 'products'. As a preliminary to the next two chapters, it is enough to note that the ups and downs of the popularity of religion in Britain (and in other European societies) do not fit what we would expect if competition were the crucial variable. In the Middle Ages a single church dominated the entire society. While there were many pious people, the involvement of the laity was not much desired or expected. The church did religion on behalf of the entire people, who were expected to support it financially, not defy it, and cooperate in its glossing of major rights of passage. With increasing dissent from the national church and increasing competition, there was an increase in the extent to which some ordinary people were involved, but there were a corresponding and greater number falling away. Instead of a whole society being religious, there was a society composed of lots of religious people and a large number who were not terribly involved. To an extent this period does fit the 'competition leads to increased religion' model, if we take the modern Protestant view that religion is a question of individual knowledge and commitment.

But during the twentieth century there has been a dramatic decline in popular involvement in religion, and the free-market model does nothing to explain that. Competition has increased as eastern religions and new religious movements have been added to the cafeteria. Competition has become fairer as the state churches have lost the last of their privileges, but, instead of religious becoming more popular, it has become patently less so. Every index of religious interest or involvement continues to point sharply downwards.

Human Capital and Individual Decision-Making

Although the assumption that individuals engage in 'maximizing behaviour' is fundamental to the supply-side explanation of religious activity, some of the work in the rational choice camp concentrates specifically on the micro-economic level. In 'Religious Practice: A Human Capital Approach' Iannaccone turns to a variety of phenomena more closely related to individual religious decision-making. He claims that an economic approach can explain denominational mobility, the typical age of converts, the typical pattern of inter-religious marriage, and the levels of participation found in different sorts of marriages.[40]

The notion of 'investment' is used to explain why most Americans stay in the churches in which they were raised, return to that church if they have drifted away (as they typically do in early adulthood), and, if they move, ideologically travel only short distances. Typically, Southern Baptists stay Southern Baptists; if they change, it is to something very similar, such as the American Baptist Church. All of these patterns are explained, Iannaccone believes, by the fact that the person has already invested a certain amount of human capital (time and effort) in acquiring the beliefs of one tradition and mastering its liturgical or ritual procedures. To move a long way requires a lot of new investment and wastes previous effort. Hence there are not many Baptists becoming Catholics.

Here again we have the common phenomenon of a body of data fitting an alternative explanation every bit as well as its fits a human capital approach. We could suppose, as most sociologists of religion have done previously, that beliefs *sediment* so as to shape our receptivity to future alternatives. That you have held for some time a Baptist view of religion may not stop you ceasing to be religious, but will make it likely that, if you remain religious or wish to return to a supernatural faith at some later stage of your life, you will find most *plausible* beliefs that accord with the residues of the earlier stage of belief. Through considering what makes beliefs more and less plausible, we can understand the pattern demonstrated by Iannaccone perfectly well without recourse to the unlikely idea that people wish to maximize the return on their investment of human capital.

Iannacconne believes that data on the typical age at which people experience religious conversion also support his model:

The human capital model predicts that religious switching, like job changing, will tend to occur early in the life cycle as people search for the best match between their skills and the context in which they produce religious commodities. Across time, the gains from further switching will diminish as the potential improvement in matches diminishes and the remaining years in which to capitalize on that improvement decrease.[41]

Again, the presented data fit the 'prediction' but the prediction does not offer a severe test of the theory because the same data are readily compatible with a quite different explanation: that the plausibility of beliefs is a product of social interaction with other like-minded believers and the extent to which those beliefs produce a satisfactory understanding of the world and one's place in it. Both of these are likely to produce increased plausibility over time. Fifty-year-old Scottish Presbyterians do not become Moonies, not because they know they have few years left in which to recoup their new investment but because their long involvement with Presbyterianism makes them ill-disposed to believe Moon and his representatives.

Like so much of the rational choice approach, the human capital propositions sound plausible when told in abstractions and ridiculous when put into claims about specific people and actions. Iannaccone assumes that beliefs and liturgical practices are hard to learn. Perhaps the religious virtuoso who wishes to master the entire Shorter Catechism will be discouraged by the thought of the effort, but most Christian churches are similar and, as researching sociologists regularly prove, their rituals can very quickly be picked up by imitating the person in the pew in front.[42] Furthermore, Iannaccone regards learning as a cost, which misses the point that it can be viewed as an enjoyable challenge. After all, the main consumers of evening classes are the elderly and retired. Knowing that they do not have enough life left to become another Picasso or Constable does not prevent thousands of old people taking up painting.

The explanation of data on the effects of inter-religious marriages is even less persuasive. We know from a variety of sources that, where a couple belong to the same church or religious tradition, they are more likely than those in 'mixed' marriages to be regular church attenders, to give money to religious work, to raise their children in the faith, and so on. Iannaccone claims:

A household can produce religious commodities more efficiently when both husband and wife share the same religion. Single-faith households benefit from 'economies of scale': the same car drives everyone to church; there is no question as to how time and money contributions will be allocated to different religions; it is not necessary to debate the religion in which one's children will be reared.[43]

There is no doubt that conflict between spouses about religious beliefs and affiliation can be painful and hence no surprise in the data Iannaccone presents to show that people tend to marry within the same denomination. People can imagine the disputes and act to avoid them. But a much simpler explanation of the pattern is that churches provide an excellent venue for young people to meet others who are similar not only in religion but also in social class, culture, and ethnic background.

Better evidence for Iannaccone's model is data that show that shared-faith marriages have higher rates of church attendance than interdenominational marriages, but again nothing in this 'tests' or especially supports the claim that the pattern arises because 'partners of the same religion can produce religious commodities more efficiently'. There is an alternative that Iannaccone dismisses when he says that 'a shared faith should have only indirect effects on individual beliefs'.[44] Let us reintroduce the idea of strength of beliefs. An axiom of sociology is that reality is socially constructed, maintained, and changed. To add to one's own internalized beliefs a significant other who reinforces such beliefs will have a profound impact on the strength of one's faith and hence on the enthusiasm with which one participates in collective expressions of such beliefs. It would require book-length treatment to fill in all the gaps in the above argument, but I hope I have done enough to show that, contrary to Iannaccone's assertion, the sharing of a faith is very likely to have sufficient effect on the strength of belief to explain why the church involvement of same-faith marriages is higher than that of cross-faith marriages.

Furthermore, there is a problem with the direction of causality. Iannaccone's data do not establish which of (*a*) couples sharing the same faith, and (*b*) extensive religious involvement, comes first. For his human capital model to have any value it must be that (*a*) precedes (*b*), but the reverse is equally, if not more, likely. It is precisely those people who are most committed to their faith who will make a point of considering only fellow-believers as suitable marriage partners. It is the true believers who take seriously Paul's injunction 'Be ye not yoked with unbelievers' and who have a narrower view of what range of alternatives counts as 'true beliefs'.

Conclusion

To summarize, the rational choice approach challenges previous thinking on two points: the reality of secularization and the role of diversity. According to Stark and his associates, secularization is impossible because the human condition gives us a persistent need for compensators and only religion can provide compensators big enough to do the job. To the extent that we can identify times and places where the demand for supernatural compensators does not appear to be high, this is a result of the failure of the market to provide an appropriate range of alternatives, and of the officials of those providers to do their work with sufficient enthusiasm and a weather eye for the market. In this chapter some specific reservations have been offered. In the next two chapters I will consider in detail the religious life of a wide variety of societies and in Chapter 5 I will draw together my criticisms.

Pluralism and Religion: USA and Britain

HAVING outlined the rational choice approach and made some critical comments, I would now like to look closely at the evidence for it presented by its exponents. In this chapter I will consider what is known about the effects of diversity on religious vitality in the USA, Canada, Australia, and Britain. The focus of the next chapter will be the European situation.

The United States

The basic ideas of the supply-side approach were first introduced by de Toqueville in his observations about religion in colonial America.[1] Drawing a contrast with the rather moribund nature of the Catholic Church in his native France, de Toqueville noted an apparent connection between the number of competing Protestants sects and the vitality of religious life. However, those who have revived de Toqueville have failed to notice that his impression of variety was formed while *travelling* around the colonies. Considerable diversity at the national level was accompanied by considerable degrees of concentration in particular places. This is important, because elements of the supply-side story operate on different geographical and social planes. Diversity within the nation state may determine issues of state subsidy and regulation, but, unless it is repeated lower down, in the places where ordinary people live and purportedly engage in maximizing behaviour, then it can hardly increase the opportunity for individuals to 'maximize their utility'. What Gaustad's geography of religious affiliation in the USA shows is that many parts of America were remarkably homogenous. He uses the term 'domination' to refer to the situation where half or more of the people belonged to one religion: 'there were in 1950 amazingly few counties that were not dominated by one or another ecclesiastical bodies . . . in approximately one-half of the counties of the nation, a single religious body accounts for at least 50% of all the membership in the county.'[2] This unity was reinforced by the clus-

tering of similar counties: almost all of the many southern counties dominated by Baptists were bordered by other Baptist counties. Britain is often
the implied contrast, but even in 1851, the year of the Census of Religious
Worship, England and Wales looked remarkably like Gaustad's America. Just
over half the counties were dominated by one religious organization. It may
be that Gaustad underestimates the extent of variation and hence its importance, because he reports his results in ways that give equal weight to all geographical units and thus misses the point that Americans were increasingly
concentrated in towns and cities. But if we look at urban England and Wales,
where half the population lived, we find that in only a quarter of towns and
cities did half or more of those who worshipped on census day in 1851 do so
in an Anglican church. To put it no more strongly than this, the de Toqueville
contrast is rather superficial and ill-informed.

Better evidence for the link between pluralism and vitality was presented
by Finke and Stark when they used the 1906 US Census of Religious Bodies
to examine the relationship between church membership and religious
diversity in the 150 largest towns and cities of the USA.[3] The results were presented as strong evidence that competition in religion, as in car production,
increased rather than undermined consumption. However, as commentators
were quick to point out, their own statistics cast doubts on their claims. Taken
on its own, the link between diversity and vitality was very strongly negative.
The more diverse places had the lower rates of church membership. There was
a very strong link between the proportion of Catholics and church membership (but that may well have been because all baptized Catholics were counted
as 'members', an assumption that is often unwarranted). Finke and Stark
only managed to produce statistics that suited their argument by 'controlling'
for the percentage Catholic in their regression equations. The experts will
understand the problem of multi-collinearity.[4] The rest of us can simply
note that the procedures come close to cooking the books. When others tried
to replicate Finke and Stark's work, they failed. Land and colleagues analysed
county-level data for over 700 counties and for a subset of counties that
contained the 150 cities studied by Finke and Stark.[5] In both cases they
came to quite the opposite conclusion. For the large sample they found that
diversity was associated with low rates of church adherence, even when 'percentage Catholic' was figured into the regression equation. On the smaller
sample of just the counties containing the big cities, they found that the direct
effect of diversity was negative, until they entered the percentage Catholic into
the equation, when it became positive but only very weakly so. When they
added data from the 1920s and 1930s so that they could see the effects of diversity on church membership over time, they found that the negative effect
of diversity was even greater. Only for a small sample containing the big

cities could anything like the relationship posited by Finke and Stark be found and that was so weak as to be statistically insignificant. As the team put it: 'Our conclusion is that religious monopoly—not diversity—fuels religious expansion . . . [and] ethnic homogeneity is also conducive to religious expansion.'[6]

Breault applied the Finke and Stark model to 1980 data and found that religious diversity had a persistent, negative, and statistically significant effect on the rate of adherence. After exploring a number of other possible explanations, Breault concluded that the difference between his results and those of the supply-siders was simply that they had used a biased and limited sample and allowed their results to be distorted by the presence (and greater than average religious activity) of Irish and southern European Catholics.[7]

In subsequent exchanges, the supply-siders have tried to answer these criticisms but they have failed to satisfy other scholars that the statistical manipulation of the data that produced their confirming results was justified.[8]

Without such sleight of hand, studies of the relationship between pluralism and religious vitality in the USA have found either no connection or the negative effect I would expect.

Canada and Australia

According to the labels that people claim when completing the census forms, religious identification in Canada fell from 95 per cent in 1901 to 74 per cent in 1991. The proportion of Canadians who told social surveyors that they had attended church in the previous week fell from 67 per cent in 1946 to 30 per cent in 1996. Those declines in the indices of religious vitality occurred over a century when Canada was becoming culturally and religiously more diverse and when the state was removing itself from any part in the religious market.[9]

In a painstaking study of diversity and religious affiliation in Canada in the 1990s, Olson and Hadaway were unable to produce the results expected by Finke and Stark. To answer the supply-side case that others had failed to reproduce their results because they had used units of analysis (such as counties) that were too large, Olson and Hadaway studied census divisions and subdivisions. The 290 divisions were typically larger than a US county; the 56,313 subdivisions, with a median population of just 902 people, were somewhat smaller than the towns and places used by the supply-siders. For both sets of data, the relationship between diversity and religious adherence was strongly negative. Olson and Hadaway concluded: 'the high rates of North

American religious involvement persist in spite of, not because of, religious pluralism.'[10]

Iannaccone presented results from a study of eighteen west European countries and their colonial offshoots but, even after dropping Ireland from his sample (presumably because it fitted even less well than the countries that he kept in), he could find only weak and statistically insignificant relationships between diversity and indices of religious interest such as weekly church attendance and stated belief in God.[11] Again this study has been subjected to critical scrutiny and found seriously wanting. Chaves and Cann concluded that, if there was any variable that was related to religious vitality, it was not pluralism but state regulation and even that connection was very weak.[12]

Furthermore, detailed studies of some of the countries used by Iannaccone, based on more accurate information, signally failed to find the results predicted by the supply-siders. For example, Australia, which has very little state regulation and a high degree of religious diversity, has very low rates of church involvement.[13] More damaging to Iannaccone's case, if we look at Australian churchgoing over a long time period, we find quite the opposite of the supply-side prediction: as the state has responded to increased cultural pluralism by reducing its interference in religion, public interest in religion has declined.

Britain

The recent history of religion in Britain (and in this it resembles most west European countries) is a problem for the supply-siders; as the religious market has become more diverse and as the state has relaxed its grip, so the power, popularity, and presence of religion have declined. But a longer historical perspective creates even more difficulties for the rational choice approach. First, because there was then no flourishing free market in ideas, it must be the case that Europeans of the Middle Ages were not terribly religious. Secondly, because Stark and Bainbridge's functionalist theory of religion does not permit secularization, it must be the case that modern Europeans are *really* quite religious (or at least demonstrate a religious yearning). To sustain their critique of the secularization thesis, the supply-siders need a radical revision of British and European history.

Put briefly, most British social scientists, historians, and church leaders think that Britain is now not very religious and was once markedly more so. There are disagreements about the extent, timing, and causes of the changes implied in such comparative description. Some historians remind us that in places urbanization was accompanied by an *increase* in informed personal commitment to the churches.[14] Others draw attention to previously neglected causes of decline. Gill, for example, has challenged the Victorian notion that the churches were short of space to accommodate the growing population and makes a better case for the deleterious effects of overprovision. Unnecessary church-building, driven by denominational rivalry, saddled many religious organizations with crippling debts and ensured that churches would be half-empty, which in turn had a profoundly demoralizing effect on congregations and discouraged newcomers.[15] Others argue that, though formal religion has declined drastically, there is something else, often called 'implicit' religion, worthy of study.[16] None of these views is incompatible with the secularization thesis advanced here. But Stark and Iannaccone so thoroughly revise our views of the past and the present that they construct an image of Britain quite incompatible with the prevailing orthodoxy, which is, of course, their intention. Such iconclasm is, I will argue, misplaced.

The Pre-Modern Past

Stark and Iannaccone caricature the conventional wisdom about Europe in the Middle Ages when they say, sarcastically, that 'Everyone knows that religion has crumbled since medieval times when all Europe walked secure in faith and grace'.[17] We must recognize that, in comparing the past with the present, we are not comparing like with like.[18] The supply-side model distracts us from this crucial point, but any long-term account of religious change must encompass change of kind as well as of quantity. In pre-modern societies, religion was not a particularly personal matter. A professional clergy performed a calendrical diet of rituals for the benefit of the entire people and not just for a self-selecting group of members who took a strong personal interest in the rituals (although there were many such people). The spoken and sung offices were held to glorify God, even if few lay people attended or comprehended. Most churches had no seating for the congregation, and the offices were spoken in Latin, often by a priest with his back to the congregation. The notion that the church's professionals could glorify God independent of the laity's involvement seems foreign to our very individualistic culture. It rested on the implicit assumption that religious merit could be transferred from the religiously observant to those who were less so. Unless we accept an unusually narrow view of religion, one that would exclude most of the human experience of the phenomenon, this does not mean that our ancestors were not religious; it just means that most were not evangelical Protestants. They were certainly superstitious and most churchmen were happy to link their religion to the wider culture of superstition. Saints and their associated shrines were held to offer powerful remedies for ailments: 'In 1543, when a storm burst over Canterbury, the inhabitants ran to church for holy water to sprinkle on their houses so as to drive away the evil spirits in the air and to protect their property from lightening.'[19]

Though the records of church courts show widespread failure to live up to the high standards set by some clergy, historians are agreed that the common people had a decent grasp of what were then regarded as the fundamentals of the faith, viewed the world through Christian lenses, and generally conformed to the Church's requirements. Most knew by heart the Lord's Prayer, the Hail Mary, and could make the sign of the cross. They knew the Ten Commandments, the four cardinal virtues, the seven deadly sins, and the seven works of mercy. They paid their tithes, brought their babies for baptism, and married in church.[20] They believed sufficiently in hell, the power of the church, and the unique status of Holy Writ for the swearing of oaths on the Bible to be an effective means of social control. They avoided blaspheming. They spent considerable sums of money supporting large numbers of priests whose sole function was to say Mass for their benefactors. 'Most people seem to have accepted that it was necessary to make reparation to God for serious and wilful sins either in this life or in the next.'[21]

What is known of church attendance in the Middle Ages? We can certainly find examples of places where few people attended church and some clergy complained about irreverent behaviour from those who did attend, but my overall estimate is far from the one Stark and his colleagues present by citing only Thomas's most lurid examples of bad behaviour. Hamilton in his general review says

a quite high proportion of laymen in the later Middle Ages did consider that they should put in an appearance at mass on most Sundays. . . . [if] nobody communicated mass only lasted half-an-hour. Nevertheless laymen become bored and wanted to know how much of the mass they needed to attend. . . . The one part of the mass in which lay people wished to share was the Elevation of the Host. The congregation knelt in complete silence when handbells were rung.[22]

It is important to appreciate what is being said here. The laity of the Middle Ages thought it sufficiently important for their souls to stand in an unheated building where men spoke or sang words that they could not understand and, at the important point of the service, to fall silent and kneel. In their unseemly haste to latch on to Thomas's evidence of casual and inattentive behaviour in church, the supply-siders have missed the bigger point. In 1580 the ruffians were in church; in 1980 they were not.

Stark and Iannaccone poke fun at Peter Laslett for claiming that 'All our ancestors were literal Christian believers, all of the time',[23] but cite no authorities who reject his overall depiction of seventeenth-century England, which is worth quoting at length:

With only sixteen exceptions every person in the parish [Goodnestone] known by their priest to be qualified for the sacrament had actually taken it at some time during the festival . . . 128 people communicated out of a population of 281. Even the defaulters promised to make amends at Whitsuntide, all but the one family in the village which was nonconformist. . . . the priest-in-charge, was evidently a devoted pastor, for he could give an account of each individual absentee. Mrs Elizabeth Richards, the widowed head of one of the households of gentry, was excused as 'melancholy', and Barbara Pain as well since she was 'under a dismal calamity, the unnatural death of her husband'. . . . This rather exceptional record of communicants draws attention to a feature of the village community . . . which has scarcely been mentioned so far. All our ancestors were literal believers, all of the time. Their beliefs were not only religious, of course, since they believed in witchcraft, evil and benign, and gave credence to many propositions and practices condemned by theologians as heathen survivals. But it would be very difficult to maintain that such superstitions ever went to make up a religion which, as a religion, was a rival to Christianity, and the unreflective villager seems not to have noticed any inconsistency within the range of his beliefs and half-beliefs. Christianity had a grasp of their subjective life which it is difficult for us to imagine, accustomed as we are to the notion of a really convinced religious person as an individual of a particular kind, a convert, an enthusiast. This was not so in the pre-industrial past.
. . . Not everyone was equally devout, of course, and it would be simple-minded to suppose that none of these villagers ever had their doubts. Much of their devotion must have been formal and some of it mere conformity. But their world was a Christian world and their religious activity was spontaneous, not forced on them from above.[24]

There is no definitive way of closing this argument about the 'Age of Faith', but we can note that Stark and Iannaccone's case rests on a misunderstanding of Thomas and that the work of most British historians sits better with Hamilton's conclusions and with a judicious reading of Laslett or of Thomas himself. A reasonable summary is offered by David Martin (who, curiously, is often claimed by the supply-siders):

The difference [between pre-modern laxity and present-day indifference] is simply this: that what is possible and indeed quite frequent in pre-modern societies is probable and nearly universal in the modern situation. . . . a pre-modern society can be marked by hostility to religion and indifference, and a modern industrial society can be marked by high practice and a favourable appraisal of religion . . . but the reverse polar case is nevertheless much more frequent.[25]

The Modern Period

Crucial to Stark and Iannaccone's revision are their estimates of church membership: 11.5 per cent of the total population in 1800, 16.7 per cent in 1900, and 15.2 per cent for 1980. They conclude that these figures show no dramatic decline. Although the sources are not specified in detail, it seems the data come from Currie, Gilbert, and Horsley.[26] What is not made clear is that the 1800 figures were estimated by, among other techniques, working backwards from later figures for communicants per clergyman and that for the nonconformists the clergy totals were guesses. I have no better estimates and simply note that some specialists prefer to avoid the exercise altogether for this early period. The data improved after the Methodists popularized the practice of head-counting. So that sceptics may check my working out and because the variety of organizations is important for a later point about diversity, Table A3.1 in my Appendix includes enumerations for 1850 and 1900 based, not on the Currie, Gilbert and Horsley summary table, but on the detailed figures for each organization given in the appendix to their book. As almost all of the bodies listed record as members only adults, I have taken as the baseline, not the entire population, but the population aged 15 and over. This gives us figures of 18 per cent for 1800, 27 per cent for 1850, and 26 for 1900. Figures for 1990 are given in Table A3.2 of my Appendix. These show that church membership had fallen to 14 per cent. By the end of the century it was 12.5 per cent.[27] Near halving of church membership since 1850 is a pretty good initial reason for talking of secularization.

Brierley, who spent thirty years professionally compiling British religious statistics, offers 30 per cent of adult population as the total Christian membership in 1900 and 19 per cent for 1990. As he notes, this disguises the extent of decline because it counts all baptized Catholics as church members, irrespective of subsequent involvement. For the Protestant denominations—until recently the bulk of British Christianity—he offers a decline from 22 per cent of the population in 1900 to 7 per cent in 1990. Over the century, penetration fell by two-thirds. In the same period the Catholic population increased from 2 million to 5 million, but, of these latter, only a third attended Mass.[28]

Incidentally, it is no help to the supply-side model that church membership grew and then fell between the start and the finish of the period Stark and Iannaccone cover. That is important for the qualifications to the secularization approach offered by some historians, but it does not support Stark and Iannaccone's general claim that the secularity of modern Britain has been exaggerated.

Stark and Iannaccone inflate the impact of their membership figures by adding: 'the British may be far less inclined than are Americans and

Canadians to actually see to it that they are signed up as church members, since a far larger percentage of the British population claims to attend church with some frequency than are counted on church rolls.'[29] This is simply not the case. As already noted, Catholic figures flatter to deceive because they count everyone who has ever been baptized. The actual Mass attendances are far smaller, declining over the century from 47 to 33 per cent of the Catholic community. Similarly, the Anglican churches always had more people on the electoral rolls than attended. In the nonconformist denominations and sects there is a switch. It occurs at different points for different organizations but let us put it at 1900 and say that, during the period of growth and in a climate of religious seriousness that preceded that date, many non-members often attended. Thereafter many members failed to do so. A 1997 survey of twenty-two congregations of the Presbyterian Church in Wales showed that fewer than half of their recorded members attended on a particular Sunday in November. A major survey of English rural religion in the 1980s found that, of 150 people selected for interview from the Church of England's own rolls, 20 per cent said they never went to church![30]

There is actually no need to guess about church attendance in the nineteenth and twentieth centuries. Data based on church censuses have long been available and widely discussed.[31] There are technical problems in interpreting the 1851 Census of Religious Worship. Especially for Scotland, where the returns were less complete than for England and Wales, there are doubts about some of the original figures. The Census counted attendances rather than attenders; most people went more than once on a Sunday. In summarizing the figures, some scholars add morning, afternoon, and evening attendances. This leads to some people being counted more than once, but that could be justified on the grounds that the disappearance of multiple attendance is itself a mark of declining commitment and one to which we should attend. Others take only the figures for the best-attended service, whichever that was for any particular congregation. That has the disadvantage of missing out those who went only to the less popular services. There is also the issue of whether one follows Horace Mann and leaves in Sunday school scholars. These problems explain why one gets varied reports, even from the same commentator. For example, in one place Brown estimates 'attendances at church to represent 60.7 per cent of Scottish population and 58.1 per cent of English and Welsh population'[31] and in another says that the Scottish figure 'was in the region of 30–35 per cent'.[32]

The quality of the information in the 1851 Census is such that there cannot be a definite resolution, but, in an extremely sophisticated and painstaking examination of a wide variety of competing assumptions, Crockett concludes: 'one can estimate that between 61.5 % and 65.1% of the "potential congregation" attended worship on census Sunday.'[34] Even allowing for the effects of the original numbers having been rounded up, he estimates that the best assumption lies between 57 and 61 per cent.

Gill has brought together an impressive array of local and church-based surveys. In rural Northumberland, Anglican attendances 'reached their peak in 1866 and decline thereafter'. Roman Catholic attendances peaked earlier: 'Their combined Easter Mass attendances were 234 in 1849, 480 in 1855, but had declined to 297 in 1861, to 187 in 1892, and to just 109 in 1899.' Gill's own 1980s census of the remaining twenty-nine buildings in use (out of a total of forty-five in 1901) found that only 9 per cent of the total population attended morning services.[35] The timing may have been slightly different for urban areas, but the general trajectory is the same: 'Free Church attendances overall have declined since the 1880s. In Greater London they declined from 13 per cent in 1887, to 11 per cent in 1903, and to 4 per cent in 1979.'[36]

Based on mass survey information, Stark and Iannaccone offer the figure of 24 per cent for at least monthly church attendance and 14 per cent for weekly attendance for the 1980s. Gerard concurs: 'no more than one person in seven attends church weekly.'[37] Conducted a decade later, the 1991 British Social Attitudes (BSA) survey gives slightly lower figures for church attendance: the data for 1991 and four earlier runs of the same survey are presented in Table 3.1.[38]

Remember that these survey data represent *assertions* about behaviour rather than direct evidence of it. Motivated by the difficulty in reconciling what Americans say about their church attendance with what the churches know, Hadaway, Marler, and Chaves compared clergy-generated and survey-based data and concluded that, for the county of Ohio they studied, the survey method exaggerated attendance by 80 per cent.[39] Based on responses from the clergy, Brierley's 1989 English Church Census put the attendance on a typical Sunday at 10 per cent. Of course, as with any other source of information, we need to consider the likelihood of error, but the relevant point here is that, while social researchers have often doubted clergy estimates on the grounds that they might exaggerate, no one has suggested that they would systematically underestimate their congregations.

One important measure of interest in religion has rarely figured in these debates and that is the number of full-time clergy. Given that funding regimes vary from time to time and place to place, we cannot infer directly the popularity of religion from the number of religious officials, but again the likely variation runs in the direction that strengthens rather than weakens the inference I wish to draw. All the British churches were able to use the interest from capital acquired during more popular and affluent times to support a staff greater than that which could have been employed on current donations.

TABLE 3.1. *Church attendance, Britain, 1983–1991* (%)

Frequency of attendance	1983	1985	1987	1989	1991
No religion	31	34	34	5	5
Once a week plus	13	11	12	13	11
Once in 2 weeks	3	2	2	3	2
Once a month	6	6	6	5	6
Twice a year	10	11	12	12	13
Once a year	6	6	5	6	7
Less often	6	6	4	6	4
Never	24	23	24	48	49
Varies	1	0	0	1	1
Refused to answer	—	—	—	0	0
Not answered	1	1	0	1	3

Notes: Until 1989 the church-attendance question was not asked of those who had earlier said that they had 'no religion'. From then it was asked of those in that class who had been brought up in a religion. Hence the shift of a large number of respondents from 'no religion' to 'never'.

Source: BSA surveys.

Hence the actual fall in popularity should be greater, not less, than that indicated by the following figures. Between 1900 and 1984, when the population increased by 35 per cent and became considerably more affluent, the Anglican clergy halved, from just over 20,000 to just over 10,000. In the largest dissenting body—the Methodists—there was some growth from 1900 to 1950—from 3,800 to 4,700—and then a rapid decline, so that in 1999 there are only some 2,500 ministers. In 1900 there were about 3,600 ministers in the various Scottish Presbyterian Churches; in 1990 no more than 1,450. As with the Church of England, the number of religious professionals halved in a period when the total population increased; in this case, from 4.5 to over 5 million. And the shrinkage was as great in the voluntary as in the state churches.

Popular Beliefs

Vital to the supply-side case is evidence that, despite lack of involvement in formal religion, the British remain religious. Stark and Iannaccone report that 74 per cent of Britons believe in God and only 4 per cent are atheists. The 1991 BSA survey data are presented in Table 3.2. Some awkwardness results from a single question trying to tap both the substance and constancy of belief. It is indeed the case that 75 per cent claim to believe in God but only 59 per

TABLE 3.2. *Belief in God, Britain, 1991* (%)

I don't believe in God	10
I don't know whether there is a God and I don't believe there is any way to find out	14
I don't believe in a personal God but I do believe in a higher power of some kind	13
I find myself believing in God some of the time but not at others	13
While I have doubts, I feel that I do believe in God	26
I know God really exists and I have no doubts about it	23
Don't know/no answer	2

Source: 1991 BSA survey.

cent claim consistent belief in a Christian divinity; 13 per cent dither and the same proportion prefer the vague 'higher-power' formulation. The same survey asked again about God in a question about change in beliefs. This time only 52 per cent claimed to believe in God and twice as many had ceased to believe as had come to believe.

We can get another perspective on what we hope is the same phenomenon from various surveys that ask a more direct question about the nature of God. Those data for various years are reported in Table 3.3. They show that by 1987 the 'higher-power' formulation was actually more popular than the conventional Christian view. This finding has been repeated in a major survey of the Nordic countries.[40] The 1991 BSA survey asked how close people felt to God: 'not close at all', 'not very close', 'somewhat close', or 'extremely close'. Only half of those who believed in God felt 'somewhat' or 'extremely' close to God and almost a quarter of these theists felt 'not close at all'. Finally, Stark and Iannaccone offer a 'claimed atheist' figure for Britain of only 4 per cent; the 1991 BSA figure is 10 per cent.

A further claimed sign of enduring religiosity is the number of respondents who describe themselves as 'religious'. Stark and Iannaccone say that 56 per cent of Britons do so. The BSA survey offered seven options: 'extremely', 'very', and 'somewhat religious', 'neither', and the same three options for 'non-religious'. Only 41 per cent of the BSA sample claim any of the three religious labels and almost all of those chose the weakest. Together, the neutral and the non-religious easily outnumber the religious. Had such a survey been conducted in 1900, 1850, or 1800, would that have been the result?

Stark and Iannaccone cite survey data on specific supernaturalist beliefs as evidence of enduring religiosity. Two points should be made. First, in all cases the 1991 BSA figures are markedly lower than their figures: for example, rather than the 54 per cent whom they claim believe in life after death, the 1991

TABLE 3.3. *What is God?, Britain, 1947, 1957, and 1987* (%)

	1947	1957	1987
There is a personal God	45	41	37
There is some sort of spirit or vital force which controls life	39	37	42
I am not sure that there is any sort of God or life force	16	—	—
I don't know what to think	—	16	—
Don't really think there is any sort of spirit/god or life force	—	6	—
Other/neither/don't know	—	—	21

Sources: George H. Gallup Jr., *The Gallup International Public Opinion Polls; Great Britain 1937–1975* (New York: Random House, 1976); Michael Svennevig, Ian Haldane, Sharon Speirs, and Barrie Gunter, *Godwatching: Viewers, Religion and Television* (London: John Libbey/ Independent Broadcasting Authority, 1989).

survey gives only 27 per cent. Secondly, and this is vital, where we have a series of results, the pattern is clearly one of *decline*. Gill, Hadaway, and Marler have painstakingly collected together all the available survey data from the 1930s to the 1990s.[41] They conclude that that there has been a marked decline in traditional religious beliefs (and particularly those with a clear Judaeo-Christian connection), a persistence or slight increase in 'New Age' beliefs, and a general increase in disbelief in both areas. Though some supernaturalist beliefs remain more popular than active involvement in the institutions that promote them, this can hardly be claimed as evidence of a stable and enduring latent demand for religion, because they too are in decline. But most importantly, even if we take at face value the survey reports that a quarter of modern Britons say they believe in the devil and hell, can we really suppose this is comparable to the omnipresent pre-modern fear of the Devil and other evil spirits described by Thomas?

Religion and Social Ceremonies

In the Middle Ages almost all babies were baptized. The ritual was thought sufficiently important for midwives to be taught a simple formula so that sickly babies would not be deprived of the essential ritual for want of a priest. Even at the start of the twentieth century, baptism was nearly universal. By the end of the century only 50 per cent of live births were baptized.[42]

At the start of the twentieth century, almost 70 per cent of English couples marrying did so in the established church and almost all the rest were married with a religious ceremony. By 1995 less than half the weddings in England and Wales took place in a religious building.[43] In Scotland in 1876, 99 per cent of weddings were solemnized in churches; in 1990, it was only 57 per cent. The same changes can be viewed from the other end. In 1971 40 per cent of marriages in Great Britain were civil rather than religious and that had increased to 47 per cent by 1990.[44]

In looking for evidence of religious sentiment beyond the churches we might consider the popularity of religious broadcasting. In 1968 40 per cent of respondents deliberately turned on to watch a religious programme and over half said they paid attention when a religious programme was on. 'By 1987, this was found to have changed, with only seven per cent of people saying they deliberately turned on when a religious programme was being shown.'[45]

Let me summarize the case for a secular Britain. The social, political, and economic changes that combined with the ideological consequences of the Reformation to create the modern world produced a profound change in the nature of religion that (with all the attendant dangers of over-simplification) we can conceptualize as a shift from religion as state and community matter to religion as individual commitment. At the same time, as many people became better informed about their faith and more personally involved in the churches, the influence of Christian doctrines and presumptions declined, as did the presence of the supernatural in the material world. A Christian society was replaced by a society with some highly committed Christians. In turn, personal involvement in formal religion declined. What makes the case for secularization compelling is the failure of *any* index of religious involvement or sentiment to show growth. Alone no one of the above indices would be terribly significant, but taken together they show a very clear picture. Whether we take the size, influence, or popularity of the churches, the willingness of survey respondents to claim Christian beliefs or to describe themselves as religious, or the use of religious offices for rights of passage, whenever we can measure such things the measures point downwards.

Pluralism, Supply, and Demand

So far I have challenged the supply-side depiction of the past and the present. I now want to challenge that account of what happened in between. The new perspective on Britain reverses the temporal and causal sequence of the interaction of increasing cultural diversity and state toleration. As they must do in order to maintain that supply takes precedence over demand, the supply-siders assert that religious pluralism is a consequence of the state giving up attempts to regulate the market. Desacralization precedes 'the rise of a vigorous religious pluralism'.[46] This is straightforwardly wrong for Britain (and for Australia, New Zealand, and Canada).

An important point that is overlooked by the supply-siders is that the UK was a multinational state that supported four separate (and at times very different) state churches: one each for England, Scotland, Wales, and Ireland. The initial impulse of the seventeenth and eighteenth centuries was to try to homogenize religion throughout the 'united' kingdom. At times episcopacy was forced on the Presbyterians of Scotland and the north-east of Ireland. For one brief period in the 1640s, Presbyterianism was even imposed on the church in England. Thereafter an awkward fudge was arranged that allowed the monarch to be the head of the Episcopal Church of England while in England and then mysteriously become the head of the Presbyterian Church when visiting Scotland. Furthermore, after failing to reform the church supported by the native Irish, the state tried to reach an accommodation that involved funding the Catholic seminary in Maynooth.

From the time of the Reformation there was an impressive array of alternatives within British religion and, if one remembers Ireland, a huge division. First, as the eminent historian of British religion, Obelkevitch, notes: 'while the established churches in Britain were comparable to those in Europe, there was also, as in America, an array of competing independent denominations.'[47] By the eighteenth century, England had a wide range of Independents and Baptists and the Quakers were flourishing. As can be seen from Table A3.1 in the Appendix, in the nineteenth century the Methodists made considerable inroads into Anglican support. Scotland in 1806 had *seven* nationally distributed alternatives to the state church, not including Roman Catholicism. Gill's meticulous reanalysis of the 1851 Census and other data show that there were many parts of England and Wales where attendances were 'predominantly Free Church attendances'.[48] The diversity shown by the 1851 Census compares well with that of the USA, especially when one recalls that, because it came from linguistic and ethnic duplication, much of the American diversity was more apparent than real.

Superficially there were considerable penalties on nonconformity. 'By contemporary standards, however, Britain enjoyed a large measure of religious freedom. Minority churches were neither suppressed nor expelled, as still sometimes happened on the continent, and enforcement of the law was often lax.'[50] The penal laws were inconsistently applied and could be evaded by occasional conformity: attending communion once a year was usually sufficient. Some dissenters regularly conformed. As one Lincolnshire peasant put it to his curate: 'We come to the church in the morning to please you, sir, and goes to the chapel at night to save our souls.'[50] When sanctions were strictly applied, as they were to Quakers at various times in the eighteenth century, they only encouraged dissent! When a landowner denied the people of Strontian land to erect a Free Church building in 1843, they had a floating church built in a Clyde shipyard, sailed it into Loch Sunart, and worshipped tantalizingly beyond their laird's control.[51] This sort of popular activism challenges the rather pathetic view of the laity assumed by the supply-siders when they suppose that there must be changes in the structure of the market to affect the supply before latent demand can become active participation. The history of dissent in Britain is littered with examples of ordinary people organizing their own formal shared expressions of that faith. Where they have wanted to, the laity have created their own supply.

As an aside, it is worth adding a small but significant note about the way in which the supply-siders measure diversity.[52] By treating the Church of England, for example, as a single homogenous unit, they overlook the considerable degree of internal variation that characterized most 'national' churches. As I will argue below in the case of Scottish Presbyterianism, formal schisms and re-unions, which in the supply-side counting method are represented as major changes, may have been no such thing if they were merely official recognition of slow and subtle changes that had already had their effect on the ground. Either side of the big changes, there were varying degrees of diversity within the major organizations. There was also considerable overlap: Jones rightly says of the apparently competing Welsh nonconformist groups of the Victorian era: 'what they had in common was more important than what they disagreed about.'[53]

To summarize, from at least the late eighteenth century Britain had a flourishing market in religion and the voluntary sector and the state sector rose and fell together. One cannot explain the supposed contrast between American vitality and British irreligion by saying that the British lacked alternatives to the state churches.

Furthermore, the history of British churches shows that clerics of the state churches were quite capable of rising above the demotivating aspects of their state-supported status and working vigorously to become popular. The Church of England of 1800 may have been complacent and slothful. Revitalized by the evangelical revival and the High-Church movements, the Church of 1880 was anything but. Obelkevitch on south Lindsay, Yeo on Reading, Cox on Lambeth, and Green on west Yorkshire furnish many examples of a committed cadre of professional clergy working hard to win the support of their parishioners.[54] Primarily what had changed was not state support for religion but its class associations, and those had changed because diversity had weakened the power of the church just as economic modernization had weakened the power of the gentry. At the start of the nineteenth century in many Church of England parishes, 'the incumbent was often a relative of the squire or his wife, or was a man specially selected for the congenial nature of his religious and political views, and perhaps for his interest in sport'.[55] By the end of the century such a parson was a rarity and a figure of fun.

One good measure of the lack of interest in affairs spiritual that the supply-siders impute to the clergy of a state church is absenteeism. It was common in the eighteenth century for Anglican clergy to hold a number of lucrative benefices and to serve in only one (or none) of them. A small part of the income was used to hire curates to perform the religious offices. The ending of this practice would look like good evidence for the benefits of competition, except for the fact that it had started to decline long before the 1851 Census dramatically demonstrated the gains that had been made by Methodism. Absenteeism fell from nearly half of all beneficed clergy to under a sixth between 1810 and 1850, and it did so largely because Anglican clergy were themselves being influenced by the same social and cultural trends as pro-duced the rise of Methodism.[56] The evangelical and Tractarian movements in the Church of England were not self-interested changes promoted to spite the increasingly confident dissenters. They were autonomous spiritual responses to the decline of the old agrarian community and the increasingly individu-alistic and voluntaristic nature of society. Although some leaders in the An-glican Church attempted to use the state to defend its privileges, many saw that the Church had to adapt to the new world and promoted internal reforms that were independent of the state.

To summarize, Stark and Iannaccone believe that, as demand is pretty much constant, changes in religious behaviour must be explained by changes in supply. The behaviour of providers—the firms—and even the existence of firms is determined by state regulation of the market. Hence 'desacraliza-tion' at state level is a precondition for the emergence of invigorating pluralism. In privileging stories about supply over those of demand, the supply-siders posit a causal sequence at odds with what happened in Britain. There we see increasing social complexity causing the dominant religious culture to fragment, which in turn forced the state to become more even-handed in its treatment of the churches. British governments did not remove the privileges of the state churches because they thought toleration a good idea. Diversity forced the state to accept that such important national issues as social control, social welfare, and education could be addressed only by secular institutions.

It is regrettable but understandable that the supply-siders should know nothing of the history of religion in Britain. It is more curious that they do not notice that the history of colonial America offers no support for the posited relationship between regulation and pluralism. A number of British colonies had established churches and even those colonies established by

dissenters could be extremely intolerant. Oliver Cromwell, no liberal himself, was openly critical of the New England Puritans.[57] The Puritans of the
Massachusetts Bay Company wanted freedom for their own programme but
were loath to extend it to anyone else. Of the thirteen small 'nations' that made
up the 'many' out of which the 'one' of the United States was supposed to
come, nine had established churches. It was because each faced significant
dissent within its own boundaries and because, taken together, they were not
the *same* church—that is, because there was religious diversity—that the
founding fathers drafted a constitution that thought religion a good thing but
did not support any particular form.[58]

The British colonies in Australia, New Zealand, and Canada followed
similar routes to state indifference. Initially the Episcopalian Church was given
a privileged position in the Australian colonies, but this became hard to defend
when it was supported by only a minority. The New South Wales Church Act
of 1836 added the Catholic, Presbyterian, and Methodist churches to those
supported by the state, but this experiment in plural establishments was soon
abandoned and in 1862 the colonies moved to the US model. The historical
record is quite clear. State regulation was abandoned because the state had
become religiously diverse.[59]

Diversity and Vitality in 1851

In addition to trying to argue that the people of Middle Ages were no more
religious than those of the late twentieth century, the supply-siders have
applied their talents to the 1851 Census of Religious Worship. Before I discuss
their findings, and at the risk of losing the reader who has little interest in statistical procedures, I would like to make two related observations about the
measure of religious diversity used by the supply-siders. We could just take
the relative size of the largest religious provider in an area as an index of the
extent of choice. If everyone is a Catholic, then there is no 'option' other than
Catholicism on offer. If half the population are Catholics, then there is a 50:
50 chance that people will be something else. In preference to that rather crude
measure, the supply-siders use the Herfindahl Index, developed by linguists
and economists to describe the extent to which a market is concentrated or
diverse. Because its effects are crucial to understanding why scholars can come
to such different conclusions about the same real world, it is worth explaining how the Index operates. The statistic is $[1 - 1(a/z)^2 + (b/z)^2 + (c/z)^2 \ldots]$
where z is the total number of churchgoers and a, b, c, etc. are the numbers
in any particular organization. The closer the number is to 1, the greater the
degree of diversity. The important point about this method of describing
diversity is that it gives greater weight to popular choices than to unpopular

ones. For example, if a town has five equally large denominations, it will score 0.8. But if it has one large denomination to which half the people belong, three that each have 10 per cent, and four others that each have 5 per cent of the population, it will score only 0.61. That is, the second city will be described as less diverse than the first, even though it has on offer a wider range of choices. In that sense it does not so much describe the possibilities for choosing as the effects of choices having been made.

This way of measuring diversity could be defended as being superior to simply counting variants if we supposed that very small religious organizations might be unknown or hard to find and hence less readily available to be chosen than larger competitors. However, in the cases of towns and cities, this seems an unnecessary compromise of the basic idea of options for choice. Distance would not have been a problem and many very small religions advertised widely (or were advertised widely through being demonized by their critics). A better reason for preferring the Herfindahl Index over a straight count of alternatives would be that we supposed people more likely to choose churches that were already popular than unpopular ones. But this goes against the spirit of the supply-side case in two respects. First, it introduces 'non-rational' elements of choice and brings the supposedly radical theory back towards the common sociological ground. Secondly, it contradicts one of the substantive claims of the rational choice model in implying that bigger is more attractive.

Crockett has identified a further problem with the Index: it is scale specific.[60] This is actually a simple difficulty. Imagine a town made up of five parishes. In each parish there is a Church of England outlet and two dissenting sects. Each parish will score 0.667 on the diversity index. If the dissenting sects are not the same in each parish (for example, in one parish there may be Baptists and Quakers; in another Wesleyan Methodists and Primitive Methodists) and we take the town as the unit of analysis, we get the markedly different diversity score of 0.8. Thus the impression one gets of religious pluralism depends on the size of the unit you use to describe the society. To illustrate the point Crockett calculated the Herfindahl score for his sample of parishes as 0.6. When he used the same places but took the much larger registration districts as the unit of analysis, he got an average score of 0.66. Simply changing the scale of the analysis increased the apparent diversity by 10 per cent. And, given the weak relationships that have been found in most of the studies that have used the Herfindahl Index (when any at all are found), such variation is quite enough to produce entirely different conclusions.

For all my doubts about the validity of the Herfindahl Index, I used it to compute a measure of diversity and applied it to the church attendance figures in the 1851 Census. My conclusion was the opposite of that predicted by the supply-side model: diversity was negatively associated with church attendance, as was the extent of urbanization and the percentage Catholic.[61]

Stark, Finke, and Iannaccone replied with their own analysis of the 1851 data. After much vitriolic criticism of my crude statistical methods, they were forced to conclude that evidence of the supply-side relationship also alluded them: 'Bruce is correct in his claim that the cities and towns of England and Wales do not reveal the predicted positive impact of diversity on religious participation.'[62]

Having failed to make their case from England and Wales, the supply-siders take Wales on its own and offer three justifications for preferring it as a test case. First, the registration districts were smaller. This is not true. The mean size of the 576 English registration districts was 226 square kilometres; the mean size of the Welsh districts was 442 square kilometres.[63] Secondly, there were fewer of those troublesome Roman Catholics. This is true. Thirdly, 'Wales would seem to be less diverse in terms of class and cultural differences.'[64] That depends on what they mean by class and cultural differences. The gulf between rural north Wales and industrial south Wales was as great as between Tyneside and rural Northumberland. Far from being a more culturally homogenous place, outside Liverpool and other north-west areas of England where the Irish conflict was replayed in a minor key, Wales was the one part of England and Wales where religious affiliation was a politically charged issue. 'By the middle of the nineteenth century the majority of the Welsh people were members of the Protestant nonconformist churches or at least associated with these Churches. Consequently there was a growing feeling that the established Anglican Church in Wales was enjoying privileges that its minority position could not justify.'[65] The dissenting denominations were the main repository of the Welsh-language, which was otherwise given no official recognition. The four main Welsh-language publications of the period were all edited by nonconformist clergymen. One of them, William Rees, the editor of *Yr Amserau*, was so active in support of the European nationalist revolutions of the 1840s that in 1848 a Hungarian nationalist deputation visited him to thank him on behalf of the Hungarian nationalist Louis Kossuth for his support. M. D. Jones entered the ministry of the Congregational Church in 1850. Five years later he succeeded his father as Principal of Bala Theological College. Throughout a long and distinguished career he combined the roles of Christian teacher and leader of Welsh nationalism and he was a staunch advocate of the disestablishment of the Anglican Church (which finally occurred in 1920). He would have been astonished to read that Wales was less culturally divided than England.

As a final note, we might observe that the disestablishment of the Anglican

Church, the main change in the regime of state regulation in Wales, came almost 100 years *after* the growth of the nonconformists had radically changed the degree of religious diversity. It was a response to, rather than, as the supply-siders would have it, a cause of, pluralism.

In common with others (such as Marxists) who believe that they have a theory of everything, Stark and his associates always respond to damaging evidence, not by questioning the value of their fundamental ideas, but by adding a further 'proposition' to their already convoluted theory. Their failure to find what they wanted in the 1851 Census material caused them to add a coda that is worth quoting at length because, though it is presented as merely fine-tuning, it actually concedes entirely the point that I and many other critics had made: 'Assume a society having a rigid caste system of a dozen castes . . . The Herfindahl Index for such a society would indicate an extra-ordinary level of pluralism . . . Yet, because it is impossible for any person in this society to shift religious affiliation, since eligibility is entirely limited at birth, there is no religious competition whatsoever. . . .'[66] Correct. It is soci-ologically unrealistic to suppose that individuals make 'rational choices' solely on the basis of their personal estimations of where their greatest return lies. People often make choices (and in many cases there is little or no choosing in it) on the basis of national, ethnic, and social identities into which they have been socialized.

A further concession has been made by Finke, who argues that Catholics do not benefit from diversity because they already have a great deal of 'inter-nal' diversity. In many US cities there were a variety of parishes with very dif-ferent ethnic identities. 'The local parish appealed to a specific immigrant group or social class, and the diversity of parishes appealed to a broad spec-trum of the population.'[67] Again, quite so. But such qualifications fundament-ally undermine the rational choice approach, which its advocates advertise as universally applicable.

Many of the technical weaknesses of my attempts to test the supply-side argument with the 1851 Census and the supply-side reply have been ably addressed by Crockett, who computerized the data from the entire Census at registration-district level and for a large sample of parishes from fifteen registration districts. In addition, he constructed a large amount of socio-economic data for the parish samples, including such information as population density, annual population growth, household size, main type of occupation, and the like. His investigations go far beyond my concerns here. It is enough to note that, using far better information than I or the supply-siders did, and with far greater statistical sophistication, Crockett concludes: 'it is very difficult to argue that there is a strong and consistent relationship between religious diversity and religious practice. The two vari-ables were never particularly closely associated.'[68] Many of the findings, most especially that there was a long-term impact of religious pluralism upon the rate of religious practice, 'contradict the . . . rational choice theorization of religion'.[69]

What Crockett found was that the lowest rates of church attendance were at the extremes of population density: for 'highly urban' and 'urban' districts but also for 'remote rural' areas. The high rates of attendance were found for the mixed districts that were part urban and part rural and for the 'rural' ones. The impact of diversity, such as it was, was similar. There was a weak positive link with attendance in rural, mixed, and urban areas, but they were negatively related in highly urban and highly rural areas. Gilbert's explanation, offered before computers allowed such sophisticated tests, concentrated on the stability of communities and the power of the landlord interest:

Not only did the pastoral agriculture and domestic industry of 'highland' regions encourage more diffuse settlement patterns than were normal in arable farming areas, but the relative weakness of the landed interest in such regions, and in mining and quarrying districts, reduced both the influence of the clergy and the basis of their financial support.[70]

This is important, because it recognizes the complexity of the links between community and social behaviour. It recognizes the one plausible element of the supply-side approach. People can attend churches only if there are some, and remoteness constrains the ability of people, not only to take advantage of the national church, but also to make their own provision. But Gilbert sensibly avoids extending this into a general explanation of religious behaviour in all settings.

To return to Wales, arguing over whether diverse or homogenous parishes had higher levels of church membership or attendance is nit-picking in the context of the changes that have occurred in Wales since 1851. Jones says of mid-Victorian Wales that 'maybe half of the population attended places of worship'.[71] Brierley estimates the churchgoing population in 1995 as just under 9 per cent.[72] That collapse of popular support has been mirrored in the change in culture. Jones could say of nineteenth-century Wales:

It was religion that provided the intellectual, spiritual and moral framework for the lives of the vast majority of persons, and the prevalence of superstition, or belief in magic and omens, and the readiness of townsfolk as well as country people to resort to witches and 'wise-men' co-existed, so far as ordinary people were concerned, with the truths of revealed religion and the high status accorded to ministers of religion.[73]

No one would now claim that the lives of the majority of the people are much influenced by witches, wise-men, or revealed religion. Since 1900 the number of clergy has halved, which hardly suggests their high status has been maintained.

To summarize, the history of religion in Britain offers little or no support for the supply-side thesis. Contrary to the causal sequence that Stark and his associates derive from their general stress on the structure of the market, a relaxation of state regulation and the removal of state subsidy did not precede the flourishing of diversity. It followed it and was caused by it. Despite the considerable degree of pluralism, religious vitality declined in Britain.

Religion and Diversity in Aberdeen

Many of tests of the supply-side model suffer from being too remote from their subject matter. Social scientists who know very little about the religious life of the times and places they wish to comprehend take statistics of varying validity, feed them into a computer program, and then massage them until they produce some sort of pattern. They have usually had no role in the initial data collection or compilation and do not even observe closely the workings of their statistical analyses. The published tables for the 1851 Census are already three removes from the reality they purport to describe (the reporter, the census enumerator, and the compiler). Had the supply-siders been involved enough to read those tables closely and calculate the Herfindahl Index by hand, they would have noticed that their favoured measuring device describes diversity in a rather strange way. But in most such studies, an assistant types in the numbers and regression equations drop out of the printer, patterns are discovered, and from those implausible tales are told. At best this is looking at the world through opaque glass; more often it is staring at a blank wall and allowing the mind to create patterns.

Even if we could be confident that the statistical descriptions used by the supply-siders were reliable, we could still reasonably object that most of the studies described above do not form terribly good tests of the approach because they are not dynamic. Showing that, in the same year, places that differ in religious diversity also differ in religious vitality is interesting, but the claim that deregulation of the religious economy creates diversity that in turn creates religious vitality is better tested by studying one place over many years. In this section I will consider how well the changes in the religious life of Aberdeen in the nineteenth and twentieth centuries fit the supply-side model.

To make sense of the details we need a rough grasp of the history of Christianity in modern Scotland.[74] The people of the Lowlands, who were most influenced by England and northern Europe, embraced the Reformation. Formally the national church, became Protestant, but large parts of the Highlands (Gaelic-speaking in culture, feudal in social organization, primitive in subsistence farming) remained unreformed. Periodically, monarchs made anxious by the radical potential of church democracy tried to impose episcopacy on the Scottish church, but mostly it was Presbyterian in structure and Calvinist in theology. At the start of the eighteenth century, Scotland had a national Presbyterian Church, a large Roman Catholic remnant in the Highlands, and a small body of Episcopalians left from those periods when the whole church was forced into the English mould. There was also, in the south-west of Scotland, a radical Protestant block of 'Covenanters' who refused to accept the national church.

The Covenanters were not in any sense liberal. They were Calvinists who wholeheartedly endorsed the idea of the state imposing the true faith on the people; their only objection to the Kirk was that it was not the true faith. The second major schism from the national church was also far from liberal. Through the eighteenth century there were a number of disputes about the degree of congregational autonomy. To simplify, the parish-church structure was financially supported by a tax on landowners: 'patrons' in England and 'heritors' in Scotland. The Presbyterian system allows no distinction between minister and elders. The minister was one of the elders and the elders were chosen by the congregation. However, in 1712, Queen Anne's Patronage Act restored to the major landowners, who paid most of the tax, the right to select the minister. Many heritors used this power wisely and consulted their congregations. But disputes were bound to arise because there were emerging class differences in religion. Evangelicalism was popular with the strata that furnished the influential men in many congregations, but the major landowners were not known for their personal piety.

In 1733 Ebenezer and Ralph Erskine and two others ministers seceded from the Kirk over the imposition of unpopular ministers. Generally, the Seceders recruited 'the responsible and the convinced while the parish churches drew the poor and dependent'.[75] Within nine years there were twenty Seceder ministers; within thirteen years, forty. Like the Covenanters, they wanted state-imposed religion so long as it was their religion.

The first serious challenge to the national church from the liberal wing came in 1751 with the expulsion of Thomas Gillespie for refusing to take part in the intrusion of a minister against the congregation's wishes. He may have been singled out for punishment because he had been less than constant in his support for the Kirk. While studying for the ministry he had defected to the Seceders. After ten days of instruction with them, he left for England, where he studied at Dr Doddridge's famous nonconformist academy in Northampton and was ordained by the English Independents. Curiously, when he returned to Scotland he was accepted into the ministry of the Kirk. When that relationship ended for the second time, Gillespie did not return to the Seceders because, although he supported their evangelical theology, he could not accept the Calvinist notion of a state church. He had become a 'voluntary'. The Relief Presbytery that formed around him grew, but less quickly than the Seceders.

As the Secession expanded it also divided along two dimensions. The decline of feudalism, the growth of a class of independent farmers, and the rise of towns and cities were contributing to a climate of increasing personal autonomy. In that climate it was inevitable that people who were enjoying a degree of independence in their work lives would begin to question the propriety of imposing religious conformity. There was also a theological dimension: a liberal 'new licht' movement was challenging 'auld licht' orthodoxy. In 1747 the Seceders split into Burgher and Anti-Burgher wings over the Burgess Oath, a statement of loyalty required of inhabitants of burghs of a certain social and legal standing. In 1799 the Burghers split into Auld and New Licht wings; in 1806 the Anti-Burghers followed suit. In 1820 the two liberal groups merged as the United Secession. Nineteen years later, the Auld Licht Burghers rejoined the Kirk. The delightfully named Auld Licht Anti-Burghers stayed separate until 1852, when most joined the Free Church and a few thousand continued as the Original Secession Church. A further tidying-up resulted from the liberal Relief Presbytery joining the United Seceders to form the (optimistically entitled) United Presbyterians.

One reason for listing these fractures and re-unions is to repeat the two important points made in the earlier discussion of religion in England that are difficult to reconcile with the supply-side model. First, from the second half of the eighteenth century there was considerable religious dissent and diversity in Scotland. Secondly, far from following the relaxation of state control of the religious market, the fragmentation of the Scottish Church was a direct result of unhappiness with specific aspects of that control.

Patronage and state interference in the Kirk were the cause of the largest split. In 1843, after decades of argument with liberals and moderates, the evangelicals—about half the elders and a third of the ministers—left the Church of Scotland. As with the Covenanters, the Free Church was in favour of state-supported religion but wanted the church rather than the heritors or parliament to determine what that religion should be.

So, by the time of the Census of Religious Worship of 1851, the religious situation in the north-east of Scotland could be described as follows. Most people were Presbyterians and Presbyterianism was divided into three. The Kirk was the established church, the Free Church wanted to be the established church, and the United Presbyterians wanted an end to establishment. There were also small numbers of Catholics, Episcopalians, Covenanters, and Original Seceders. In addition to these locally produced variants, there were also branches of Protestant movements that had begun in England: Quakers, Unitarians, Independents, Methodists, Adventists, Brethren, and Pentecostalists all made their appearance in Aberdeen. However, none had any great impact, which reinforces an observation made earlier: there seems a limit to how much diversity is required to satisfy local demand. There are a number of well-rehearsed arguments within Christianity and hence a small number of common lines of fragmentation: religious freedom versus state imposition; congregational autonomy versus centralized structure; ethical versus liturgical religion; a learned and trained ministry versus a spiritually adept lay ministry; the relative weight of the Holy Spirit; and adult versus infant baptisms. With the exception of Pentecostalism's 'gifts of the spirit', Scottish Presbyterianism provided variants of all these positions and hence left little space to be colonized by the organizations that were produced in England in arguments over the same issues. While there is some merit in the notion that a range of religions will better serve the spiritual needs of a diverse population than a single tradition, there is a point beyond which adding new varieties adds nothing to the practical choice.[76]

The centre of the fertile farmlands of the north-east and a major seaport, Aberdeen is the third largest city in Scotland. In 1851 it contained around 72,000 people. By 1950 it had grown to 183,000 and by the end of the twentieth century there were over 200,000 inhabitants. Making generalizations from any one case is always precarious, but there seems nothing about Aberdeen that should exempt it from the social processes identified by the rational choice theorists. Indeed, it is probably an exemplary site to test the supply-side claims, because, unlike Glasgow, Edinburgh, or Dundee, Aberdeen saw very little inward migration, except from its own immediate hinterland, until the oil boom of the 1970s. Changes in degrees of diversity were largely the result of schisms and unions within a single people with a common religion. This removes from the equation the role of religion as guarantor of ethnic identity and allows us to see more clearly the impact of diversity.

The citizens of Aberdeen have never been short of religious options. In 1797 there were at least eleven competing organizations. By 1851 this had grown to at least fifteen and in 1991 there were at least forty-one. How did religious vitality vary over the same period? Unfortunately for the rational choice approach, in so far as it can be measured by church attendance or church membership, it declined drastically.

In 1851, the first measurement point after the great Disruption, membership stood at 45 per cent of the adult population (see Table A3.4 in the Appendix). It rose quickly to 60 per cent in 1871, fell back to 51 per cent in 1891 and varied between 49 and 54 per cent until 1961, when it began a thirty-year precipitous decline. The picture for church attendance is very different (see

Table A3.5). In 1851 about 60 per cent of Aberdeen adults attended church. By 1878 that had fallen to 37 per cent and by the end of the nineteenth century it was around 30 per cent. We do not have good data for the first three-quarters of the twentieth century so we cannot be sure of the trajectory of decline, but the figures for 1980, 1984, and 1995 were respectively 13, 12, and 11 per cent of the adult population, which puts Aberdeen firmly within the range of typical British cities and reminds us of how implausible is the claim that British secularization is a sociological myth.[77]

Although we may contest the accuracy of any particular set of figures for any particular year, we need not doubt the overall pattern of change, which is ably documented in any number of local histories and biographies of Aberdeen church leaders and given ample concrete illustration in the large number of churches that have been converted into flats, warehouses, or night clubs, or simply demolished.

How is the decline of religious vitality related to diversity? Clearly, over the period as a whole, it is very strongly and negatively correlated—exactly the opposite of what the free-market model would require. If we group the Brethren assemblies into two 'organizations'—Open and Exclusive—there were fifteen options in 1851. This rose slowly and steadily to twenty-one in the first quarter of the twentieth century, to twenty-five in 1951, and by 1991 had reached forty. Thus we see a considerable increase in the number of available options (very few of which would exclude any ethnic or linguistic group) and considerable decline in religious vitality.

If we describe pluralism by the Herfindahl Index and correlate it with either church membership or church attendance, we see a very strong, and strongly negative, relationship.[78] As I have severe reservations about its value, and as its proponents could argue that the Herfindahl Index is not terribly useful for describing very limited changes within what is overwhelmingly a religious monoculture, I am quite happy to leave that aside and explain what happened in Aberdeen with words and specific organizational histories.

As noted, church membership and church attendance varied largely independently of each other and represent different expressions of religious interest or commitment. While church attendance appears to have changed in only one direction (downwards), membership first rose, stayed on a plateau for almost half a century, and then fell sharply. Over the period, the relationship between membership and attendance switched. In the early nineteenth century, full members were a subset of those who regularly attended a church. By polarizing Presbyterians, the Disruption gave a new importance to membership. In the twentieth century the increasingly democratic tone of the wider society was reflected in a more participatory style of religious organization. This combined with the decline in evangelical fervour in Scottish Presbyterianism to create a much more inclusive attitude to formal membership. It was more easily asked for and granted. Membership became the less rigorous of the two ways of describing church involvement. For the mainstream churches, regular attenders became a subset of members.

The explanation for the very low church-membership levels at the start of the period is simple and does owe something to a supply-side account. Aberdeen was unusual in the success of the 1843 Disruption. All fifteen parish ministers and most of their elders walked out of the Kirk and the Free Church began with an impressive membership that then failed to expand in line with population growth. While the adult population increased by 87 per cent between 1851 and 1891, the Free Church grew by just 42 per cent. Having lost all its ministers and almost all of its buildings, the Kirk had to rebuild from scratch, and over the same period it grew from around 5,000 to around 23,000 members, an expansion of 360 per cent, well ahead of population growth. Obviously at the point where its organization was in ruins, the Kirk had difficulty 'supplying' its members. Counting them, collating the figures, and passing them to the Presbytery and to the General Assembly were not the highest priority. At least some of the growth that followed the rebuilding of the Kirk's organization in Aberdeen was simply a matter of improved record-keeping and data collection. Of course, there was also real growth. As the Free Church gloated over its success, those who remained loyal to the national Church felt a new impetus to show their affiliation by not only attending but also joining formally. At least for the Kirk, competition did not lead to innovation or a more acute attention to meeting the needs of supporters. Thus it could not have brought in people who had previously been outside the churches because there was not a product well suited to them. What competition did do was to strengthen the commitment of existing supporters to the preferred brand of Presbyterianism.

As this distance we cannot be sure of the reasons for the Free Church's failure to grow beyond its founding numbers, but historians such as MacLaren suggest two reasons.[79] First, the Disruption had been long in coming. For at least two years before the split, it had been heatedly debated, and, by the General Assembly of 1843, anyone who felt an attraction to the evangelical cause had been recruited. Unlike the Erskine secession, which started small and then won people to its cause, the Disruption was a well-prepared and advertised event that left no penumbra of potential recruits for future growth.

Once it was the master of its own destiny, the Free Church developed in such a way as to limit its appeal. In Aberdeen the split had a class basis. The Kirk kept the top and the bottom: the rich businessmen, landowners, and their workforces. The Evangelicals who came out at the Disruption were likely to be lower middle class. As the newly autonomous congregations built their new churches, they expressed their upward social mobility by shifting to the better parts of town.

It was self-evident that the more wealthy members a church could attract the better would be its financial position and its resultant status in the country. It was early realization of this simple fact which undoubtedly played a large part in influencing the choice of building sites for both Greyfriars and Trinity Free churches. Both of these congregations deserted what were primarily working-class parishes and built their churches with fifty yards of one another in fashionable Crown Street.[80]

All three of the Presbyterian churches charged pew rents and all had to press members for funds, but to build quickly a national structure of churches, manses, and schools that could rival that of the Kirk put enormous strain on Free Church congregations and the constant pressure to be generous doubtless put off many potential members. The Free Church's attempt to impose its moral values on the working class also alienated many. By the middle of the nineteenth century, the fragmentation of Presbyterianism had largely destroyed the ability of kirk sessions to maintain social control. Unless they were so poor as to need its charity, those who found criticism of their behaviour onerous could simply walk away from any particular church. Despite the obvious death of Presbyterian discipline, the Free Church congregations of Aberdeen insisted on aggressive enquiries into the morals of their poorer members (the better-off either had better morals or immunity from inspection). As one of the offices for which marginal adherents would come to church was baptism, kirk sessions could expend their civilizing zeal on badgering the poor about their 'ante-nuptial fornication'. Not surprisingly, the objects of such attention found the easier or less intrusive morals of the Kirk more congenial.[81]

As can be seen from Table A3.6, from its foundation to its 1900 merger with the United Presbyterians the Free Church grew only slightly (about 8 per cent per decade) and well behind the general population. Between that merger and its re-union with the Church of Scotland in 1929, the dissenting wing of Presbyterianism grew by between 13 and 15 per cent per decade, again well behind the general population. After its initial growth in the decades from the Disruption to 1881, the Kirk also fell behind the city's expansion. Despite the re-union of 1929, the trend for the first half of the twentieth century was remarkably stable, between 7 and 5 per cent growth per decade. For the decades ending 1951 and 1961, the Kirk added only 5 and 2 per cent and thereafter it experienced a net decline of 17, 10, and 18 per cent for the decades ending 1971, 1981, and 1991.

We can now revise some of the claims of the supply-side model and see how well the Aberdeen case fits them.

First, as can be seen from Table A3.4, the popularity of the non-Presbyterian options changed hardly at all throughout the 150 years of our survey. However we are to explain the decline of popular interest in religion, it cannot be because the market was inadequately supplied with a variety of options. If Aberdonians stopped consuming one sort of religious product because it no longer satisfied them, they had many other outlets for their religious potential. They could have gone elsewhere; they did not.

Secondly, the only growth that exceeded (or came close to matching) the expansion of the city was in the established Church of Scotland and not in the dissenting and more sectarian organizations that should, according to supply-side predictions, have been the main beneficiaries of competition. The difficulty in critically evaluating the supply-side model is that its plethora of propositions allow any outcome to fit. More will be said about this in Chapter 5, but the rational choice theorists are fond of the general notion that, the more people pay for something, the more they will value it. Possibly so, but MacLaren is sure that the Free Church's high financial demands discouraged many potential members. Those demands resulted from the desire to compete with the Kirk in the provision of not just churches but manses and schools and theology colleges and teacher training colleges—a duplication that became entirely redundant just eighty years later. We might conclude that here competition damaged the cause of religion by unnecessarily inflating the costs of provision. However, the supply-siders could argue that, had there not been a state-supported national Kirk, the Free Church would not have expended so much money and energy on duplication. But then, if everything fits the rational choice model, it explains nothing.

Thirdly, the idea that religious behaviour is strongly related to market structure gains no support from the Aberdeen's trends in church membership and church attendance, which were remarkably stable despite the structure of Presbyterianism changing abruptly twice. Prior to the 1900 merger, the United Presbyterian membership hardly changed. Over the thirty years of its existence the United Free Church growth fluctuated only two percentage points. In the five decades from 1901 to 1951, the Kirk's growth rate also varied by only two percentage points.

This stability further defies supply-side expectations, because it endured during a time when both the status and the financial structure of the Church of Scotland were radically altered. The growth of dissent and the fracture of the Disruption led to the Church of Scotland losing almost all of the privileges associated with being the national church. The re-union of Presbyterianism was possible because the two dissenting strands gradually ceased to be sectarian and the establishment ceased to be, in the sociological sense, a church. All three converged as denominations. In 1874 patronage was ended.

In 1921 parliament formally gave up its right to control the Kirk. In 1925 the tax obligations that had supported the Kirk were commuted into one-off capital sums and the Kirk was set on a par with the United Free Church, depending on a combination of income from investments and current giving. Yet, as the religious market become more free and the competition between the various providers more fair, church membership and church attendance declined.

Fifthly, the finally reunited Kirk's cultural hegemony and social power declined with its membership. By the last quarter of the twentieth century thousands of Aberdonians were, by lack of any other attachment, free to join new religious movements (or older sects such as the Mormons, the Seventh Day Adventists, or the Witnesses). The Kirk could no longer effectively stigmatize such apostasy. But very few people took advantage of their new freedom to choose.

In all this attempt to find evidence that changes in supply materially affected the popularity of religion in Aberdeen (and failing to do so), I have made almost no mention of those changes that have extremely strong links to church involvement: industrialization, population growth, the rise of egalitarian democracy, the increase in personal autonomy, and a rise in prosperity. The statistical connections are so strong that I do not need to labour the point by detailing the correlation co-efficients.[82] We may wish to argue about the relative causal weight of the modernizing factors historians have conventionally associated with secularization, but there is nothing in the Aberdeen example to lead us to abandon that approach in favour of the supply-side theory.

Conclusion

In this chapter a very large amount of evidence about changing patterns of church involvement has been examined for evidence to support the rational choice approach. Very little has been found. It is clear from the tone of their writing that Stark, Finke, and Iannaccone relish their status as iconoclastic revisionists. It is clear from the evidence I have presented here that, dull as it may be to say so, with regard to the Anglo-Saxon world, the old orthodoxy was by and large right.

4

Pluralism and Religion: Europe

THE previous chapter considered the application of the supply-side model to religion in Britain and its former colonies: the USA, Canada, and Australia. I would now like to consider the very different societies of continental Europe: de Toqueville's old world of Catholic, Lutheran, and Orthodox churches. What light, if any, does the rational choice approach shed on the recent history of religion in Europe?

As we can see from Table 4.1, church-attendance rates vary considerably across Europe. As always the data vary considerably in quality but if, for the time being, we take them as broadly reliable, what explains the relative placings? The Nordic countries are at the foot of the table and there is a preponderance of Catholic states at the top, but then France, Belgium, and Czechoslovakia are in the bottom half. A sensible starting point is to note simply that the countries of continental Europe have very varied histories and their religious cultures are hardly likely to be comprehended with one or two simple principles.[1] In order to get some analytical purchase, I will group the cases along the conventional lines suggested by historians and political scientists and hope that some degree of systematic contrast within and between clusters will allow patterns to become visible.

As a very broad starting point we could say that European religion falls into two patterns: some societies have largely given up religion while others are fighting with and about it. Where the history of nation-building has left a stable and increasingly prosperous democratic nation state, then interest in religion has declined and it has done so whether the nation is religiously diverse (Great Britain), religiously homogenous (Scandinavia, Belgium, or France), or religiously 'pillarized' (Holland). Of the five settings mentioned, Britain has the greatest diversity, but it also has the first and most secular culture. Nor does the nature of the religious tradition, taken alone, have much effect. In the bottom half of the table we can find Catholic France (which did its fighting over religion in the eighteenth century) and Belgium and the Lutheran Nordic states. The situation in France has been summarized as follows: 'All the criteria measuring the degree of attachment to institutional

Pluralism and Religion: Europe

TABLE 4.1. *Church attendance, Europe, 1990–1993* (%)

Country	Attend church 'at least monthly'
Ireland	88
Poland	85
Northern Ireland	69
Italy	51
Austria	44
Switzerland	43
Portugal	41
Spain	39
Slovenia	35
Hungary	34
West Germany	34
Romania	31
Belgium	31
Holland	30
Great Britain	24
Czechoslovakia	21
East Germany	20
France	17
Norway	13
Finland	11
Denmark	11
Sweden	10
Latvia	9
Iceland	9
Bulgaria	9

Source: Ronald Inglehart, Miguel Basanez, and Alejandro Moreno, *Human Values and Beliefs: A Cross-Cultural Sourcebook* (Ann Arbor: University of Michigan Press, 1998).

Catholicism show decreasing figures, whether it be baptisms, catechism classes, professions of faith, religious weddings, attendance at religious services, or even belonging to the Catholic Church.[2] In Catholic Belgium regular church attendance fell by half between 1967 and 1990: from 43 per cent to 18 per cent. The demand for a religious gloss to rites of passage remains higher than the demand for regular worship, but it too shows marked decline. As one might expect, the demand for church funerals has changed least (from 84 to 81 per cent), for church weddings most (from 86 to 59 per cent), and the demand for baptisms falls between the two (from 94 to 75 per cent).[3] In Holland, the proportion of the population that belongs to no church has risen steadily since the end of the Second World War. In 1958 it was just under a quarter. By 1975 it was 42 per cent, and in 1992 it was 57 per cent.[4] Of those who do claim a church affiliation, fewer attended. In 1975 71 per cent of Catholics and 50 per cent of Dutch Reformed members attended at least once a fortnight; in 1991 the figures were respectively 36 and 43 per cent. In common with other west European countries, there is a considerable generational difference. For those over 51, the unchurched proportion rose from 23 to 41 per cent, but the corresponding figures for adults under 30 changed from 20 to 72 per cent. Unless there is an unprecedented religious revival among that cohort as it ages, the Dutch churches will shortly collapse.[5]

According to the supply-side model, the decline of the dominant traditions should be followed by a wave of religious innovation. More latent demand will be unmet. The former orthodoxy will lose its power to stigmatize new religions as threateningly deviant. So start-up costs will be lower. So new religious providers will enter the market to meet the untapped demand and religious vitality will increase. This has not happened in the stable societies of western Europe. Stark and Bainbridge claimed that the more secular countries of northern Europe had an unusually high rate of cults. Indeed, they went so far as to claim that new religious movements were more popular in the 1980s in Britain (with 3.2 such groups per million population) than in the USA (2.3 per million).[6] On closer inspection, it turned out that this counter-intuitive finding was produced by counting, not members, but the number of offices or bases set up by new religions. As most movements with any ambition set up a missionary outpost in every major capital city, this way of measuring distribution grossly exaggerates the popularity of new religions in small countries and deflates it for large countries.[7]

But there is another Europe. In places, nation-building has been incomplete. The state is unstable and its sovereignty is questioned. Ethnic and national groups compete within or across borders. In those sorts of settings, where it has played a major role in preserving communal identities, religion has remained vibrant. Ireland and Poland remained two of the most actively religious parts of Europe because, until the struggles for national liberation succeeded (fully in the case of Poland; only partly in the Irish case), the Catholic Church served as one of the main repositories of national identity.

The rest of this chapter will examine the fate of religion in first the stable democracies of the Nordic countries and then in the countries of the former Soviet Union and the Moscow Pact and consider the relative influence on it of religious market structure and ethnic conflict.

Nordic Religion

Denmark, Norway, Sweden, and Finland can be grouped together as Protestant nations that differ importantly from England and Scotland in having state
churches that were the product of the Lutheran strand of the Reformation
rather than the more radical Calvinist wing.[8]

As Norway was a Danish colony, we should begin with Denmark. From
1536 to 1849, the Evangelical Lutheran Church was the state church because
it was the church of the royal family. When the power of the monarchy was
revised with the democratic constitution of 1849, the status of the Lutheran
Church was subtly altered by being rested now on the people. As part of that
extension of democracy, people were permitted to withdraw from the Church
and, more importantly, they were allowed to form their own societies within
the Church. The result was an extremely broad national church that, unlike
the Church of England, managed to accommodate the two big revivalist
movements of the nineteenth century: the Grundtvigians and the Home Missions. At the end of the twentieth century only the head of the Danish state
is required to belong to the folk Church, but 90 per cent of the population
still remains in membership.

From 1523 to 1814 Norway was a Danish colony. It was then granted home
rule and joined in a union with its neighbour Sweden, which lasted until 1905.
With the exception of the Sami and the Kven in the far north, who formed
about 1 per cent of the population, Norway was ethnically homogenous. It
was also very poor until the mid-nineteenth century. Since then its success
in extracting for export raw materials (first trees and now oil) and in high-
technology engineering has made it one of the richest countries in the world.
Like Denmark, nineteenth-century Norway experienced a number of pietistic revivals. In clear echoes of John Wesley, the Reverend Lars Levi Laestadius
attracted a large following for his preaching against wealth, self-indulgence
(particularly, alcohol abuse), and the spiritual decay of the clergy. Also like the
Danish case, the Norwegian Lutheran Church managed to accommodate the
Laestadians.[9]

As part of the reform of relationships within the Danish empire, and
between people and sovereign, the position of the state church was relaxed.
Hans Nielsen Hauge (1771–1824), the founder of an evangelical revival movement, was prosecuted under the Conventicles Edict, which allowed the
Lutheran Church to control religious gatherings. The Norwegian parliament
unanimously abrogated the Edict in 1836, on the plea of the Haugeans but
also with support from the 'true believers', a pro-Lutheran movement with
strong anticlerical sentiment. The government vetoed the bill twice, but the
constitution meant that any bill passed three times became law. As in Scot-

land and England, initial moves to liberality were timid. Many of those who supported the repeal of the Conventicles Edict did not support the wider-ranging Dissenters Bill of 1845; they were willing to liberate tendencies within Lutheranism but not to extend religious liberty to other Christian groups. Even the Dissenters Bill put awkward limits on religious freedom. Only those over the age of 19 were permitted to leave the state church, which resulted in a number of Baptists in the 1880s being fined or jailed for recruiting under-age Lutherans. Five years after the 1875 formation of the evangelical Free Church had significantly extended religious diversity, there was a further relaxation when the list of those who had to be members of the state church was shortened to the King, the Royal Council, judges, theology professors, teachers, and senior civil servants. Finally, in 1964 the constitution was revised to guarantee 'all inhabitants of the realm free exercise of religion'—a provision almost identical to one that had been proposed in 1814, in the very brief period when Norway was free from Denmark and not yet linked to Sweden.

Changes in Sweden and in Finland, which from the Middle Ages until 1809 was a Swedish colony and then became a Grand Duchy of Russia until independence in 1917, were similar. Lutheranism was the state religion because it was the religion of the throne. With the rise of democracy this was recast as the religion of the 'folk' and the requirements gradually eased. In 1860 the Swedes were allowed to leave the Lutheran National Church but only to join another Christian body. In 1951 this final obstacle was removed and Swedes were permitted the freedom to have no religion.

Until the end of the nineteenth century all Finns were required to belong to either the Lutheran Church or the much smaller Orthodox Church. The Nonconformity Act of 1889 gave official status to a number of Protestant organizations (the Baptists and Methodists were the first to benefit) and permitted Finns to leave the state churches for those bodies. When Finland gained its independence from Russia after the First World War, as part of its formalization as an autonomous democracy, it permitted citizens complete freedom to belong to any religious organization or none.

As one would expect of a national church that was closer to the Catholic than the Anglican models, the late nineteenth century saw some elements of the organic split found in Catholic societies. The Lutheran clergy attacked the labour movements and nascent social democracy parties as anti-Christian and many industrial workers became openly anticlerical. However, unlike the case in Spain or Italy, where the parties of the left enjoyed only a brief period of power before being overthrown by fascist movements, the Nordic left-of-centre parties were fortunate to preside over a period of rapidly growing wealth, and were thus able to lay the foundations for welfare states and a social democratic consensus that the national churches came to endorse.

The Nordic countries remained far more homogenous than the USA (because they had very little inward migration) and than Britain (because they industrialized far later). None the less there was a variety of revival movements and schisms. These were smaller and less hostile to the folk churches than was the case in Britain and were more easily accommodated within the national churches. They still created pressure for relaxation of state regulation and this occurred, slowly and haltingly. Internal pressures for relaxation were given additional weight in the constitutional discussions of the last part of the nineteenth century by the fact that the idea of religious liberty was becoming widely established as part of what it meant to be a modern country.

What has happened to popular religious participation over the twentieth century? The available data are summarized in Tables A4.1–A4.5 in the Appendix. In Finland, the proportion of members taking communion once a year fell from 55 per cent in 1912 to 20 per cent in 1962,[10] and has since halved again. The measure might be different but the trend is the same; in Sweden average Mass attendance fell from 17 per cent at the start of the century to 2.7 per cent in 1965, and remained at that level for the rest of the century.[11] In Finland 'participation in Sunday worship services has been steadily falling over recent decades. Between 1980 and 1985 the number of attendances fell by more than a quarter.'[12] Fewer than 3 per cent of members attend weekly. Denmark shows the same pattern of decline. In 1927 church attendance in rural areas was between 7 and 13 per cent; in 1967 it was 2 to 7 per cent. In 1964 only 1.7 per cent of Copenhagenners attended church. Other measures of religious interest show similar results.[13]

The most unusual feature of the religious life of the Nordic countries is that, despite it having been easy to withdraw from church membership, and thus save on taxes, for decades very few people did so.[14] Stark and Iannaccone casually denigrate the Nordic people by asserting that 'social pressures are such that 90% retain official church membership', which rather misses the point that the 'social' would press for itself to stay in the church only if most (or at least the most influential) of the 'social' saw something good in church membership.[15]

The second supply-side observation is also misguided. Stark and his associates persistently talk about state churches as though the financial relationship between citizens and churches was obscure. Stark and Iannaccone say: 'In most of Europe's Protestant nations the state continues to offer "free" religion—or at least religion that the consumer already has paid for through taxes.'[16] This is coupled to the general claim that people value most what has cost them dearest to argue that state religion is undervalued because the people have not 'paid' for it. Stark says: 'religion is perceived to be "free" in that it is provided by the government . . . people tend not to value what they perceive to be free.'[17]

Leaving aside the highly contentious claim that financial cost is the major determinant of social valuation, the supply-side case rests on the belief that the consumers of state religion are unaware of what it has cost them. This shows considerable ignorance of how taxation works. In England, before 1836, when the church tax or 'tithes' could still be paid in produce, farmers knew exactly what they paid and had plenty of opportunity to be awkward about it—a Hampshire farmer once told the tithe-owner that he was about to lift his turnips: 'When the tithe-owner's men and wagons were gathered by the field the farmer appeared, drew ten turnips, gave one to the tithe-owner's man, and said he would let his master know when he would draw any more.'[18] In Wales, where the tithes paid by dissenters went to support what was seen as the 'English' Episcopalian Church, they were a major cause of rioting in the 1840s. Secondly, the supply-siders betray their politics when they assume that people have markedly different levels of awareness of costs that they meet directly and indirectly. What is presented as science is no more than propaganda for *laissez-faire* capitalism. Were they more familiar with life in social democracies they would appreciate that tax-payers are very well aware of the fact that they are taxed and have strong views on levels of taxation and state spending.

This makes the Nordic position even more of a paradox. Most uncommitted or marginal Norwegian Lutherans, those who do not belong to other churches, are not quite in the position of British dissenters, who were taxed to support a church they opposed. But they are consciously willing to pay to maintain an organization they do not attend terribly often and to support spokesmen for beliefs they no longer hold. The explanation can be discerned from the fascinating material in the 1997 Religion and Moral Pluralism (RAMP) study. Respondents were asked to rank the importance of various church activities. There was a surprising degree of agreement between the four countries. The activities rated most important in all four countries were funerals, baptisms, and weddings. Next, and surprisingly close, came the preservation of old church buildings and the celebration of Advent and Christmas. Those all came above the midway level. Below and in declining order of importance came 'church music and singing of the choir', the 'celebration of Easter', 'well-known hymns', and the 'ringing-in of the Sabbath'. The two least important occurrences were 'regular Sunday services' and 'holy communion'! So the most important things the folk church could do were to provide a religious gloss to significant personal and community events and to maintain the national heritage by preserving historic church buildings. Marking the Sabbath, regular worship services, and what (even for Protestants) should be the most important part of church life, holy communion, were ranked lowest.

Another question asked people to rank ten activities on which the church could spend its resources. The most popular was social work with the old and sick, second came upkeep of cemeteries, and third came 'keeping churches open for private prayers'. Fourth was international aid and emergency relief, and fifth was the preservation of church buildings. Arranging activities for children and young people was sixth, then came 'arranging services in the national language abroad'. Eighth in order of preference was aid to Christians abroad, ninth holding services every Sunday in all parishes, and last in the list was international missionary work. With the exception of keeping churches open for private prayers, there is a very clear ordering here: what have traditionally been regarded as the principle activities of the church, trying to spread the Christian message and regularly worshipping the Lord, were the last two items in order of preference, and secular community activities came at the top.

Interpretation

Taken over a long period, the Nordic countries offer a major challenge to the supply-siders. The thing we are trying to explain—religious vitality—has changed a great deal over the last two centuries: all the indices of the power, popularity, and presence of religion show decline. Yet there is little change in the structure of the religious market, despite the steady relaxation of state regulation. As the tables in the Appendix show, for all the growth in alternatives, the Lutheran Churches continue to dominate the religious life of the Nordic countries.

Of course the supply-siders could say that European countries are still not very tolerant and nowhere near as liberal as the USA. This is true. But the supply-side model does not say that there is some cut-off point at which the benefits of deregulation begin to flow. It says that, the less regulated a religious economy, the greater the diversity and the greater the levels of religious vitality. Irrespective of how the religious markets of the Nordic countries compare with that of the USA, the uncontestable fact is that they are less regulated than once they were. Yet there is no religious revival.

The difficulty of interpretation is to know what things would have been like otherwise. Viewed from the USA, it may seem obvious that state support kills religion. But from Britain a very different interpretation suggests itself. The levels of belief and personal involvement are similar in the Nordic countries and Britain. That is, 'demand' for the ideological core of religion is very weak. However, the established status of the Lutheran Churches and their tax base for fund-raising allow them to provide social and liturgical services to the population at large. The homogeneity of the societies allows the national churches to be truly national while the multinational character of Britain prevents the churches playing such a role.

If comparisons of the Nordic states over time fail to support the supply-side case, comparisons between them also fail to support Stark and his colleagues. On most measures the Finns appear to be both more rigorous and more orthodox than their neighbours. The RAMP study showed the remarkably consistent figure of 33, 34, and 32 per cent for the proportion of Norwegians, Danes, and Swedes who 'never' attend church; for Finns it is only 19 per cent. Equally consistently, 9, 9, and 8 per cent of Norwegians, Danes, and Swedes attend at least monthly, while the figure for Finns is 13 per cent. Half of Finns pray at least once a month, as compared with a third of Norwegians and a quarter of Danes and Swedes. Finland also has the highest number of people who believe in God and believe in a traditional Christian version of that God. Only 3 per cent of Swedes and 7 and 8 per cent respectively of Danes and Norwegians believe that the Bible is 'the literal word of God', but 18 per cent of Finns take that view. On the issue of how important were a variety of church activities, the Finns consistently scored higher than the others. The average scores (out of 10) for all items were 4.4 for Finns, 4.1 for Danes, 3.8 for Norwegians, and 3.7 for Swedes. A very clear difference is visible in the answers to the question 'How important is God in your life?' used in the World Values Survey (WVS). Denmark and Sweden rank lowest with scores of 18 and 19, Norway scored 27, but the Finns scored 42.[19]

Whatever distinguishes them, it is not the structure of the religious economy, which in all four countries is similar. Finland was an exception, but only because it spent the nineteenth century under Russian rule and so the liberalization that occurred elsewhere in the mid-nineteenth century was delayed until after the Russian Revolution. That the country slowest to liberalize its religious economy is also the most religious goes directly against the supply-side expectation.

Nor is diversity (in the sense of people being free to choose between a range of religions) relevant. Finland was more pluralistic than its western neighbours in that it had a dual establishment of recognizing both the Lutheran and the much smaller Orthodox Church, but membership of these was determined by geography and ethnicity: almost no one moved from one to the other. In terms of plausible choices, Finns were slightly more constrained than their Nordic neighbours because Finland was less influenced by the pietistic movements of the nineteenth century and suffered fewer breaks from the folk church than its neighbours.

A more promising line of explanation concerns economic development. All four countries are now similar in prosperity: the 1990 gross domestic product of Norway was $23,830 per head, Finland's was $24,540, and Sweden and

Denmark fell in between. But this represents a recent change. In 1957 Norway, Sweden, and Denmark were all between $1,057 and $1,380, but Finland was only at $794. Even in 1970 the Finnish GDP was only three-quarters of the average for the other three. So we are looking at a country that for a long time lagged behind the economic development of its neighbours. There is also a significant difference in urbanization. In the 1990s Denmark and Sweden were the most urban of the four with 85 and 83 per cent of their people in large towns and cities, then came Norway at 73 per cent, and Finland was the least urban at 64 per cent.[20] These data are consistent with the conventional secularization view that economic modernization is likely to be associated with a decline in religious commitment.

However, there is another vital difference between Finland and its neighbours that is hinted at in the RAMP data. Those surveyed were asked to respond to ten versions of the statement 'The National Church should be present …' where the sentence was completed by such options as 'at the celebration of the National Day' and 'at festivities among the royal family'. All four countries are united in accepting the autonomy of politics. On a scale from 1 to 7, 'at the national conventions of the political parties' scored only between 1.5 for Denmark and 1.9 for Finland. However, over all the possible items, the Finns averaged 3.2 against 2.0 for the Danes, 2.4 for the Norwegians, and 2.5 for the Swedes. While no other country scored more than 4 on any item, Finland scored over 4 on three: the celebration of national day, national festivities, and the end of school year ceremonies. And the greatest disagreement between the four countries concerns the question of whether the church should be present at a regiment's jubilee celebrations. The Danes scored only 1.7, the Norwegians 1.9, and the Swedes 2.1. But the Finns scored 3.7.

These results suggest that the greater religiosity of the Finns may be related to issues of national integrity. Denmark and Sweden were themselves imperial powers and since their demise and democratization they have been relatively free from external interference. Norway has been relatively untroubled by predators since the introduction of home rule in 1814 and full independence in 1905. But Finland was under Russian rule through the nineteenth century and, although it gained its freedom in 1917, it did not regain Karelia. Finland fought two wars against the Soviets and was forced to pay heavy war reparations after it had made a truce in September 1944. For the rest of the twentieth century it had to maintain cautiously polite relationships with a threatening superpower neighbour.

The result was a strong desire to maintain a very clear national ethos. Although it is primarily carried by the Lutheran Church, it is also expressed by the Orthodox Church, which is affiliated, not to the neighbouring Russian

Orthodox Church, but to the Greek Orthodox Church. For the vast majority of Finns, Lutheranism is what distinguishes them from the Slavs next door. That ethnicity has played a major part in Finnish religiosity is further suggested by an interesting internal difference. The west coast of the country shares the Gulf of Bothnia with Sweden and there is a significant population of Swedish-speaking Finns. The RAMP data suggest that, although this is the least urbanized and industrialized part of the country, its inhabitants are less religious than the average Finn. That, given their greater distance from Russia, is what we would expect if national autonomy was a major consideration.

However, Lutheranism did not distinguish the Finns from the Swedes on the west coast of their country and on the other side of the Bay of Bothnia or the Norwegians to the north. As the Swedish empire had been Lutheran, religion could form an enduring part of national consciousness only after Russia (and then the Soviet Union) had become the major threat, and hence the religio-ethnic bond, though closer than in the Scandinavian countries, was never as strong as it some of the countries to be discussed below.

To summarize this section, the supply-siders offer the Nordic countries as a prime example of the deleterious consequences of religious establishment: regulated markets prevent the satisfaction of latent demand for religion. However, as I argued in the previous chapter, this is hardly persuasive when the evidence of revival movements and religious dissent shows that the Nordic peoples were quite capable of making their own religious provision when they found that of the state church unsatisfactory. Furthermore, the free-market model fails to explain the changes of the twentieth century. In all four countries, increasing religious liberty has been accompanied by increasing secularity. It also fails to explain the differences between the Nordic states. The most plausible explanations for the marginally greater religious vitality and orthodoxy shown in Finland are, first, the relatively late arrival of industry and prosperity and, secondly, the fact that for Finns the assumption that 'Nordic people are Lutheran' takes on a slightly more urgent and insistent tone in the country where national autonomy is recent and precarious. Helsinki is close enough to St Petersburg for Russian musicians to busk in the streets of the Finnish capital. That is close enough for religion to acquire an additional ethnic charge.

Religion in the Communist World

One of the absurdities of the supply-side approach to religion is that it is so convinced of the virtues of the free market that it pays little attention to major differences in the *intentions* of state regulation. These can change, even in a relatively short period of time. The Greek Orthodox Church has traditionally played an important part in sustaining Greek culture and was heavily implicated in nationalist movements of the nineteenth century and in the opposition to the Nazis in the Second World War. During the dictatorship of the Colonels (1967 to 1974), the state tried to draw the Church into an even closer alliance in defence of 'Greek Christian values', which caused major divisions within the Church. The restoration of democracy in 1974 returned the Church to something like the relationship the Lutherans enjoyed with the Nordic state or the Catholic Church had in the Republic of Ireland. But, when the socialists came to power in 1981, relations again became strained as the government introduced civil marriages and attempted to nationalize church property.

The greatest contrast with the state support for the Nordic Lutheran Churches is the suppression of religion that occurred in most Communist states. The story of the churches in eastern Europe is extremely complicated, but we can gain entry by starting with the relatively simple cases of the Baltic states and using their fate to raise general points of interest from other countries in the former Communist world.

Lithuania, Latvia, and Estonia

The three Baltic states are interesting because their political histories are similar but their religious histories are very different. For centuries they changed hands between German, Polish, and Russian rulers. At the end of the First World War, the unprecedented simultaneous collapse of the German and Russian empires allowed all three to enjoy a short period of independence. The fledgling democracies were undermined by economic depression and in 1926 a military *coup* in Lithuania created an authoritarian regime that lasted until 1940. For one year the Soviets occupied the country and then there were four years of German occupation before the Soviets again took the country, which they kept until the collapse of Communism. In 1991 Lithuania was again recognized by the international community as a sovereign state.[21]

Modern national consciousness emerged in Latvia in the second half of the nineteenth century when it was nominally a Russian province but effectively run, as it had been for centuries, by Baltic Germans. Ironically for what later transpired, Latvians welcomed the Czar's moves to 'russify' the country because they wanted to see the Germans weakened. Like Lithuania, Latvia enjoyed a brief period of autonomous democracy between 1920 and 1934, when a *coup* brought to power a mildly authoritarian regime that survived until the Soviet occupation of 1940. Latvia suffered an intensive campaign to destroy any social institutions that might resist Soviet rule. In the first year of Soviet occupation around 34,500 Latvians were killed or deported to Siberia. As a result, when the Germans pushed back the Soviet troops, they were welcomed. When the Soviets returned in 1944, over 100,000 Latvians fled to the West. The effects of Soviet russification can be seen in the ethnic make-up of the country. In 1935 Latvia was full of Latvians: under 10 per cent of the population was Russian, Belorussian, and Ukrainian. Fifty years later these groups had grown to 42 per cent. The story for Estonia was similar. In 1934 80 per cent of the people were ethnic Estonians; by 1989 this had fallen to 69 per cent. This in contrast to the situation in Lithuania, where at the end of Soviet rule the population was still some 80 per cent Lithuanian.

One major difference between the Baltic states is the degree of industrialization. In the late nineteenth century Western firms built factories in Latvia and Estonia in order to get behind protective Russian tariff barriers. Lithuania's loss of Vilnius to Poland in the post-First World War settlement meant that it no longer had a border with the Soviet Union, which significantly reduced trade and allowed it to remain predominantly agricultural.

All church-membership figures need to be treated with caution, but even if we doubt the exact numbers there is no reason to suppose that the figures given in Table 4.2 place the three countries in the wrong order. Indeed other

TABLE 4.2. *Religion, ethnicity, and development, Baltic states, 1990s*

	Lithuania	Latvia	Estonia
Church membership (%)	46	23	15
At least monthly church attendance 1996 (%)	31	16	9
Religious composition	72% Catholic	15% Catholic	1% Catholic
	3% Orthodox	8% Orthodox	20% Orthodox
	1% Lutheran	15% Lutheran	14% Lutheran
Religio-ethnic bond	Strong	Weak	Weak
Ethnic cohesion (% titular ethnicity 1989)	80	52	62
Religious diversity (Herfindahl Index)	0.18	0.77	0.56
Industrialization	Low	High	Middle
Urbanization (%)	68	69	71
GNP per capita $ (1990)	2,710	3,410	3,810

Sources: Peter Brierley, *World Churches Handbook: Based on the Operation World Database by Patrick Johnston* (London: Christian Research Association, 1997); Inglehart, Basanez, and Moreno, *Human Values and Beliefs*.

sources put the figures for active church participation for Lithuania even higher.[22] The 1995/6 WVS gives the following figures for 'at least monthly' church attendance: Lithuania—31 per cent; Latvia—16 per cent; and Estonia—9 per cent. How might we explain these differences? One obvious consideration is the level of industrialization just mentioned. The Soviet Union continued the policy of industrializing Latvia and Estonia, while Lithuania remained predominantly agricultural.

A bigger difference concerns the role of religion in political dissent. In the nineteenth century, the Catholic Church in Lithuania was vital in sustaining a sense of national identity, especially in preserving the language, which the Czarist regime tried to suppress in favour of the Cyrillic script. As Hiden and Salmon put it: 'In Lithuania, as in Poland, the Catholic Church led the campaign against the russification of the schools.'[23] Commenting on the later Soviet period, Senn says of it that 'the Catholic Church . . . constituted a legal haven for people wanting to display some sort of resistance to the regime, and many dissidents in fact could not distinguish between their own religious and national feelings'.[24] The Church of St Casimar in Vilnius might have been a Museum of Atheism (from 1956 to 1988), but the clergy remained resolute and the underground publication of *Chronicle of the Catholic Church* was one of the most potent acts of anti-Soviet defiance of the 1970s.

Muizneks notes, 'Unlike their Lithuanian counterparts, Latvian dissidents lacked an organizational base such as the Catholic Church.'[25] Despite it accounting for about a third of the population, the Catholic Church in Latvia did not play a significant role in opposing Communism. The equally large Lutheran Church was also absent from nationalist struggles (its Cathedral in Riga was turned into a concert hall), as was the smaller Orthodox Church (which is not a surprise as it was the church of the Soviet Russian settlers). Like its Nordic neighbours, Estonia was historically Lutheran, though the growth of the ethnic Russian population had created an Orthodox population that in 1995 was estimated to be larger than that of the Lutherans.

Going back one step, it is obvious that the ability or willingness of a church to act as a guarantor of national identity owes a great deal to the balance of ethnic groups. But there is also a complex set of links between state repression, popularity, and ethnic identity. If we introduce the extreme case of Poland, we can more clearly see the point. The Catholic Church in Poland was thoroughly Polish and had for centuries acted as the repository of national identity. It was so popular and institutionally strong that the Communist government had very little success in its efforts to control it and the Church had little difficulty recruiting and training its clergy. Between 1937 and 1980 it doubled the number of its places of worship and also doubled the number of full-time clergy. In the late 1960s half the population claimed to attend Mass every Sunday and 75 per cent claimed regularly to join religious processions.[26] The Church provided an important source of moral support for the merging Solidarity movement in the late 1970s. The election of the Polish Cardinal Karol Wojek to the papacy in 1978 gave a massive boost to anti-Communist sentiment, and during his visit to Poland in 1979 there was a small but import-ant sign of the autonomy of the Church: the massive crowds that turned out to greet him were policed not by the state's security forces but by stewards from Catholic youth organizations. When the Communist Party acted to pre-empt Soviet interference by imposing martial law in 1981, 'the Polish religious institutions once again assumed the role they fulfilled in the partition period . . . its institutional infrastructure provided a base from which some form of organized resistance to martial law could emerge'.[27]

The Church in Lithuania, though almost as popular as its Polish counter-part, was more heavily constrained by the Communist Party. This was poss-ible because Poland's longer history as a powerful independent state (at times having itself been the hub of an empire) made it less easy for Soviet commun-ism to dominate (as did its distance from Moscow). That greater autonomy (reflected, for example, in the stronger sense of nationalism in the Polish Communist Party) made it less easy for the party to control the Catholic Church. In contrast, Lithuania had a far shorter and less impressive history of autonomy and was more easily incorporated by Soviet Communism (as seen in the weaker sense of national autonomy in the Lithuanian Community Party). This in turn meant that the Catholic Church was more easily bullied by the secular state. Its lack of resources discouraged the middle classes from joining the clergy, and, just as the Catholic Church in England made up its shortfall of clergy recruits by enlisting Irish priests, so the Church in Lithua-nia recruited Poles. This in turn weakened the association between the Church and Lithuanian national consciousness. None the less the ties remained strong and the dissident movement relied heavily on the Church.

Although it is possible for the same religion to claim both sides in a war, the close combination of religious affiliation and national identity works best when there is a clear division between the godly and the ungodly. Lithuanian Catholicism took strength from opposing russification and attempts to impose the Orthodox Church in the Czarist era. It was more divided in the years between the two world wars, when the attempts to increase the sense of national cohesion led to restrictions on the civil liberties of Poles (who were also Catholics) within Lithuania's boundaries. But the Lutheran Churches in Latvia and Estonia were even more constrained in their ability to link faith and national integrity. 'Up to the turn of the century the churches were almost exclusively staffed by German colonisers as well as being under Scandinavian influence and were thus identified with political and cultural domination by a foreign minority.'[28]

To recap thus far: religion may remain popular if it is part of a religio-ethnic identity that is threatened. Where the church is deeply rooted, it can resist state repression. The growth of the Russian population (and the division of Latvian natives between Catholic and Lutheran churches) left the Lutheran Churches in a much weaker position in Latvia and Estonia than was the Catholic Church in Lithuania (and more so in Poland). None the less, one might have thought that both the size and the historical relationship with the native population should have allowed the Latvian and Estonian Lutheran Churches to play some role in sustaining national identity. That they did not suggests that at least some of the pattern we see is to be explained by the nature of the religious traditions in question, a suspicion that is reinforced by the descriptions summarized in Table 4.3.

Like all such propositions, this involves massive simplification, but we can

TABLE 4.3. *Church attendance and confession, former Communist countries, 1990s*

Country	Attend 'at least monthly' (%)	Dominant confession
Poland	74	92% Catholic
Croatia	36	73% Catholic
Slovenia	33	84% Catholic
Hungary	32	63% Catholic
Lithuania	31	72% Catholic
Romania	31	74% Orthodox
Armenia	30	64% Orthodox
Georgia	27	45% Orthodox
Moldova	23	45% Orthodox
Czechoslovakia	21	62% Catholic
Ukraine	18	31% Orthodox
Latvia	16	15% Catholic
		15% Lutheran
		8% Orthodox
Serbia	15	80% Orthodox
East Germany	9	80% Lutheran
Bulgaria	9	37% Orthodox
Estonia	9	20% Orthodox
		14% Lutheran
Russia	8	93% Orthodox

Sources: Church attendance data from WVS and Inglehart, Basanez, and Moreno, *Human Values and Beliefs*. Relative confession sizes calculated from the 'community' figures in Brierley, *World Churches Handbook*.

note some major differences in the relative ability of the main strands of Christianity to remain distant from the state. This is partly a consequence of their attitudes to the world implied in their theology and partly a matter of organizational structure.

The 'unreformed' Christianity of the Catholic and Orthodox churches combined a universal incorporation of the people with considerable toleration of laxity, provided it was not accompanied by criticism of the church's status and religious authority. The radical wing of the Protestant tradition did not tolerate laxity and sought to make all people into committed religiously observant members. Except in the highly unusual circumstances of settler societies such as the Afrikaners in South Africa or the Scots Presbyterians in Northern Ireland, the sectarian impulse led to such organizations losing a grip on the society as a whole and becoming self-selecting sects.[29] Between these two extremes falls the Lutheran tradition, which is largely Protestant in theology but also accepted the pre-Reformation church structures and the relationships with the wider society and the state implied in them. Where the Calvinists who influenced the Presbyterian tradition tried to impose the standards of the religious virtuosi upon the whole population and use the state (or the 'civil magistrate' as Calvin called it) to promote the true religion, the Lutherans accepted a notion of 'two kingdoms': that there was a proper sphere for the church and a proper sphere for the state. Though they should be mutually supportive, they need not be the same.

The sect form of religion has the advantage of presenting a radical challenge to the secular power (Communist or otherwise); the Confessing Church in Nazi Germany and the Baptists in the Soviet Union are good examples. However, because such sects are not national in scope (and cannot be because of the rigour of their demands on members), they cannot form a strong bond with ethnic or national identity and thus serve as a base for sustaining opposition to the state.

Czechoslovakia

The above themes can be pursued through other examples of former Communist states. One thing that becomes obvious as soon as one looks closely at Czechoslovakia is that we are unlikely to understand changes in religious vitality in many countries if we simply take the nation state as defined at any one time and use gross statistics of church membership or affiliation for that unit in international comparisons. Although, for most of the nineteenth and twentieth centuries, Czechoslovakia was more or less a single state, its internal divisions were so great that any consideration of the links between religion, ethnicity, and politics has to take its component parts separately.

What became Czechoslovakia was Christianized primarily through the work of Saints Cyril and Methodius in the ninth century. In the early years of the fifteenth century Bohemia became a centre for the Reformation. The leader of the rebellion against the corruption of the Church, Jan Hus, was burnt at the stake in 1415, but his followers continued as a Reformed presence in the Czech lands, despite the general success of the Counter-Reformation. Slovakia remained primarily Catholic, although there was a sizeable Lutheran element. Thus Catholicism and Protestantism competed, prevented any one religious tradition becoming uniquely associated with the national myth, and 'in the struggle weakened their popular acceptance'.[30] After the First World War, some 19 per cent of the Catholic Church in the Czech lands left in protest at continued links with the hated Hapsburg monarchy.[31] In the 1920s a large group of priests split with Rome because they wished to use the vernacular in services and to marry. Initially calling itself the Czechoslovak Church, it was severely compromised by the state and it declined considerably under the Communist regime.[32]

In Slovakia, the Catholic Church retained the support of the peasant Slovaks. Although many of the clergy opposed it, the puppet Slovak state established by the Nazis was led by a Catholic priest, Fr Josef Tiso, and from the end of the war Slovak Catholics were vulnerable to accusations of unpatriotic collaboration. Despite that division, the Church remained sufficiently popular for the incoming Communist Party officials to describe the Slovaks as suffering from the 'Polish disease'.[33]

The history of the Uniate or Eastern-Rite Church (which, to simplify, can be seen as falling between the Catholic and Orthodox traditions) shows heavy-handed repression backfiring. The Communist government that took full control in 1948 followed the Soviet model of dividing and ruling by favouring the smaller Hussite and Evangelical churches and persecuting what were seen as the major challenges to its authority. Until the Second World War there were some 550,000 Uniates, but, when the Soviet Union annexed Carpatho-Ukraine, that number fell to 270,000. Although they were only a small part of the population of around 15 million, that the Uniates had their base in an ethnic group that was not entirely encompassed by the national borders made the Party see them as a significant threat and in 1950 the government forced the Uniate Church to merge with the Orthodox Church. The majority of clergy refused and many were imprisoned, among them Bishop Gojdič, who died in prison ten years later, and his auxiliary, who was held in a psychiatric hospital until 1963. During the brief liberalization of 1968's 'Prague Spring' the Church was rehabilitated, and individual parishes held elections to decide whether to remain Orthodox or revert to Catholicism. Almost all chose the latter option. Despite (or, more likely, because of), persecution, the Uniates appear to have grown at a time when other Czechoslovak churches were declining. The Vatican's own figures show 355,000 Uniates in 1985—an increase of almost a third since the Second World War. Ten years later the *World Churches Handbook* showed a community of almost 200,000 and an active membership of 172,000. Whether this represents a subsequent real decline or merely disagreements in counting methods is not clear, but, if we were to split the difference, the Uniate performance would still be markedly better than that of Christianity in general in Czechoslovakia. Walters suggests that in the Communist era the Christian churches overall lost two-thirds of their members.[34] Chrypinksi has no doubt that the survival of the Uniates is due to the fact that for both Slovak and Ukrainian members 'the Church became a major force in the striving for national independence'.[35]

In 1948 the state confiscated all the property of the Catholic Church, thus depriving it of almost all of its income, closed all its schools, and ended religious instruction. The Vatican responded by excommunicating all Communist Party members and readers of the Communist press. At the same time as the state hindered the Church hierarchy by, for example, refusing it permission to fill vacant bishoprics, it also encouraged malleable clergy to join the state-sponsored *Pacem in Terris*, and then sought to promote those people to high church offices. Supported by the Vatican's refusal to accept such nominations, the Church rejected state attempts to control its affairs.

The fragmentation of the population prevented any religion claiming to speak for 'the people', who were themselves hardly united in what was always a state of two halves. In particular the Catholic Church was hindered in that anti-communist propaganda based on appeals to Slovak nationalism alienated Czech Catholics and liberals, who saw in it dangerous reminders of Fr Tiso's Nazi state. None the less, in the latter days of communism, the Church's refusal to be co-opted did form a focus for anti-state sentiment that had very few other outlets. In 1984 Cardinal Tomasek invited the Polish Pope to Czechoslovakia to celebrate the 1,100th anniversary of the death of Saint Methodius. The Pope accepted, but the visit was blocked by the government. The Cardinal's invitation and the Pope's acceptance were widely circulated in *samizdat* form, and a petition requesting the government to change its decision attracted 17,000 signatures. In 1987 Catholics in Moravia started a petition calling for religious freedom that eventually gathered half-a-million signatures. Cardinal Tomasek signed it and had it promoted in Catholic churches. The following year, as Gorbachev's reforms weakened the grip of the Soviet Union on its satellites, Tomasek increased the pressure with demands for greater church autonomy and finally defied the state by appointing unapproved candidates to vacant bishoprics. In contrast, the Lutheran Church played little part in anti-communist movements. A small number of

Evangelical Church laymen and clergy were imprisoned for their involvement in the human-rights movement Charter 77, but they were given little or no support from any official church body.

The purposes of this history are to illuminate the differences in religious vitality of various European countries and evaluate the supply-side view of the role of state regulation. The virtue of Czechoslovakia is that for most of the twentieth century it had a single regime of state regulation (though that changed considerably over the period). Although we must always be critical of religious statistics (especially from countries where the state had a considerable interest in muddying the waters), the available evidence suggests that the Slovak part of the state (though the less diverse) remained considerably more religious than the Czech part. In 1967 46 per cent of Czechs but only 12 per cent of Slovaks claimed no religious affiliation.[36] In 1995 the respective proportions were 38 per cent and 20 per cent (see Table A4.6). The extent of secularization may well be far greater than suggested by those figures. A Catholic Church source estimated that only 5–10 per cent of the people of Bohemia were 'believing' Catholics.[37]

As with the Nordic and Baltic states, the two most likely explanations are the level of industrialization and the part played by religion in national integrity. The Czech lands were far more industrialized and prosperous than Slovakia (which was one of the major reasons they split in 1993). Although Slovakia was predominantly Catholic, the Catholic Church did not manage to achieve the role it played in Poland or Lithuania. In the absence of a strong church link to solidaristic opposition to communism, the churches declined. In 1950 94.6 per cent of the Czechoslovak population was described as Christian. In 1985 it was about 30 per cent.[38]

Divided Germany

The contrasting fates of religion in the capitalist West and Communist eastern parts of Germany can shed further light on the consequences for religious vitality of state actions. Prior to the First World War the Lutheran and Catholic churches in the states that merged to form the united Germany enjoyed a relationship with the government similar to that of the churches in the Nordic countries, with the difference that the German Lutheran Churches continued to be a group of regional organizations rather than a single unified body. The end of that war saw an interesting example of how a cultural practice that had evolved because it was functional in one setting could be imposed on another, not because it was needed, but because it had come to be seen as a good thing in its own right. When the Allies constructed the constitutional foundations for the Weimar Republic, they broke with the previous German tradition and established a secular state. The UK and US experience of diversity requiring a separation of church and state, and the very different French experience, which had created a secular state as a reaction to the Church's support for the wrong side in the 1798 Revolution, combined to make it an article of faith that a modern democracy should not be entangled with religion. There was also some interest in keeping weak any institution that might strengthen German nationalism. Under Hitler, the Third Reich attempted to recreate the older model with the emphasis shifted from church and king to church and people. Some Catholic Bishops signed a concordat with Hitler; the Lutherans did not, though the main opposition to the regime came not from Lutherans but from the much smaller 'Confessing' Church, which was freer to adopt critical postures because it saw itself less as a national church and more as a sect of self-selecting believers.

After the war the Lutherans reformed as the Evangelische Kirche in Deutschland (EKD) with a structure that covered both halves of Germany. At this point the levels of religious observance in the two parts were comparable. The greater number of Catholics in the Federal Republic of Germany (FRG) made for higher rates of church attendance, but the commitment levels of Lutherans were similar on either side of the 'Iron Curtain'. However, if we look again at the data in Table 4.1, we find that forty years later the two parts had diverged drastically. In both parts of Germany we see decline, but in what used to be the German Democratic Republic (GDR) interest in religion has plummeted. Lemke says that church membership in the east fell from 90 per cent in 1950 to 36 per cent in 1989—less than half that of the FRG. In the Lutheran Church of Mecklenburg there were 12,000 confirmations in 1950, 6,000 in 1970, and only 2,000 in 1982.[39] Two surveys conducted for *Der Spiegel* in 1967 and 1992 showed that, while all indices showed traditional Christian beliefs to have lost support, the change in the former GDR was markedly greater than in the FRG.[40]

The explanation does not lie in diversity. Being evenly divided between Catholics and Lutherans, with the split between two organizations, and with substantial numbers of other Protestants, the FRG was more diverse than the GDR.[41] Taking state regulation in the way the supply-siders use the notion, the FRG had more of it than the GDR, in that the state legally and formally protected the Lutheran and Catholic churches while in East Germany the state was officially neutral and equally opposed to all religion. A much more likely explanation lies in the way that the Lutheran Church in the GDR responded to its new and difficult position.[42]

The gradual worsening of relations between the two parts of Germany, culminating in the erection of the Berlin wall in 1961, led to the Lutheran Church being divided. Unlike other Communist governments, the GDR regime did not greatly oppress or persecute the Church. Although the state system of tax support was ended, as was religious instruction in schools, the theological faculties in state universities were left alone, as were church hospitals: 'for pragmatic reasons—not the smallest of these being the hard currency assistance from the FRG—the Church was never exposed to the harsh treatment experienced by Christians in other Communist-ruled states of Eastern Europe.'[43] In return for state permission to open new churches, increased access to state broadcasting, and greater freedom to import religious literature from the West, the Lutheran leadership endorsed the state. As Bishop Schönherr put it: 'We do not want to be a church against or alongside, but in socialism.'[44] With rather more subtlety than the Czech regime, the GDR Communists encouraged those clergy who could be manipulated into striking increasingly anti-Western postures. While the anti-militarism of the Lutheran Churches and their support for the reunification of Germany annoyed the government, that same anti-militarism was a useful stick with which to beat the West when it was developed into a strong pacifist platform. The Church regained some ground in popular affections in the 1980s when it confronted the government's cynical support for its peace campaigns. When the government refused to permit 'social peace service' as an alternative to conscription in the military, Bishop Krusche published a critical open letter and had it read in all the churches of the Evangelical Union. In the resulting state crackdown, a pastor was given three years in prison and ten peace activists were deported to the West.

Hungary

Hungary was liberated from Turkish rule by the Austrian Hapsburg monarchy, which imposed Counter-Reformation Catholicism on a largely Protestant population and thus created a strong association between confession and social class and a political culture in which church served state. Had Catholicism remained only the faith of the nobility, Reformed religion might have become closely associated with movements for national autonomy, but the Protestants were themselves divided between the Calvinist and Lutheran traditions and Catholicism became sufficiently popular for Catholics to form the majority population. Church and state enjoyed a close relationship during the rule of Admiral Horty in the interwar years.

 Although the Communist domination that was imposed by the Soviet Union after the war will always be remembered for the brutal repression of the 1956 rising, the Kadar regime pursued a much more accommodating policy towards the churches than did many other Communist governments and the churches reciprocated. It had a particular problem with the strong-willed leader of Hungary's Catholics, Cardinal Jozsef Mindszenty, who was tortured and given a show trial. He enjoyed a brief period of freedom during the 1956 uprising and then had to take refuge in the American Embassy in Budapest, where he stayed until 1971, when he left the country and went to Rome. In 1974 the Pope removed him from office, ostensibly because his authoritarian and aristocratic views were incompatible with the liberal spirit of the Second Vatican Council but also because his continued opposition to Hungarian communism was an embarrassment to the Vatican's *rapprochement* with the Hungarian state.

The Lutheran Church enjoyed equally cordial terms with the state, far more so than did its sister church in the GDR. Bishop Zoltán Káldy, who led the Lutherans from 1967 to 1985, wholeheartedly supported the regime: 'There is no "third way" for travellers between socialism and capitalism. Our Protestant churches are not neutral: we stand unambiguously on the side of socialism.'[45]

In the late 1980s, as the Communist world fell apart, church leaders became more aggressive in their demands for autonomy but they took little part in wider movements of opposition. Although I would not want to offer an exaggeratedly simple explanation of religious change, the contrast between the popularity of the Catholic and Lutheran churches in Hungary and the Catholic Church in Poland and Lithuania suggests that, whatever short-term institutional advantages the churches gained by it, such positive support of communism cost Hungarian Christianity dearly. Again we have to acknowledge the weakness of the statistics, but, while noting that the reform of Communist rule in the late 1980s permitted the expansion of church activities, Nielsen says of the Catholic Church: 'attendance dropped drastically during the 1960s and 1970s and has by no means recovered.' Of some 6 million baptized Catholics, not more than 1.5 million remain in any sense active and 'probably only one-third (half of them over fifty-four years of age) . . . attend services regularly'.[46] According to the 1981 WVS, 51 per cent of Hungarians 'never attended' church.[47]

Localism and Autonomy

Although the Orthodox tradition has some commitment to ecclesiastical structures that cross national boundaries, such cosmopolitan links do not have the same theological justification in Orthodoxy as does the primacy of the papacy in Catholicism. Hence Orthodoxy tends to split along national and ethnic lines, with the Orthodox in this or that country claiming the right to autonomy. This is why Orthodox churches are much more likely than Catholic churches to become closely associated with a particular country or society.

Even more so it explains why Lutherans are readily suppressed or co-opted. Although the Lutheran Church in Estonia or Latvia shares a common tradition and 'fraternal relations' with the Evangelical Lutheran Church of Finland, for example, neither in practice nor in the theory of Lutheranism is there a strong external dimension that aids Latvian Lutherans to rise above their local circumstances.

Rich people the world over may keep a reserve of gold in a Swiss bank. Whether or not they call on that reserve will depend on how secure they feel in their own countries. The internationalism of the Catholic Church may give it greater *potential* than its rivals for avoiding the close embrace of the state, but it does not always, or often, take advantage of that reserve power. The Church remained distant from, or opposed to, the state in Poland and Lithuania and became a focus for popular nationalist opposition to Communism. In Czechoslovakia it was heavily persecuted. But in Hungary it struck a conciliatory pose and lost a great deal of popular support as a result. In Italy, France, Spain, and Portugal, and most countries of Latin America, the Church has been quite happy to cooperate with the secular authorities when they have been right wing and willing to support the privileges of the Church. The Spanish crown was traditionally strongly linked with the Catholic Church. Under the terms of a 1753 concordat the monarch had the right to appoint bishops. As was the case with pre-Revolution France and with Italy, the strong organic model of church, state, and landowner generated its countervailing anticlericalism, which came close to victory in the years prior to the Civil War of 1936. When General Franco and his Falangists came to power, the Church resumed it close relationship with the state. Only in the early 1970s, when the stubborn refusal of the Falangists to democratize was becoming an intolerable embarrassment to the Catholic Church internationally, did the Church seek to distance itself from the state. As happened in Greece, the first post-dictatorship left-of-centre government saw church–state relations becoming strained as each side tried to establish its primacy. The government appointed as an ambassador to the Vatican someone of whom the Church disapproved. In turn, the Vatican offended the government by canonizing a number of right-wing 'martyrs' of the Civil War. Again, because it refutes the supply-side expectations, it is worth noting that the increased liberalism and toleration of the democratic era has not been accompanied by an increase in signs of religious vitality. The *World Churches Handbook* estimates that the Christian community declined from 92 per cent in 1960 to 68 per cent in 1995. Church membership fell from 9.7 million in 1960 to 9 million (a fall of 8 per cent) over a period when the population grew by 33 per cent. Church attendance figures for Spain as a whole are not available, but in the 1960s between 60 and 80 per cent of various social groups such as students, middle-class professionals, and farmers claimed to attend Mass every Sunday. As we would expect in a Catholic country, the figures for urban industrial workers were far lower.[48] According to the WVS, 'at least monthly' attendance declined from 53 per cent in 1981 to 37 per cent in 1995.[49]

As with previous examples, it is difficult to distinguish various sources of secularization. Doubtless some rejected the Church because of its previous support for fascism (but then many Spaniards still support conservative political parties). Since its entry into the European Union, Spain's economy has prospered and much of its traditional culture has been eroded. But, whatever the details of the explanation of decline, the sure fact is that the Catholic Church has declined at a time when state support has been reduced and very few of those leaving the Church have joined any of the many but still very small alternatives.

Religion Post-Communism

The rational choice theorists believe that state control of the religious market suppresses diversity by inflating the start-up costs for new religions. Thus the relaxation of state control should lead to increased diversity of religious products and then to increased consumption. In what I have shown above to be a mistaken chronology for Britain, Stark and Iannacconne assert that changes in state regulation may precede the proliferation of religious innovations by some time. It is, of course, true that many sorts of changes require some considerable time for their full effects to be worked out. By 1999 a full decade had passed since the fall of Communism, enough time for some sign of the changes predicted by the supply-siders to have appeared. As the grip of the Soviet Union on its constituent parts and on its neighbours relaxed in the 1980s, and as Communist regimes collapsed in country after country, there should have been a proliferation of religious initiatives and an increase in religious vitality.

This has not happened. There has been a considerable improvement in the infrastructure of religious organizations but that has largely benefited the previously hegemonic suppliers. In Hungary under Communist rule there was a slow but steady growth of Protestant churches that were too small for the state to bother to regulate them. The weakening of Communism gave the Catholic Church the chance to re-establish its national organization, to reclaim its privileges, and thus to threaten the advances made by the Protestant churches. Church attendance rose from 8–10 per cent in 1973 to 12–16 per cent in 1993, but this growth was almost all in the Catholic Church.[50] And it had nothing at all to do with a former monopoly being forced by increased competition to work harder. It was simply the removal of artificial constraints on its activities, allowing a popular organization to service enduring demand. In Latvia, Estonia, and the Ukraine, the relaxation of state control has led to open disputes among the major churches, associated with major ethnic groupings. In the former Yugoslavia, the collapse of the state has greatly increased religious vitality, but, again, this has come about by competing ethnic groups mobilizing their competing religious identities as part of their struggles for land and political power.

Changes post-communism suggest that in some settings we need to distinguish between the clergy and the tradition. Even where the Communist state managed quite successfully to corrupt the leadership of the Orthodox Church, the historic tradition could remain a latent focus for dissent and a resource for creating an autonomous identity. For example, despite having been co-opted by the Communist Party and suffering a thoroughly corrupt leadership for a decade, the Georgian Orthodox Church quickly regained popular affections when the liberalization of the regime allowed a reforming generation to displace the discredited leadership.[51] Something similar could be said of the Russian Orthodox Church, which had been made a department of state by Peter the Great. When the Soviets took power, it found itself being used by atheistic rather than Christian civil servants. Its church buildings were preserved as tourist attractions in Moscow and Leningrad and allowed to decay elsewhere. Its officials were sent abroad to pretend to the rest of the world that the regime was not totalitarian. As we can see from the WVS figure of around 8 per cent for 'at least monthly' church attendance, the Orthodox Church lost most of its popular support, retaining primarily only the allegiance of the very old.[52] Nevertheless, after the collapse of Communism, it not only regained many of its resources but it also regained its old role as a major plank of Russian national identity, and by the late 1990s was also regaining public support.

Of course it may be that supply-side predictions will be fulfilled at some time in the future, but, writing in 1999, I see very few signs of it happening and such signs as there are suggest otherwise. In those places where the external threat has been removed, the end to the need for religious supports for national integrity has been followed by a decline in the popularity of religion. In Poland the Catholic Church is increasingly being seen not as a uniquely Polish institution that deserves the loyalty of all Poles but merely as one interest group among others. In the Republic of Ireland active involvement in the Church is declining precipitously. A 1998 survey showed 69 per cent of people claiming to attend Mass weekly—down from 90 per cent in the 1960s.[53]

A Summary

As I have repeatedly argued that we cannot comprehend the changing fortunes of religion in Europe within such simple principles as those of the supply-side model, it is only consistent to begin my summary by admitting that no short summary will be easy. I am almost tempted at this stage to bow to historians such as Hugh McLeod, who argue that sociological explanation for such a broad phenomenon as religion over such a broad range of countries is impossible.[54] However, I will try to bring together the main points I have made.

First, we must accept something of McLeod's stricture: we cannot avoid an interest in the specific political history of particular countries. Even within what looks from a distance like a unitary phenomenon—Communist repression of religion—there is considerable difference in the detail of how particular regimes attempted to suppress, control, or co-opt the churches and those details are important. We also need to appreciate that certain elements of an explanation are entirely contingent and cannot form the basis for useful generalization. One reason the Lutheran Church in the GDR did not aggressively play the nationalist card (usually the best hand against international Communism) is that German history is teinted by the Nazi extermination of the Jews. The Catholic Church in Czechoslovakia had similar problems with the Nazi state of Fr Tiso. We could unite the two experiences in the general proposition that 'The church of a people with a recent history of genocide will find it awkward or counter-productive to stress its nationalism', but that does not take us very far. When historical contingencies have such a major impact on popular perceptions and on a church's freedom to present itself in one light rather than another, it is crass to suppose we can find the cause of major variations in religious vitality in a regression equation.

In so far as we can generalize, we can note that, although confession does not make a difference for the stable countries of western Europe, it does have an effect in contested societies through the likelihood of a religion becoming closely associated with an ethnic group or a national myth. Put very simply, the Calvinist wing of the Reformation (and, although no examples have been pursued here, even more so the fundamentalist and Pentecostal varieties) is less readily amenable to serving the purpose of group identification than the more communal religions of Catholicism, Orthodoxy, and Lutheranism. And, of those, Lutheranism, the more reformed and hence individualistic, is a less likely candidate for the role of cultural defender than the other two. Or, to put it in the terms used at the start of this book, Reformed religion is far more likely to produce sects than to sustain the church type of religion. However, even this complex observation needs to be qualified by recognizing that the greater localism of Lutheranism and its central concept of the religious and the secular sphere as two separate kingdoms may allow it greater freedom to swing to the left or to the right and thus to remain a 'national' church despite the state changing its political complexion. The Finnish Lutheran Church was strengthened by its support for the Wars of Independence, weakened by its association with the bourgeois 'Whites' in the 1917 revolution, regained some ground during the Second World War, and finally re-established itself as the folk church by its support for the social democratic consensus of the last quarter of the twentieth century. In a united country, it was forgiven the difficult middle period and allowed to present itself as having consistently been the church of the Finnish folk. In contrast, the Catholic Church in Spain has failed to make the same adjustment.

However, in the struggle against Communism, the international dimension to the Catholic Church provides a degree of protection against co-option that Lutheranism lacks.

A second safe generalization is that what follows when the state attempts to repress rather than support religion depends on the public perceptions of the church and the relationship between it and the 'state'. The church type of religion can come to terms with the state or it can provide an effective opposition, if it is genuinely popular and the state in question is not. The most obvious examples are when changes in regional powers introduce a regime that is perceived as foreign. Thus the Catholic Church in Poland, Ireland, or Lithuania very effectively performed the role of guarantor of national integrity. The Orthodox Church in Russia was also a custodian of national identity but that led it to being easily co-opted first by the czars from Peter the Great onwards, then by the commissars of the Soviet period, and on into the Yeltsin era, when it enjoyed a revival of its old role as the spirit of Mother Russia.

Thirdly, we may note that how any particular religion, ethnic identity, and state combine depends on the coincidence of the boundaries of the first two and the third of these entities. The common nationality of the Lutherans in the FRD and GDR allowed the Lutheran Church in the East greater power in resisting the regime than its sister church in Latvia.

That leads to the fourth generalization: religious diversity prevents any one religion becoming closely associated with national identity. And, contrary to the supply-side case, such closeness appears to be more often an advantage than a constraint. Repeatedly we have seen that the popular religions are those that have remained 'churches' in the sense of encompassing an entire people and legitimating its interests. Particularly in circumstances of overt state repression (but even in the Nordic countries where national integrity is not much threatened) a religious organziation has prospered when it has been able to claim to represent the nation or the ethnos.

Finally, I will return to one of the other observations about the 'deep struc-ture' of secularization explored in Chapter 1. For all that the surface structure mechanics described in this chapter are causally implicated in the fate of reli-gion, none the less levels of industrialization remain highly significant. A lot of the variation within and between societies is explained by levels of indus-trial development and prosperity. Whatever the starting point, as Inglehart's cross-national data show, as societies have become more prosperous, so indices of commitment to conventional religion have declined.[55]

Conclusion

First I should stress the most important point of this survey: in almost every European country, the twentieth century has seen the power, popularity, and presence of religion decline. Although the data presented here vary consider-ably in reliability and validity, they show patterns that are consistent with what we learn from histories, biographies, and personal experience. In the stable countries of the West, religion has waned. The picture in the East is more complex. Overall, Communism had some considerable success in deliberately creating secular societies, more so when the big stick was accompanied by a few small carrots (Hungary and Czechoslovakia are examples). Where Com-munist regimes tried to suppress genuinely popular churches (the Uniate Church in Czechoslovakia or the Catholic Church in Poland), religion increased in popularity but then (clearly so in Poland and there are signs of it in Lithuania) declined once national integrity found a secular vehicle in an independent state. The third pattern is the least easy to distinguish from other changes, but it seems likely that there has been an increase in popular involve-ment in religion in those countries where the churches have belatedly reasserted their autonomy and been able to re-establish their previous facili-ties. We do not have to accept the free-market approach to religious behav-iour to appreciate that the state may, by destroying the infrastructure of churches and denominations and by penalizing people for expressing their faith, artificially drive down indices of religious sentiment.

Or, to put it in terms of the question I raised in Chapter 2's criticism of the supply-side model, what is to prevent 'auto-supply' servicing demand that supply fails to meet? This is a vital question that the rational choice theorists overlook. A complete answer will have two elements. First, theology is vital. Having no grand theory of Apostolic Succession or ecclesiastical authority, Protestants who are alienated from the dominant church (or who have their church suppressed) can make their own provision; if they are able. That is the second element. People need a degree of political freedom, self-confidence, personal autonomy, and literacy to provide their own religious offices. The Cornish tin-miners of the 1830s had those characteristics. The Russian peasants of the 1830s or even the 1930s did not. Hence, in so far as we recognize that the extent and nature of supply are sometimes relevant, the effects of any changes in that sphere will vary depending on the nature of the religious culture and the degree of social development of the population.

We would expect that, once churches in the former Communist states are allowed to operate at a level that reflects their popularity, marks of religious interest and involvement will rise to something like what they would have been had the state not artificially suppressed religion. The old will do more publicly and more often what they did rarely and covertly. Where the liberation of a dominant ethnic church has occurred in the context of war with a neighbour of a different religio-ethnic complexion (as in Slovenia and Croatia), the revival of religion can be considerable. However, at the risk of sounding like a stuck record, I would repeat that, in so far as there has been an increasing interest in religion, it has come about, not through competition among suppliers, but by traditional customers becoming more committed to their traditions.

To return to the key proposition of Chapter 1, modernization erodes religion except where it finds or retains social functions other than its central task of mediating between the natural and supernatural worlds. The exceptions to the general expectation of decline can largely be encompassed by the notion of cultural defence. Where, as in Ireland, Poland, or Lithuania, religion had been and could remain a vital part of ethnic or national identity, it remained popular. There is nothing new in this observation. In 1978 Martin wrote: 'A positive overlap with the national myth is a necessary condition for a lively and widespread attachment to religion.'[56] The churches retained vital social functions that inhibited such threats to religion as privatization and relativism. In the organizational language of the first chapter, religion is strongest where it can remain in the 'church' form and not be forced into the confines of the 'sect' or the compromises of the 'denomination'. Note that I say 'strongest' rather than 'strong'. In many settings where the dominant religion remained in the church form until late in the twentieth century, and was forced to become more denominational only by the requirements of modern democratic theory, religion has still declined.

In Chapter 1 I specified the primary requirement for the church form: ethnic homogeneity. To quote Martin again: 'Cases where it is very difficult for the national myth to coalesce with religion arise where there are several highly distinctive religions within a national border.'[57] In relatively homogenous countries, industrialization generates diversity and egalitarian democracy and the combination of the two forces the church (and the sects) to become denominations. Where industrialization (and the class formation that accompanies it) occurred late, after the principle of democratic accountability had been established, the religious innovations that are associated with social differentiation could be contained either within or very close to the state church because the state church had by then accepted the basic notions of egalitarianism, democracy, and toleration. England's dissenters of the seventeenth and eighteenth century were driven out of the church. The Nordic revivalists of the nineteenth century mostly remained within their respective state churches.

I would like to add one final set of thoughts about the implied connections between religious vitality and cultural defence. A number of times I have criticized the rational choice approach for resting on quite implausible assumptions about human behaviour and I would like to clarify my own basic assumptions here so that my cultural defence alternative is not open to similar criticism. It would be easy to offer a thoroughly cynical interpretation of many illustrations of the links. When, in the aftermath of the collapse of the state in Albania, we find Albanians who had previously been Communist Party cadres stressing their Muslim identity and leading attacks on the ethnic Greeks (who are Orthodox Christians) in order to solicit economic aid from Turkey, we may rightly suspect this belated rediscovery of Islam. Likewise, when we find the political and military leaders of the Bosnian Serbs—Radovan Karadzic and General Ratko Mladic—being photographed taking communion from an Orthodox bishop, we might suppose that their interest in religion owed much to their desire to win Russian support. However, I do not want to suggest that such instrumental manipulation of religious affiliation underpins all or even much of the cultural defence role of religion. When they erected a statue of the Virgin Mary and conspicuously heard Mass, the Gdansk shipyard workers who formed the basis for the Solidarity movement in Poland were neither cynics nor the dupes of cynics. My explanation rests much more on the large social structural advantages that can be enjoyed by ethnic religion.

A shared religious belief system can explain 'our' virtues and 'their' vices and thus legitimate material interests. It can give hope for the future. Especially when the religious tradition has itself survived for centuries and through a range of political upheavals, its very continuation can give its adherents hope that their present trials will similarly be survived.[58] By adding an additional dimension to the bonds to which one should be loyal, it strengthens interaction within the ethnic group and reduces links across boundaries. Where the state itself rests its legitimacy on ethnic or national identity, the common religion can benefit from government and community support for religious socialization and rituals. My point is not that people do religion in order to attain secular goals. It is that the fortuitous combination of religious and secular goals adds plausibility to the religious belief system. Unlike the rational choice model, my approach offers an explanation of why people believe, not an assertion that secular considerations create religious behaviour.

The close ties between religion and ethnicity explain why the fall of totalitarian Communist regimes has not been followed (as the supply-side approach would predict) by a flowering of new religious options. The relaxation of state control in former Communist countries has made it possible for new competitors to enter the religious market. And many organizations have done just that. American evangelicals have spent huge sums of money training citizens of the former Communist states so that they can promote 'Bible-believing' Christianity. But such innovations have made little impact on the overall picture, because the collapse of Communism has been followed, not by the creation of liberal individualistic tolerant and stable democracies (the sort of setting in which people might seek to 'maximize'), but by a series of national and subnational struggles in which loyalty to the Communist state has been replaced by the much more powerful demand of loyalty to the ethnic group.

Under Communism there may have been large practical obstacles, but arguably there were fewer psychological barriers to religious dissent. The old regimes, at least in theory and sometimes in practice (especially for small religious traditions that were not seen as a threat to the state), confined religion to the private sphere. In some parts of the Communist world, as in eighteenth-century England, 'occasional conformity' and lip service to the ideology of the state could be accompanied by private indulgence of one's spiritual preferences. The ethnic group, especially when engaged in war, does not easily permit private reservations.

Finally, after all the descriptive detail and the abstract summaries, I would like to claim that the fate of religion in Europe offers little or no support for the key propositions of rational choice theory. The effects of state support (and of state repression) are not uniform and they are not uniformly bad. Religious pluralism either is irrelevant or weakens the power of religion. Whatever explanatory value the concentration on the structure of the religious market has for understanding religion in the USA, it has no useful application for Europe.

5

Rational Choice: The Basic Errors

THE previous two chapters have looked very closely at the recent fate of religion in a wide variety of settings. In addition to considering the British and US data that the supply-siders have themselves advanced to support their rational choice approach, I have tried to test the general claims about the effects of diversity and state regulation on religious vitality by looking at a range of continental European societies clustered so that their salient features could become apparent. With all due recognition of the considerable variation in the quality of the available data, I conclude that the observations made by Stark and his colleagues that are useful are invariably those also made by scholars outside the rational choice perspective. Those ideas particular to the 'new paradigm', as it advertises itself, find little or no support in the evidence presented here.[1] I now want to pick up the critical threads from the end of Chapter 2 and pursue them to the point where we can understand in what sort of society the rational choice approach might work and thus come to a clear understanding of why it fails to work in most of the settings described in Chapters 3 and 4.

Plausible Story Lines

One general criticism that can be made of the economic approach to religion is that it has little resonance with the understandings of the people whose behaviour it must explain. Sociologists are divided over whether this matters. I take the view that there are no structures that are not created by the behaviour of individuals. While the positivist search for patterns in action is a useful place to start doing social science, the interpretation of such regularities as we find rests in the end on a convincing explanation of why members of this or that group do what they do. It is perfectly sensible for Durkheim to begin his study of suicide by comparing the suicide rates of various groups of people, but for his explanations to be plausible he must provide a reasonable story of why this sort of person is more or less likely to commit suicide than some other.[2] It does not follow that the people in question must be aware of all the causes of their actions and every aspect of the environment in which they act, nor is it necessary that they use the same terms as the social scientist. But our explanatory models cannot rest on implausible stories about our subjects and we would do well to be sceptical of theories that, when unpacked, turn out to rely on people acting in ways we cannot imagine of ourselves.

So I do not object to the rational choice approach on the ground that it identifies as causes of peoples' actions things of which they are ignorant. Even less do I object (as some believers might) on the ground that the language of economics somehow debases the behaviour it describes. What I resist are implausible biographies. When Stark and his colleagues move from abstract assertion to illustration, the crassness of their claims is exposed. Can we take seriously Iannaccone's 'same-religion' couple who go to church more often than their 'mixed-religion' neighbours because the single journey saves on petrol? I have already mentioned Stark's assertion that, because they are paid irrespective of their popularity, 'the German clergy are better off with empty churches, which place little demand on their time, than with full ones'.[3] Had Stark said of himself that he would be better off if his courses were so unpopular that no students took them because he was paid irrespective of student numbers, he would, we may presume, have noticed the narrowness of motive allowed. Doubtless there are some employees of US universities who would like to be paid to do nothing, but to suppose that of the typical academic, as of the typical German Lutheran minister, betrays the blinding cynicism of the free-market economist. Stark's own actions defy the motives he imputes to others. He does not flood the sociology journals with articles preaching his supply-side gospel because it earns him any money; he is already at the top of his profession. I presume he does it because he is driven by a conviction that he is right and that others should believe him. He wants to persuade. He wants followers. He has pride. As does the typical German Lutheran minister.

Studies of actual clergymen tell us the obvious: irrespective of the security of their salary, they want to be popular. One detailed study of rural Church of England vicars showed that, for all they tried to put a brave face on their dwindling congregations, they were troubled by very small congregations: 'If it gets very small—say five—I am disappointed' and 'It's annoying two or three Sundays a year if no-one comes'. Apart from the psychological problems of being confronted by indifference to what one holds dear, as voiced by the man who said 'It hits you when nobody turns up', small congregations inhibit performance: '16 people without a choir trying to do Anglican chanting is a pretty dismal experience.'[4]

I might add that almost every motivational link in the rational choice model can be similarly challenged by reason and by evidence. Stark and his associates present their theorems and propositions as if they rested firmly on what every sensible hard-headed person knows, but each is thoroughly contestable. To pursue the above example, the assumption that state-funded clergy will work less hard than those dependent on private giving not only demeans the civil servant (that is standard for free-marketeers) but valorizes the entrepreneur and misses the point that entrepreneurs have their own 'inefficiencies'—deceiving their customers and cheating the taxman being the two most common. In the entrepreneurial world of US fundamentalism, faith-healers lie about their curative powers and cynically sell snake oil, television evangelists solicit donations of Third World poverty aid and use them to pay their broadcasting bills, and pastors use tax-free church resources to subsidize extravagant lifestyles. Of course no one would claim him to be typical, but it was US television evangelist Jim Bakker, not some German Lutheran, who used his religious activities to pay for gold-plated taps and an air-conditioned dog kennel.[5] I note this not to poke fun at US television evangelists but because it bears directly on the supply-side explanation of popularity. As it does in conventional economics, the supply-side model assumes that competition is good because it forces producers to work hard to meet the desires of consumers. But that overlooks the possibility of cheating. Some dairy men strive diligently to produce more and better milk, but others just water it down. In the absence of either a very strong moral code or a very strong regulatory framework, competition is as likely to lead to fraud as to efficiency. I am not suggesting that we balance the imputation of sloth and cynicism to the state-funded clergy with the imputation of equally invidious motives to another group of people, but it is only proper that we appreciate the extent to which the supply-side model rests on contentious assumptions. There is no more warrant for assuming that people always behave in a self-interested fashion than there is to suppose that they always behave generously. To prefer the first to the second seems a choice driven more by ideology than by evidence.[6]

The previous two chapters gave us one good reason to be suspicious of the rational choice model: that it is not supported by the evidence. Another cause for suspicion is that it is all too easily supported by the evidence. Anomalous cases cause one sort of problem, but equally awkward are cases that are accommodated too easily, where the accommodation suggests an inappropriate lack of specificity in the propositions. Beneath the apparent rigour of hypotheses and theorems, there is a general flaccidity that allows everything to be claimed to support the theory. The supply-siders argue in one place that low start-up costs are good because they permit widespread innovation that in turn allows everyone to find a religion that suits. But they also argue that high costs are good because, the more people invest in their religion, the greater will be their commitment. Iannaccone tries to resolve the inconsistency by suggesting that the demands churches make of their members cannot exceed the benefits members receive from participating in such churches.[7] Thus demanding churches must provide a wider range of rewards or 'better' rewards. True. But we have no way of knowing in advance where the balance of demands and rewards that produces utility lies. The size of a reward (and even whether something is reward rather than cost) cannot be determined objectively and externally. There is no agreed scale. One person's penalty ('Not another two-hour prayer meeting!') is another's blessing ('Two hours of power in the Precious Blood!'). In the absence of any way of specifying utility other than by observing success and failure, the explanation become circular. If a church grows, its rewards must be higher than its costs; if it fails, costs must have been higher than rewards. This is not explanation; it is merely renaming.

Maximizing and Comparison

Thus leads us to a general difficulty in applying economistic models to religious behaviour that has not been sufficiently explored: the issue of comparability. Rationality in allocation requires that the 'ends of economic units be comparable and measurable on a single scale'.[8] So that I can know which brand of cornflakes will maximize my returns, I must be able to compare the quality and quantity of the flakes in two brands. Economizing first requires that one is able to chose between ends that are genuinely alternative. 'Economising is possible only in so far as the problematic alternative ends are comparable on some scale. When this condition is not met, there is no way of finding out which end or combination of ends will bring the greatest return and so there is no economic way of choosing among them.'[9] Although certain peripheral features of churchgoing (finding a spouse, for example) can be replaced by secular alternatives, the core cannot. In the matter of seeking salvation, ten-pin bowling is not an alternative to worshipping the Lord. Furthermore, even another religion is not an alternative to a religion in the sense that a Ford is an alternative to a Chrysler. Like some secular ideologies (but unlike consumer goods), religions generally demand the loyalty of their adherents. With the exception of Buddhism and modern liberal Protestantism, the great religions claim a unique grasp of the salvational truth. To the guardians of Roman orthodoxy, the Catholic Church is the unique repository of religious truth. Other religions are not plausible alternatives that can be examined for economizing possibilities; they are errors, false-hoods, and heresies. Or, to put it another way, we cannot hedge our bets by buying only a small amount of a religion. We may temporize, and many believers do their best to experiment with their involvement in various churches, but the absence of certainty about the ultimate returns for such involvement means that we cannot regard religious promiscuity as a form of rational diversification of investment.

Even if we could find some mechanism for comparing the rewards of invest-ing in religion rather than something else, we would run into the difficulty that the second requirement for economizing—the existence of a means of comparing costs—is absent. To one potential member of a Pentecostal church a weekend Bible study may be a price to be paid while to another it may be the answer to prayer. Becker is wrong to think we can solve that problem by using 'time' as a shadow price. People do not spend time. They spend time doing this or that. How they feel about what they are doing changes the cost of the units thus exhausted. We can know the price of cornflakes; it is impossible to know the price of being a Mormon or a Jew.

The difficulty of applying the assumption of maximizing to religious behav-iour can be seen very clearly if we consider the constraints on choices. Let us first consider the position of the producer. A distributor of Massey-Ferguson tractors who finds he is selling a duck can transfer to the John Deere company. If the agricultural sector hits the skids, he can get out of tractors altogether, sell his real estate, and buy yen. Can religious organizations do the same? Ian-naccone says: 'In competitive environments, religions have little choice but to abandon inefficient modes of production and unpopular products in favour of more attractive and profitable alternatives.'[10] He offers no illustrations to support this claim. Churches and evangelists have a long history of economic irrationality. While demand may have some effect on supply in that popular-ity may influence recruitment of candidates for the ministry, for example, there are huge cultural constraints on what churches can do to become more popular. Western European Protestant churches may envy the stability of the Catholic Church, but, unlike the tractor distributor, they cannot simply announce that the Reformation was a mistake and return to Rome. While, of course, religions change, they can do so only slowly and within rhetorical limits set by their own history and traditions.

The difference between ideologies and consumer goods can be seen very clearly in the way that their producers respond to unpopularity. When the Ford Motor Company discovered that Edsel model was extremely unpopular, it did not persist in making it and console itself with the thought that the Edsel was just too good for the ordinary motorist. It scrapped it and launched a new model. When extreme left-wing parties fail to recruit more than a handful

of members and get trounced at elections, most do not announce that socialism was a mistake. Instead they console themselves with the exalted status of
the select few who are free from the blinkers of false consciousness. Far from
abandoning unpopular lines, sectarians find solace in knowing that they are
doing the Lord's work and will get their reward in heaven if not before.

This comment should not be misunderstood. I am not suggesting that ideologues are incapable of change or that they do not consider ways of making
their ideologies popular. Church leaders agonize about the latter, and charismatic religious leaders may often radically alter their beliefs.[11] The point is
one of degree and constraint. While a manufacturing company may risk losing
customers and name-recognition advantages if it changes its lines too
abruptly, there is nothing intrinsic to its activities that prevents such innovations or even prevents a complete change of business. Religious organizations
are hugely constrained by their own belief systems.

If the producers of religious goods are constrained in their freedom to
abandon 'inefficient modes of production', to use Iannaccone's phrase, potential consumers are similarly constrained. One of the most curious features of
the rational choice model is that it treats actors as agents without identity or
history. This is very clear in the way that Stark and his associates think about
diversity. In most of their work, and in their use of the Herfindahl Index, they
count all religious organizations as being equally available to all people. But
this overlooks the fact that adding a Swedish Lutheran church to a county
makes no difference to the options available to people who do not speak
Swedish. In most large US towns there is a near-complete duplication of
Protestant denominations and sects because American religious life is still
racially segregated. Even in the 1990s, fifty years after the landmark court judgments that ended formal segregation, racially mixed congregations are
sufficiently rare for the decision of the majority white Pentecostal Fellowship
of North America (which includes the Assemblies of God congregations) to
form a new multiracial umbrella organization to be hailed as 'the Memphis
Miracle'.[12] Five years after its formation, black Pentecostal clergy reported
little impact on the extent of segregation at congregational level. Yet, in measuring and comparing levels of diversity in the USA, the supply-siders made
no reference to racial divisions.

This naïvety about race is carried over to the supply-siders' thinking about
religion in those many societies where religious affiliation has nothing to do
with personal preference. In most of the societies described in the previous
two chapters, religious affiliation is not achieved; it is ascribed at birth, as part
of ethnic or national identity. In very many of them, religious affiliation could
be changed only at great personal and social cost: being ostracized is the most
pleasant outcome and being killed is not unknown. Choosing one's religion

might be possible and even common in the USA, but in Belfast, Zagreb, and Baku religious affiliation is not a matter in which one may readily seek maximizing opportunities. The consequences of switching are far greater than the petrol saving achieved in Iannaccone's human capital model.

As I noted in Chapter 3, Stark and his colleagues have finally acknowledged the existence of cultural and social constraints on choice, although in characteristic fashion they present it as their own discovery, make no reference to those who have long criticized this basic weakness in their model, and fail to appreciate how thoroughly the admission undermines the rest of their work. They cannot have it both ways. Either the maximizing choices of individuals are the basic motor of religious change or they are not. To admit that, in many societies, social norms constrain choice and then to proceed as if this had no major implications for the entire rational choice approach is poor scholarship.

I would like to offer an aside before the concluding summary. The narrowness of my target should be noted. There is always a danger of being taken as criticizing other theories or observations that are perhaps related only by a coincidence of terms. This book is not an attack on the view that most behaviour is rational. It is perfectly proper that we should assume action to be minimally rational until we have very good grounds for arguing that, in any particular case, it is not. Were social action not minimally rational, we would not be able to identify, comprehend, and explain it. What I have been taking issue with above is the very specific claim that *economic* (as distinct from social, legal, or political) rationality provides a useful model for understanding religious belief and behaviour.

That said, my conclusions are simple. Economic or rational choice models of behaviour depend on us knowing what is the rational choice. When faced with the possibility of buying the same breakfast cereal from two outlets, it would be economically irrational not to compare the prices and buy the cheaper. But 'To the extent that we cannot tell, or cannot tell uniquely, what the rational choice would be, the theory fails . . . In a word rational-choice theory can fail because it does not tell us what rationality requires.'[13] Or to quote from Diesing's exploration of the limits of economic rationality: 'Salvation is a definite end, so it can have means and a technique of achievement; but it is not an alternative to any other end. It is priceless. The technical question, "What must I do to be saved?" makes sense and can be answered; but the economic question, "How much is salvation worth to you?" does not.'[14] We need add only that the answers to the technical question will vary from religious group to religious group and from insider to outsider. There is a dramatic switch at the point of belief. What the atheist thought was a complete waste of space becomes an extremely rewarding activity when he becomes a believer. That switch prevents us applying rational choice expectations, yet it is the very thing that economic models pretend to explain.

The last word on this topic should be given to the great American social theorist Talcott Parsons, who worked all his life to bring into creative harmony the assumptions of the various social-science disciplines but did so by recognizing that each had an appropriate sphere of relevance.

Economic analysis is empirically significant only in so far as there is scope for a certain kind of 'rationality' of action, for the weighing of advantages and disadvantages, of 'utility' and 'cost', with a view to maximising the difference between them. Insofar, for instance, as behaviour is purely instinctual or traditional, it is not susceptible of such analysis. On the other hand, its significance rests on there being appreciable scope for the treatment of things and other people . . . in a utilitarian spirit . . . as morally and emotionally neutral means to the ends of economic activity.[15]

Secularization and Choice

Parsons's final sentence allows us to see this argument in an appropriate historical or evolutionary context. Many spheres of human activity are not open to economizing behaviour because they are controlled by a culture of norms. Although it involves a crude simplification, one way of describing modernization is as the gradual shrinking of cultural limitations on economizing, as more and more activities and their products are treated as 'commodities'. Bibby has argued that the modern approach to religion is a consumerist one.[16] As yet, this seems an exaggeration. Berger is undoubtedly right that the cultural pluralism of the modern world requires even those who wish to believe to do so in a manner markedly different from that common in traditional societies. In his terms, even true believers are 'heretics' because we choose God instead of God choosing us.[17] This is true, but, having made our choices (which often means only continuing in the tradition in which we were raised), we engage in a socio-psychological process that Marxists call 'reification'. We deny our own authorship of our choices and regard our actions as inevitable, natural, and plain right. No doubt our initial involvements are often hesitant and experimental, but, having chosen, we swear lifelong fidelity and dismiss our previous involvement with alternatives as misguided youthful experimentation. That is, we form an attachment that is (and is intended to be) far deeper and more enduring than that which we have to our washing machines, PCs, and cars. The obvious parallel is marriage. We may reasonably say that divorce has become more popular as we have come to regard our marriages in an increasingly utilitarian fashion. When a particular relationship no longer satisfies us or allows us to 'fulfil our potential' or some such, then we end it and seek out another. But if we are on the road from a world constrained by social norms to the grand shopping mall of utility maximizing, most of us are not yet ready to recognize that fact openly. To pursue the marriage parallel, what for many Westerners has replaced lifelong monogamy is not promiscuity but serial monogamy. Even though we may sometimes suspect that this new union will last no longer than the last one, yet we swear undying love and promise ourselves that this is the real thing. This still seems to be the case for one section of that group of people (more common in the USA than anywhere else) who pursue their quest for spiritual fulfilment through a variety of options. Those who switch between sects are not self-consciously consumerist. With each new affiliation, they hope to find a depth of attachment closer to that which characterizes 'traditional' identities rather than identifies the limited commitments of consumerist rationality. The one group that does fit Bibby's expectation are the denizens of the 'cultic milieu' that will be discussed in Chapter 7.

Whether or not we are in some way station between a traditional world and a thoroughly modern world in which economizing is the dominant mode of behaviour in all spheres (and not just those of production and distribution) is far too large a question to be answered here. Suffice it to say that in order for us to be free to choose we must be free of loyalties and social constraints. Economistic models work well for cornflakes and cars—products for which there is a very high general demand and little brand loyalty. For those, most people will maximize. It follows that religious behaviour will be explained by a rational choice approach only when religion is no longer strongly associated with other important social institutions and identities, when it is removed from the public sphere and reduced to a matter of personal preference, when its focus is not the life of a nation but the privatized sensibilities of the individual. In a thoroughly secular society, our religion will be no one else's business. Then we will be free to choose. However, most of us will not bother.

In this chapter I have presented the two most abstract arguments against the rational choice model. First, the internal requirements for maximizing are missing from religious belief and behaviour: as we cannot know what is the rational choice, we cannot make it. Hence behaviour in this field cannot be explained by the rational choice model. Secondly, most social environments are not yet conducive to choosing a religion. In most societies, religion is too important to be a matter of personal preference.

6

Conservative Religion

A CENTRAL argument of this book is that, leaving aside the Catholic and Orthodox countries, there is a largely common pattern to the mutation of religion in the industrializing societies of western Europe and their colonial offshoots: except in those settings where ethnic and national conflict places an unusual premium on communal solidarity, the church form of religion is challenged by that of the sect and both become denominations. In the last quarter of the twentieth century, the cultic form has become more common. The denomination and the cult will be considered in detail in the next chapter. It is the impact of choice on the sectarian style of religion that concerns me here.

The role of diversity in sustaining religion is often paradoxical. The rational choice theorists overlook two grand ironies. The first was explored in Chapter 4: in many settings diversity does not occasion choice and switching between options but instead provokes conflict and forces people further back into their existing identities. The second irony is that, in settings where high levels of diversity have created a pluralistic social and political structure, sectarian religious groups may take advantage of the freedom it offers to distance themselves from competing views and from the wider society. They build social institutions that mask their choice and as much as possible deny choice to their children. Liberality at the societal level is a resource that allows the creation of local hegemonies. As I will try to show, conservative religion prospers more in the USA than in Britain, not because the US market offers greater choice and more maximizing opportunities, but because the structure of US society allows conservatives the space in which to sustain something like the church form of religion.

Conservative Success

In discussing the Stark–Bainbridge theory of religion in Chapter 2, I accepted what they present as a major source of evidence for their theory—the relative success of sectarian religion—but argued that an alternative and less contentious explanation of this phenomenon was possible. I would now like to pursue that point.

In response to a question in the 1957 census, 99 per cent of Canadians claimed a religious identity and 82 per cent of them actually belonged to a church. By 1991 the proportion ticking a religious identity box in the census had fallen to 87 per cent and less than a third of those actually belonged to a church. The interesting feature becomes clear if we compare different strands of Protestantism. For the denominational type, the proportion of those claiming an identity who also said they belonged to a congregation changed from 74 per cent in 1957 to 30 per cent in 1990 (the Anglicans) and 84 to 35 per cent (United Church). For those who claimed a conservative Protestant identity, the change was from 86 per cent to 55 per cent: a considerable decline but considerably less than that experienced by the liberals. We see a similar difference in patterns of church attendance. For all Canadians, weekly church attendance fell between 1957 and 1990 from 53 to 23 per cent. But that total masks an important difference. In 1957 40 per cent of those who said they belonged to the mainstream United Church went to church most weeks; in 1990 it was 15 per cent. The drop for the conservatives was only 3 per cent points: from 51 to 48 per cent.[1]

The broad picture for Britain is similar. Between 1970 and 1995 the Anglicans, Presbyterians, and Roman Catholics declined by respectively 32, 40, and 36 per cent. What Peter Brierley calls the 'Free Churches' (of which the large part are Pentecostal and independent evangelical congregations) lost only 10 per cent of their members.[2]

Between 1956 and 1995 the Church of England lost almost exactly half its members (about 1.5 million). The Methodist Church (which by then had become thoroughly denominational) lost 45 per cent of its 1956 total. Halfway through that period the Presbyterian Church of England and Wales merged with the majority of English and Welsh Congregationalists to form the liberal United Reformed Church (URC). Before the 1972 merger the two constituent parts had together lost about 12 per cent of their members. Far from stemming the flow, the merger accelerated the rate of decline. Between 1972 and 1980 membership fell by 22 per cent. From 1980 to 1995 it recorded a 30 per cent drop, despite taking in as a block over 2,000 former members of the Churches of Christ. Taking the whole period from 1956 to 1995, its progenitors and the URC declined from around 300,000 members to just over 100,000: a loss of two-thirds. The conservative congregations that stayed out of the formation of the URC, largely on theological grounds, did a better job of retaining their members. The Evangelical Federation of Congregational Churches showed a modest loss: 4.5 per cent. The Congregational Federation lost 10 per cent of its own members but recorded a net gain of 11 per cent over the period because it was joined by thirty-two congregations from the Scottish Congregational Union. Thus within one ecclesiastical tradition we see the liberal URC becoming rapidly less popular while the two conservative schisms declined gently.

What is almost certainly the largest decline is seen in the most liberal denomination: with 30,000 members at the end of the war and only 6,700 in 1995, the Unitarian and Free Churches lost 78 per cent of their people. Of the historic British organizations, the best performance in the second half of the twentieth century was recorded by the conservative Baptist Union, which saw a drop of only 38 per cent. Within the Baptist tradition, the more sectarian Grace Baptist Assembly showed a growth of 17 per cent between 1980 and 1995, while the Baptist Union of Great Britain declined by 6.2 per cent. Leaving aside those churches that recruit mainly from immigrant groups, the best Christian performances were recorded by Pentecostal organizations and by the 'house churches' of the 1970s. The Assemblies of God saw a 70 per cent growth between 1980 and 1995. The Elim Pentecostal Church grew by 100 per cent. The Fellowship of Independent Evangelical Churches pretty well stayed level. It grew slowly in the 1960s and had 415 congregations in 1975. Twenty years later it had gained twenty. Quantifying the 'new' churches of what Andrew Walker has called the Restoration movement is difficult, but Brierley, who put considerable effort into tracking them for his English Church censuses, suggests a tenfold growth: from a total of around 10,000 in 1980 to over 100,000 in 1995.[3] The two organizations that have grown most have been two sects outside the mainstream of Christianity. The Jehovah's Witnesses grew from 28,000 in 1956 to 131,000 in 1995 and the Mormons did even better, growing from 9,000 in 1956 to 171,000 in 1995.[4]

As these data may invite misinterpretation by those who deny the fact of secularization, I will risk labouring the point and stress the disparity in size between those organizations that have declined and those that have grown. Taken together, the halving of the Church of England, Methodism, and the URC has removed over 2 million members. Against this, the near stability of the older evangelical churches and the growth of the new churches make little impact.

That England and Canada are not alone in showing relative conservative success can be seen from Scottish examples. Scotland has the advantage for our purposes of relatively little immigration and a range of churches that are similar in organization and have equally deep roots in Scottish culture but differ markedly in theology. As we can see from Table 6.1, with the exception of the Reformed Presbyterians (or Covenanters), the fate of the Scottish churches falls into the expected pattern. Like the Church of England, the

TABLE 6.1. *Presbyterian Church membership, Scotland, 1956–1995*

Churches	1956	1995	Net change	Change as % of 1956 total
United Free Church of Scotland	24,800	6,900	−17,900	−72
Church of Scotland	1,319,600	698,552	−621,048	−47
Free Church of Scotland	25,000	19,000	−6,000	−24
Free Presbyterian Church of Scotland	4,750	4,200	−550	−12
Reformed Presbyterian Church	610	100	−510	−84
Associate Presbyterian Church	—	1,300	—	—

Sources: Robert Currie and Alan D. Gilbert, 'Religion', in A. H. Halsey (ed.), *Trends in British Society since 1990* (London: Macmillan, 1972), 407–50; Robert Currie, Alan D. Gilbert, and Lee Horsley, *Churches and Churchgoers: Patterns of Church Growth in the British Isles since 1700* (Oxford: Oxford University Press, 1977); Peter Brierley, *UK Christian Handbook Religious Trends 1998/99 No. 1* (London: Christian Research Association, 1997).

Church of Scotland has lost almost half its members, the more liberal United Free Church has suffered more, and the two sectarian Free Churches have survived best. Indeed, had the Free Presbyterian Church not split, it would have recorded a growth of 16 per cent.[5]

Similar patterns can be found in every other industrial society. We could also consider religion in Australia. In summarizing a range of data, Marler and Hadaway conclude: 'whether we look at attendance during the past month, the past two weeks or the past week, the attendance rate in 1997 is approximately one half of the rate in 1960.'[6] As with the Canadian Census, there was been a recent and very large increase in those who claim 'no religion': from 2.5 per cent in 1961 to 21.6 per cent in 1997. We might also note that the number of those who refuse to answer the question (many of whom will have declined to answer because they have no interest in the topic) has also grown from under 2 per cent to 10 per cent. Table A6.1 in the Appendix details the religious affiliations claimed in the censuses. Drawing firm conclusions from these figures is not easy because so much of the change stems from immigration rather than from the internal dynamics of church life. Over the century Australia has grown from just under 4 million to 17 million people and the population that is not identified with some non-Christian religion (that is, the Christians and those who could have been) has grown from about 3 million to over 16 million. So, to keep pace with their potential market, the Christian churches would need to have grown by some 400 per cent over the century.

The Catholic Church managed that because it recruited very large numbers of southern Europeans and the indigenous Catholic population had, until the 1970s, a much higher than average birth rate. If we look at the Protestant churches that were in place in the first quarter of the century, we find that all fell a long way behind. However, the more sectarian churches generally came closest to matching the population increase. The mainstream Anglicans grew by 168 per cent and the Baptists by 215 per cent. That the majority of Presbyterians and Congregationalists merged to form the Uniting Church makes it impossible to disentangle the relative fates of those strands of Protestantism, but what is striking is the collapse of Unitarianism and the growth, well ahead of population increase, of those sects on the fringes of Christianity: the Seventh Day Adventists, Pentecostalists, Mormons, and the Jehovah's Witnesses.

We must remember that, as for the Canadian censuses, these figures represent only an affiliation claimed by ticking a box or writing on a government form. There are not good series of national church-membership figures, but we can get some idea of the actual strength of the various religions in Australia if we consider the information on church attendance gathered from the Protestant churches in the 1991 National Church Life Survey. As Table A6.2 in the Appendix shows, there is a huge variation in what proportion of those who claim a particular affiliation in the census actually attend church. Only 5 per cent of those who call themselves Anglicans or Presbyterians go to church. For the Uniting Church it is 12 per cent. A fifth of nominal Lutherans are active. But over a third of those claiming the Baptist or Salvation Army label and over three-quarters of those calling themselves Seventh Day Adventists actively support their church. And the number of people who attend Pentecostal churches is actually greater than those who describe themselves as such in the census. A further sign of Pentecostal strength is that three-quarters of them were born in Australia, and over half of them had two Australian-born parents. Thus we are seeing indigenous expansion rather than (as is the case with Catholics or Anglicans) an immigrant influx. There are not good church-attendance data for the start of the century, but an official survey of church attendance in New South Wales in 1890 reported that 28 per cent of the people were 'habitual' attenders.[7] If 'habitual' meant fortnightly or more, it would be twice the present rate.

To summarize, the Australian picture seems typical in showing a considerable decline in the popularity of religion overall, with the more sectarian of those organizations present in the nineteenth century doing markedly better than the more liberal and mainstream churches. Although they remain small compared to the general population, the sects of the twentieth century—the Adventists, Pentecostalists, Mormons, and Witnesses—have all shown considerable growth.

As the supply-siders make much of conservative resilience and draw the bulk of their examples from the USA, I will not labour the point with additional American material.[8] I will draw this section to a close by concluding that on this one point I am at one with my rational choice opponents: although, as I will make clear below, sectarianism does not provide immunity to secularization or guarantee success, it does seem to be the case that the sectarian form of religion has survived the last half of the twentieth century in better shape than its denominational counterpart. That is what needs to be explained.[9]

The Stark–Bainbridge Account

Stark and Bainbridge explain the relative success of conservative religion by its greater usefulness. Religion is more appealing than secular philosophies because it can provide supernatural compensators, which, because they are supernatural, are bigger and broader in scope and less susceptible to refutation than secular alternatives. So, while social democracy can promise moderate redistribution of wealth through progressive taxation, Christianity can promise that the meek will inherit the earth and the rich will be as likely to enter the kingdom of God as a camel is to pass through the eye of a needle. Furthermore, while religions often promise benefits in this life (Get Saved and Save Your Marriage!) much of what they offer cannot be tested this side of death. While observation may bring us to the conclusion that Communism does not work, the promise of the life ever after cannot be similarly evaluated. As the supernatural can offer better and bigger compensators than any secular alternative, those religions that gradually accommodate to the mores and beliefs of the secular world are giving away their strongest hand and will be displaced by more traditionally supernaturalist competitors. Hence, liberal churches will decline and conservative ones will grow.

However, as I pointed out in the earlier discussion, if conservative success is to be explained by its superior appeal, it ought to be the case that liberal and mainstream churches decline because their members come to find the product unsatisfactory and the sectarian alternatives grow because what they offer appeals to the unchurched and to disaffected liberals.

There are a few changes that at first sight look like that. For example, the Congregational Federation gained thirty-two congregations from the Scottish Congregational Union in 1994, but, of course, these were conservatives who changed organizational allegiance in order to *maintain* their conservative witness when the organization to which they belonged became more liberal. They switched institutional affiliation; they were not seduced by a more attractive belief system. We see something similar with the Churches of Christ, which in 1842 had 1,300 members. The movement grew steadily and peaked with 16,000 members in 200 congregations in the 1920s. As the leadership became more liberal (expressed particularly in contributions to modern biblical scholarship and involvement in the ecumenical movement), conservative congregations withdrew, either to continue as independents or to attach themselves to the Baptist Union.

Many liberals do leave their churches because they lose interest or lose faith, but disillusioned adults are not the main problem. The two crucial points are the end of childhood and the end of life. Churches that decline generally do so because children stop attending when they are no longer brought by their parents (and leaving home to attend college is a common break point) and because members die faster than they are replaced. Although major biographical breaks (divorce or moving town, for example) and major institutional changes (a new minister or a major reorganization of parish structure) can cause people to reconsider their church involvement, those who are still active church members into their adult years generally remain so until they die. If the main cause of liberal decline was a failure to produce impressive enough rewards and compensators, we would expect to find large-scale adult defection. In almost every year since 1950 more British Methodists have 'left' through death than disaffiliation.[10]

We can also look at relative conservative resilience from the other end by asking where the more sectarian religious organizations get their members from. In the 1970s Bibby and Brinkerhoff looked at recruitment to twenty randomly selected evangelical churches in Calgary and classified sources of new members as 'reaffiliation' (the recruit having come from another evangelical group), birth, and proselytism.[11] As the title of their first paper 'Circulation of the Saints' implied, the considerable effort that these churches put into evangelistic outreach was not a major source of new members. They repeated their research at decade intervals, on the third occasion adding four new charismatic congregations to replace four of the original sample that had ceased to function, and found the pattern we see in Table 6.2.

In later comments Bibby noted one flaw in the studies, which was that they had not traced the affiliation of new members back further than one step. It was thus possible that, though almost three-quarters of new members had previously belonged to some other evangelical church, they had earlier belonged to liberal churches or had had no church connection at all. Bibby is able to throw some light on that possibility with data from a larger survey that compares the affiliation of respondents with that of their parents. This shows that 61 per cent of conservative Protestants had conservative Protestant parents, while the parents of 21 per cent belonged to mainline Protestant churches, 8 per cent were Catholics, and 10 per cent were described as having no affiliation.[12] This suggests that evangelical groups are more successful at

TABLE 6.2. *'Circulation of the Saints', Calgary, 1966–1990* (%)

Years	Source of new members		
	Reaffiliation	Birth	Proselytism
Original sample			
1966–70	72	19	9
1976–80	70	17	13
1986–90	72	13	15
Additional sample			
1986–90	71	15	14

Sources: Reginald Bibby, *Unknown Gods: The Ongoing Story of Religion in Canada* (Toronto: Stoddard, 1993), 42.

recruiting outsiders than was the impression created by the original 'circulation of the saints' research, but it none the less confirms the central point that the relative fortunes of competing religions are determined mainly by their ability to retain their own people.

A similar US study surveyed almost 3,000 members of various 'new evangelical' congregations (such as the Vineyard movement, associated with the 'Toronto blessing' and other Pentecostal manifestations). These churches modify more traditional evangelicalism with what they call 'cultural currency', by which they mean not encumbering the biblical message with outmoded dress codes and dull forms of worship. As these were new congregations, almost no members could have been recruited by birth. A higher proportion than in the Canadian research said they did not belong to any church prior to joining the one in which they were surveyed, but still only 13 per cent said they had no religious upbringing. For the Vineyard congregations, 75 per cent had switched from some other conservative Protestant church.[13]

A British study of conservative recruitment suggests something important about its dependence on the wider culture. A survey of the 249 Brethren congregations in 1978 showed that 40 per cent had seen no adult conversions in the previous two years. Ten years later, that figure had risen to 45 per cent.[14] Nowhere in the industrial world are evangelicals terribly good at recruiting outsiders, but they seem far better at it in the USA than in Britain, with Canada falling somewhere in the middle. That, conveniently, is also how we would rank the three countries in terms of their secularity. Not surprisingly, sectarians find the secular, society less fertile than the more religious. In a country where almost everyone pays lip service to God and some Christian faith is common, 'witnessing' to casual acquaintances is relatively easy and painless, and, even with their strong tendency to form their own enclaves, American evangelicals can interact confidently with the wider society. British evangelicals are in a very small minority in a largely hostile environment. Though they have far more contact with the heathen than their US counterparts, they can do little with it because even the mildest sort of proselytizing would be regarded as unacceptable in most casual relationships. It would be offensive because the evangelical must know that the object of his or her attention is ideologically light years away. In the same way that using conversational openings to try to interest American stockbrokers in Maoist communism would be aggressive, proselytizing is almost guaranteed to be confrontational. It is an obvious point, but the more secular the general culture and the further away (in ideological distance or in years from some previous biographical connection with Christianity) are those outside the sect, the harder it will be to recruit them.

We can put this in historical terms by recognizing that, as societies become more secular, so the pool of likely converts for sectarian religion shrinks, and hence that each wave of revival will be smaller than the one before. In trying to turn conventional Anglicans into committed evangelical Methodists, John Wesley had to shift them only a very short distance. Essentially all he had to do was persuade them to take more seriously things they already believed and there were a lot of people who believed those things. As eighteenth-century dissent moderated (for reasons I will discuss shortly), a new wave took its place with the formation of the Salvation Army and a variety of Pentecostal movements at the end of the nineteenth century. This attracted far fewer people and grew more slowly. The charismatic and neo-Pentecostalism movements of the 1960s were smaller still. As the mainstream churches have become more liberal and as the number of those with no church connection has increased, so the distance that any sect must persuade outsiders to travel has increased enormously. This would lead us to suppose that sects have become gradually more dependent on biological reproduction for growth, and this does indeed seem to be the case. The only obvious exception is the Mormons, who devote an unprecedented amount of effort to proselytism.[15]

Strictness and Separation

Instead of concentrating on the differing appeals of denominational and sectarian religion, we should be looking at retention and socialization. A pioneering work in this field was Dean Kelley's *Why the Conservative Churches are Growing*,[16] the thesis of which is ably summarized by Hoge:

Strong churches are characterized by a demand for high commitment from their members. They exact discipline over both beliefs and life-style. They have missionary zeal, with an eagerness to tell the good news to all persons. They are absolutistic about beliefs. Their beliefs are a total, closed system, sufficient for all purposes, needing no revision and permitting none. They require conformity in life-style, often involving certain avoidances of non-members or use of distinctive visible marks or uniforms.[17]

A very similar case for organizational strength was made by Rosabeth Kanter, who wanted to know why some communes or intentional communities succeeded while others failed. So that the effects of differences in the communities were not swamped by differences in their surrounding societies, she concentrated on communities that had been formed in one country within a relatively short time period: the USA between 1780 and 1860. She managed to identify 90 such communities: 11 'successes' that had survived twenty-five years (the conventional view of a generation) and 79 'failures' that had not. She concluded that, although there was no shortlist of properties present in all the successes and uniformly absent from the failures, there were characteristics that were common in almost all of the communities that lasted one generation and rare in the failures. The successes demanded various forms of sacrifice (such as abstinence from sex, alcohol, and dancing) from their members. They had world views that drew hard lines between the good people of the commune and the rest of the world. They had very strict definitions of membership and rigorous membership tests. New members were required to prove their commitment by investing a great deal of time and money in the enterprise, which in turn made it costly to defect. Almost all the successes bolstered this psychic and social separation from the world with geographical isolation. Kanter concluded that commitment was not a mysterious phenomenon that had to precede the formation of a utopian community. Rather it was a social property that could be engineered by the deliberate use of what she called 'commitment mechanisms'.[18]

In the style of rational choice theory, Iannaccone has taken the work of Kelley and Kanter and developed a formal model that, he claims, predicts conservative success. He begins by noting that: 'Religious groups demanding sacrifices appear more successful than those that do not. The explosive growth of the Krishnas, Moonies and other eastern cults is well-documented.'[19] Actually it is not. The more sectarian of the new religious movements of the 1970s attracted most public attention, but it was the less demanding ones that attracted and retained most members. And, for the sorts of reasons to be explored shortly in considering the typical evolution of sects, the more sectarian new religious movements have been forced to moderate considerably. But we can leave that exaggeration aside for the moment.

To lay the foundation for his model, Iannaccone begins by posing the question of why anyone would want to join a strict church: 'Why become a Mormon or a Seventh Day Adventists, let alone a Krishna or a Moonie, when the Methodists and Presbyterians wait with open arms?' Why should people make sacrifices for their religious beliefs? He then rephrases the question as a more general economic problem: 'How can burnt-offerings and their analogs survive in religious markets when self-interest and competitive pressures bar them from most other markets?'[20] The explanation for this apparent irrationality is that it solves the closely related problems of 'free-riding' and low levels of commitment.

As Iannaccone expresses the free-riding problem: 'Church members may attend services, call upon the counsel of the pastor, enjoy the fellowship of their peers and so forth without ever putting a dollar in the plate or bringing a dish to the potluck.'[21] As with his human capital model explained in Chapter 2, what seems sensible in the abstract (in this case, how does a group prevent itself being exploited) becomes ridiculous when put into an imaginary biography. Church members could indeed do all of the above, if they did not believe in God or had no interest in the goodwill of their fellows. However, they could not do them if they believed (as evangelicals do) that there is an all-seeing omnipotent God who would be insulted by such sleights to his servants. In order to set up his explanation of apparently irrational commitment devices, Iannaccone posits a quite false problem by arguing that religious groups lack effective means of externally monitoring commitment. For those who do believe, or who are sufficiently close to belief to act as if they did believe, there is a thoroughly effective internal monitoring system: the indwelling Holy Spirit. And that force is embodied in the social relationships of the group. To take his own example, very few people who wished to be respected by a group to which they belonged (or which they were considering joining) would attend a potluck supper without bringing a contribution.

What makes the free-rider problem even less of an issue for any sort of group that wishes to recruit new members is that such groups quite consciously go out of their way to cultivate a penumbra of potential members. Far from seeing free-riders as a threat, most evangelistic religious groups make strenuous (but not very successful) efforts to encourage the uncommitted to associate with them in the hope that deepening social ties to existing members and the pleasurable experiences of initially tentative and experimental involvement will result in the associates becoming true believers.

Iannaccone believes that 'less committed members threaten to swamp groups that would otherwise have high levels of participation.'[22] A grand assertion is presented as a problem and then a formal model is elaborated that proves that the thing to be explained is actually a solution to the posited problem. The assertion here is that people are better off in groups whose average level of participation is greater than their own. We can see what he means if we consider Marx's famous description of communism as 'from each according to his abilities, to each according to his needs'. Were I a member of a pension fund that set different levels of contributions according to income but paid out the same benefits to all members, I would have a clear interest in disguising the true extent of my income so that, while I enjoyed the same benefits as every other member, my contributions were as low as possible. There is no difficulty understanding the issue, but we need not accept such narrow self-serving as the general motive force of human behaviour. US economists may find it hard to believe, but there are many settings in which people are quite willing to contribute to the general good, to support redistributive tax systems, and to assume an unusually high burden for the benefit of others. But not only is the general rule suspect for patently financial matters such as tax systems, it is even less persuasive when applied to areas of human life where the costs and rewards of an activity are often indistinguishable. As I argued in the previous chapter, one of the main weaknesses of the rational choice approach is that it fails to appreciate the way that communal and solidaristic activities such as participation in a worshipping collectivity elide cost and benefit. In a world where actively engaging in evangelistic outreach is one of the pleasures of knowing that you are one of God's people, those true believers who give up long hours for the church are unlikely to resent those souls less able or willing to engage in the Lord's mighty commission.

Furthermore, most religious belief systems have built-in protection against excessive free-riding in that the benefits of belief are held to be available only to those who sincerely believe. The cynical pension-fund member who unfairly deflates his contributions will still get his pension. The cynical 'Pentecostalist' who only pretends to have been born-again and to have received the second blessing of being filled with the Holy Spirit will not go to heaven. In the nineteenth century the Free Church in the Scottish Hebrides usually had far more adherents than members. It was quite common for people to be raised in the church and attend faithfully all its services, pray daily, and carefully study their Bibles and yet still not come forward to take communion because they were strict Calvinists. An old gravestone in Esheness on the Shetland mainland says of the man buried beneath 'To all outward appearances, he was a Christian'. The author of that apparently grudging inscription did not mean the deceased was a hypocrite. He just meant that we can never be sure of our place in God's divine providence. Rather than risk insulting the Creator, many Scots Calvinists declined to take communion, despite being, to all appearances, fully qualified. The notion that religious groups are threatened by a lack of effective mechanisms for external monitoring of the commitment of members is simply a false problem.

The one empirical study that has tried to find evidence of Iannaccone's difficulty-to-be-overcome failed. Over 500 churchgoing Christians in the much-studied 'Middletown' (actually Muncie, Indiana) were asked 'What percentage of members of your church would you say receive a number of rewards from church but do not contribute much in terms of time or money?'. Almost half of those asked saw no problem at all and only 9 per cent thought it a major problem. And very few of those felt that their church life was being made less satisfying by the presence of relatively uncommitted people.[23]

But we can go back a stage and see an earlier flaw in Iannaccone's approach to strictness. He begins by assuming that burnt-offerings and such sacrifices as incurring stigma are irrational and hence need some extraneous explanation. There is actually a very simple explanation of why people give up caffeine, bang tambourines in public places, or take vows of silence. They do so because they believe these are spiritually valuable exercises that bring them closer to God or salvation or spiritual enlightenment. Like the Stark–Bainbridge theory of religion criticized in Chapter 2, Iannaccone's whole approach starts by assuming that religion is false and that the actions engaged in by religious people need some explanation other than that they believe these actions to be pleasing to God.

We need not stop our attempt to understand religious behaviour at the point of showing simply that believers think these things are sensible. That would be merely description. There is nothing wrong with asking why, in addition to the obvious reason that they think God requires it, religious people do what they do. However, if we begin with untenable assumptions about the fundamental dynamics of human behaviour and from those generate problems that are not seen as such by those we are trying to understand, we are sure to construct wrong explanations of their actions. This is what Iannaccone has done.

As noted a number of times in earlier chapters, one major difficulty with the rational choice approach is that many of its propositions, cut free from the dubious underlying theory, are unobjectionable, and I have the same response to much of what Kelley and Kanter have to say. The main disagreement is only with the suggested causal sequence, which is exaggerated in Iannaccone's particular elaboration of those observations. He is quite right to say that the sectarian form of religion enjoys a number of advantages in terms of social organization: primarily it reduces involvement with the wider world by providing alternative forms of satisfaction within the company of the faithful. He is simply wrong to suppose that this stems from an attempt to solve the problem of free-riding. In effect he is saying, with Kanter, that increased commitment comes from the group having commitment mechanisms. The sequence should be reversed. Commitment may be reinforced by being institutionalized in patterned expectations of how the committed should behave, but, in logic and in time, faith comes before the commitment mechanisms, which are an expression of it, not its cause.

That Iannaccone has the causal sequence the wrong way round is clear at the very start of his work, where he defines the sect by its behavioural requirements. For him a sect is a religious group that demands its members be radically separated from their surrounding society.[24] As with the Kanter and Kelley approach, this has the odd effect of implying that any religious belief system can be constructed in a sectarian manner. As I will elaborate in the next chapter, this is not the case. At the very heart of sectarian religion is a particular epistemological claim: that there is only one saving truth and that we have it! Without that core belief, none of the characteristics that Kelley summarizes as strictness and none of Kanter's commitment mechanisms would be possible.

A more realistic approach to strictness must begin by appreciating that, far from being initially desired for its group-reinforcing functions, separation from the wider society was often reluctantly adopted by the sect only after it had failed to persuade the rest of the world to accept its standards. Although I will shortly say something about the panoply of social institutions created by US fundamentalists, it is important to note that the authors of 'The Fundamentals of the Faith', the 1920s publications that gave their name to the movement, were not separatists. Many initially rejected the idea of 'coming out' of their denominations and setting up rival institutions and did so reluctantly only once it had become clear that they were in a minority.[25] Separation is usually an accidental by-product of trying to hold either genuinely deviant beliefs or beliefs that were once commonplace but that become deviant because the rest of the world changes.

If we start, not with patterns of behaviour, but with beliefs, and if we begin by recognizing that what most sectarians believe was once close to the dominant views of their societies (and their behaviour was once pretty normal too and hence requires no elaborate functional explanations), we can see a less theoretically elaborate but more sensible relationship between strict religion and resilience.

World views and belief systems are sustained by social interaction. People talk to each other about what they hold dear. They exchange interpretations of both serious and trivial events. In conversation, they gloss topics with an ideological coating. When people do this together in groups, they reinforce each other's faith. When we talk of 'discipline' and 'control' in religious

movements, we are usually using those terms in a very weak sense. Evangelical Christians expect each other to maintain a certain standard of 'witness',
a certain 'walk with the Lord'. Those who fall short of the standards are 'disciplined' by their fellows. Wayward evangelicals are not shot. Their friends
'have a word with them'. Their pastor takes them aside. Their relationships
with other members cool. If they cannot be restored to the straight and
narrow, they will be made to feel sufficiently uncomfortable for them to leave
the group. Those who remain take their beliefs seriously enough to wish to
see them supported in their relations with significant others. So they select
their friends and marriage partners from among those with whom they feel
comfortable and who share their vision of the world.

Even if there are no overt rules against mixing with the unregenerate, the
time and effort devoted to religious activities and the pleasure derived from
them have the effect of isolating the true believer. The committed members
of Ian Paisley's church have two or three services and a prayer meeting to
attend on a Sunday. There is also a midweek Bible Study and an early morning
midweek prayer meeting. There is an outdoor service on a mid week
lunchtime. Most weeks there are also youth club meetings and door-to-door
visitations. There is also a great deal of committee and preparation work that
can easily consume another two or three evenings a week. If one adds to this
the fact that a wide range of popular activities (such as going to the cinema,
attending dances, drinking in public houses and bars, going to football
matches, and anything that happens on a Sunday) will be regarded as unsuit-
able, we can readily see how committed believers come to form a distinctive
subculture.

Avoiding Diversity in Pluralistic Contexts

I would like now to elaborate a point made above about the environment for
sectarian success. We recognize that the sectarians have a survival advantage
in being insulated from the wider society. Such social distance is often a combination of the sect rejecting the world and the world rejecting the sect. The
sensible observation of the supply-siders is that the environment in which any
religious organization operates has a marked effect on that organization; their
mistake is taking a narrow view of what matters about the environment. There
are aspects of the structure of public administration and the operations of the
state other than the regulatory regime for religion that have considerable consequences for the survival or growth of the sect. If a degree of distance from
the wider society is beneficial, then it ought to be the case that the sectarian

form of religion does best in those societies that make such distancing easier. This does indeed seem to be the case and goes a long way to explaining the different fates of conservative Protestantism in the USA and Britain.

In order to cope with its size and internal diversity, the USA has evolved a system of regulation of such matters as education and public broadcasting, two fields that are vital to the preservation of a deviant world view, that is considerably more open and diffuse than the heavily centralized structures of the UK. In the USA it is relatively easy and inexpensive for people to start their own schools. Private schools may teach pretty much what they like and even state schools have considerable autonomy. With the exception of the schools run by the Catholic Church and the Church of England (and the latter are not numerous), the UK has only a very small and expensive élite private-school sector. Moreover, teachers are trained in public universities, accredited by public agencies, and paid at national wage rates. State schools are constrained by a national curriculum and even private schools are kept similar by the common class and educational background of their staff and the requirements of the examination boards that validate their qualifications.

Vital to any group's preservation of a distinctive world view and way of life is its ability to control information and ideas. Until the technical innovations of the 1980s that brought satellite and cable television and the liberalization introduced by the Conservative government led by Margaret Thatcher from 1979 to 1994, the British mass media were heavily constrained.[26] There were only four national radio channels, all controlled by the state British Broadcasting Corporation (BBC). Until 1982, when Channel 4 was licensed, the UK had only three television channels, two of them run by the BBC. Even the two commercial channels were heavily controlled. Individuals and organizations could not purchase air time to show their own programmes and ideological advertising was not permitted. The BBC and the commercial companies were required to provide religious broadcasting, but its content was heavily regulated so that it encompassed the broad consensus of Christian churches. As Britain has become more culturally diverse, that consensus has been broadened. Opportunities to broadcast on the BBC Radio Four's 'Thought for the Day' or 'Songs of Praise' slot are rotated around the varying religious organizations and traditions roughly in portion to their presence in the population at large, but there is a very clear understanding that spokesmen will not be provocative, will not criticize other religious positions, and will not proselytize. Since the 1970s, the space given to religion has diminished and a large number of broadcasters now fulfil their statutory obligation to produce religious programming by having secular programme-makers make programmes *about* religion.

To summarize, for most of the twentieth century UK television and radio produced common-denominator religious programmes of an essentially ecumenical character. What they did not do was allow particular religious organizations to produce programmes that represented their views.

We can see the importance of these different regulatory regimes if we consider the ability of US sectarians to construct their own world. I will use the names 'Joe' and 'Jolene' for a Baptist couple I met in Virginia in the late 1970s. He was an assistant pastor in Jerry Falwell's Liberty Baptist Church; she taught in the independent Christian school that was attached to the church. Their two children attended that school. On completion one went to Falwell's Liberty College (now Liberty University); the other went to another religious institution, Oral Roberts University in Tulsa, Oklahoma. During the holidays the students of Liberty College helped run a fundamentalist summer camp.[27] The church also supported a maternity home and adoption agency for unmarried mothers, a programme for reformed alcoholics, and a prison-visiting programme. Jolene's mother had an apartment in a church-run complex for 'senior saints'. She and her elderly friends helped out with the church bookstore and with the huge mailing operation that was attached to Falwell's television show *The Old Time Gospel Hour*. The family watched programmes on Pat Robertson's Christian Broadcasting Network (now the Family Channel) or the Trinity network and listened to Christian radio channels and programmes. The kids listened to Christian rock and country music. The family did not take a secular newspaper but subscribed to a range of weekly and monthly Christian magazines. Joe had a publication called *Christian Yellow Pages* that allowed him to make sure that he purchased his car and his refrigerator from like-minded fundamentalists.

What struck me forcefully as distinguishing this life from that of an English evangelical couple was not that Joe and Jolene spend a huge amount of time in church and church-related work (though they did) but that, even when they wanted to do something 'secular' such as attend a softball game, they attended a game between two teams of young fundamentalists watched by an audience of fundamentalists. As far as I could tell, neither Joe nor Jolene had a friend or work colleague who was not an independent Baptist fundamentalist. They lived in a world that was fundamentalist in almost the sense that England in the Middle Ages was Christian. They had constructed for themselves a culturally homogenous society to support their fundamentalist subculture. They had managed to ensure that most representations of the outside world came filtered through fundamentalist media. They had provided themselves with fundamentalist alternatives to secular institutions. They had a social life that ensured that almost all their interaction was with fellow believers, so that the mundane events of everyday life could be glossed in such a way as to confirm their fundamentalist world view.

This is the paradox that is overlooked by the rational choice theorists. Diversity, if it produces a pluralistic structure of public administration and government, allows people considerable freedom to avoid diversity. Where British Christians are offered an almost unavoidable diet of programming that insidiously undermines their particular beliefs, US evangelicals have been able to create a system that allows them to avoid what they do not want to see and produce what they want. The parallel world of US fundamentalist institutions allows a young fundamentalist to study law at a good quality conservative Protestant institution. The Scottish evangelical who wishes a career in law must study Scots law in a secular institution surrounded by non-believers.

Of course there is a degree of circularity involved in this account. US fundamentalists have the facilities to construct their own minority world because there are a lot of them. There are now so few conservative Protestants in Britain that, even when broadcasting regulations were relaxed, they could not take advantage of them. Although the regulations now permit the establishment of a Christian cable television channel, there is too small a market to make it viable.

In case this is read as an application of the supply-side approach (state-run religious broadcasting deadens the faith; a free market permits it full expression), I would like to clarify how the regulatory regimes for education and broadcasting differ from that for religion. As I have stressed, the weakness of the supply-side case for religion is that it does not plausibly explain why believers who are alienated from state religion do not make their own provision. The same objection does not hold for education and broadcasting, because in these fields the state's control is effective. Private provision of either in the UK is nearly impossible. As some churches did in Communist states, it is possible to construct *samizdat* forms of communication, and doubtless many Christians in the GDR or Hungary derived considerable pleasure from defying the state, but such private consumption could not be structured into the day-to-day life of a supportive community and could be a socially supportive activity only in the context of major political dissent or ethnic conflict.

The second way in which my treatment of regulatory regimes differs from the supply-side approach is that it is concerned with opportunities for the maximizing individual to satisfy his or her individual preferences, a thoroughly atomized view of the world. I am concerned with the space a regime allows minorities to construct communities.

To summarize: to the extent that a nation state or a society is prepared to allow people to create their own subcultures, the sect form can prosper by socializing its children in the faith. If the nation state or the society does not allow autonomous institution-building, then sectarians will find it difficult and expensive to insulate themselves from the wider secular society.

Threats to Sectarian Religion

Thus far I am suggesting that the sectarian form of religion can insulate itself against the corrosive effects of positive and warm relationships with people of alternative and competing viewpoints. In the right circumstances (and the USA has more of those than most European societies) sectarians can create culturally homogenous sub-societies in which their religious world view is as taken-for-granted and as natural as Christianity was in the Middle Ages. However, that is not the end of the story. Conservative religion faces a variety of challenges. Were it the case that sectarianism provided general immunity to secularization, then sects would neither decline nor change. Yet they do both.

One obvious problem of insulation is that the sectarians become dependent on their own biology. They can thus inadvertently commit suicide by shunning sexual activity, as the Shakers did.[28] Less dramatically, population changes in the geographical area in which the sectarian religion has its roots will have a major impact. Its concentration in the southern states, which enjoyed a major growth in population and in economic power and political prestige, was of great benefit to US fundamentalism. But demography is not always that kind. When the Free Church of Scotland merged with the United Presbyterians, 150 congregations in the Highlands and Islands stayed out. In the Hebrides the Free Church became a powerful force in social life: for decades it managed to preserve the Sabbath against the desires of the ferry company to sail on Sundays. But the Highlands and Islands have been in decline throughout the twentieth century. The young people were attracted to the cities of the British mainland by educational and career opportunities and most never returned. Most also abandoned their regional church on moving. Scots who did want a conservative form of Protestantism were not attracted to what was seen as a distinctly Highland movement. Instead they joined Baptist or independent evangelical congregations.

When a sectarian religion is already small, its relative isolation makes it particularly vulnerable to idiosyncratic problems. Our search for general explanations should not blind us to the fact that organizations (and hence the ideas carried by them) may prosper or fail because of the actions of individuals. American fundamentalism is sufficiently large and internally varied to survive easily the sexual and financial scandals of the 1980s that saw the very public fall from grace of televangelists Jimmy Swaggart (sexual deviation) and Jim Bakker (sexual deviation and fraud). For every disgraced pastor there were thousands of honest preachers to whom the disillusioned could turn. But when the Exclusive Brethren of the fishing communities of the north-east of Scotland were rocked in the early 1960s by the claims that their spiritual leader Big Jim Taylor had been a little too physical in his counselling of female followers, enough people were lost seriously to weaken the movement.[29]

The Free Church of Scotland provides a good example of a movement having become so introverted and inbred that personal conflicts seriously damaged the credibility of the movement as a whole. Donald McLeod was the Professor of Systematic Theology at the Free Church's theology college in Edinburgh and editor of the church's magazine. For many years he had been making enemies within the church for his radical political views and for his rather liberal attitudes towards some of the more distinctive aspects of Free Church doctrine and policy. In the late 1980s he was accused by two women of making improper sexual advances to them. For almost ten years his enemies (who included close relatives) pursued him through the church and civil courts and the brethren became thoroughly polarized. Of the 5,000-strong membership 1,500 signed a petition supporting him. Despite the courts clearing him in 1998, the following year McLeod's opponents were still pursuing avenues for church discipline. A number of ministers have resigned and many members have withdrawn.

I do not want to labour the point. All that needs to be said is that being relatively enclosed creates its own vulnerabilities. Among those is the difficulty of keeping up with the growth of benefits being enjoyed by those outside the closed circle. In the 1920s there was little difference in the standard of living or the range of cultural products enjoyed within and outwith the Exclusive Brethren of the north-east of Scotland. But with the expansion of the welfare state and the increase in professional white-collar work, the scope for the small businessman and the self-employed tradesman was reduced. Especially with the decline in the numbers employed in farming and fishing, by the 1970s those who declined to go to university and attain professional qualifications were being asked to give up far more than had their grandfathers. On one point Iannaccone is absolutely right and that is that the sect, if it is to keep its people while keeping them cut off from the wider society, has to be able to offer sufficiently attractive rewards. Where Iannaccone is wrong is in thinking that 'sufficiently attractive' is an objective property (like rainfall) or a matter of convention sufficiently enduring for us to treat it as if it were an objective property. It is neither. It is a fragile judgement that depends on the balance of force between the persuasiveness of the sect and the weight of alternative interpretations. Whether any sectarian continues to believe that the benefits of membership are 'sufficiently attractive' to justify the required sacrifices depends on the success of the sect's rhetoric and social interaction. More often than not, what is at issue is not the value of Brethren rewards versus world's bright lights. Young Brethren members did not weigh eternal salvation and a well-paid profession and pick the latter. They thought about the claim that salvation was available only in the Brethren and concluded that they no longer believed it. They went to the Baptists or the Church of Scotland because in those organizations they could enjoy what was available in this world and still keep the promise of the life hereafter. The Brethren's problem was not, as Iannaccone frames it, a failure to provide rewards shiny enough to compensate for the required sacrifice. It was a failure to maintain the persuasiveness of the rhetoric that asserted the Brethren's unique grasp on what was needed for salvation.

In the case of the Exclusive Brethren, the sect rather obviously lost the war with the secular world. Mostly sectarian religion adjusts slowly, as it concedes ground and builds new trench systems. Our concentration on the success of fundamentalism in the USA should not blind us to the extent to which it has changed over the century in ways that amply justify the description of 'secularization'. James Davidson Hunter has thoroughly documented the gradual decline of asceticism among US conservative Protestants.[30] Objections to social dancing, folk dancing, watching 'Hollywood-type' movies, playing pool, and studying on a Sunday have completely disappeared. In 1951 98 per cent of a sample of young evangelicals thought that drinking alcohol was 'morally wrong all the time' and 99 per cent thought the same of smoking marijuana. By 1982 the figures had fallen to 17 and 70 per cent respectively. Sex was so taboo in 1951 that the survey did not even ask about it. In 1961 only 48 per cent said that 'casual petting' was morally wrong all the time. By 1982 that had fallen to 23 per cent. The corresponding change for 'heavy petting' (one would love to know where Hunter's respondents mentally placed the dividing line) was from 81 to 45 per cent. As the distinctive mores have been abandoned, so the distinctive religious beliefs have been compromised. Hunter believes that many conservatives had taken an important step towards reducing the sectarianism of their religion by splitting the world: they continue to insist that they know what God requires of them but they are no longer so sure that he will require the same of others. They continue to seek heaven but are not so sure that those who differ are going to hell. This is not yet the toleration and relativism of the denominational ethos, but it is a significant step in that direction.[31]

Mentioning changes in American evangelicalism allows me to return to a topic introduced briefly in Chapter 1: the evolution of sects. Although some denominations began as churches, most started life as radical sects, in considerable tension with their societies, and gradually moderated. We see this with the Methodists and the Baptists. The austere commitment of the early Quakers, with their distinctive mode of plain dress (with wide-brimmed hats for the men, who conspicuously refused to doff them for the King) and distinctive forms of speech, gave way among those who came to be called 'Gay Quakers' to more conventional styles. The early Quakers would not have read a novel or attended the theatre but the Gay Quakers (usually the off-spring of wealthy merchants, manufacturers, and bankers) became more and more like the Church of England neighbours with whom they mixed as social equals. By the middle of the nineteenth century we find them crossing over into first the evangelical wing and then the mainstream of the Church of England.[32]

New sects were formed but they too gradually compromised. The Salva-tionists and the Pentecostalists followed the same path. As they grew, the Mormons became less radical and conformed to the mores of American society; they abandoned polygamy and racism. Already, in less than thirty years, we see similar changes in the Unification Church (or 'Moonies') and the Krishna Consciousness movement. Initially both expected converts to devote themselves full-time to the life of the movement. As the first genera-tion of young people have grown up and acquired children, so various cate-gories of associate membership have been created to accommodate those who wish to remain attached to the movement's ethos and some of its beliefs but are no longer prepared to commit their entire lives to it.[33]

In the general account of secularization, I explained the gradual modera-tion of the Protestant sects as a reluctant accommodation to their minority status and to the diversity that they had inadvertently created by exercising their option to dissent. I have now introduced another cause of change: increasing prosperity. I would now like to explore further the reasons why sects change.[34]

The first generation of members deliberately and voluntarily accepted the demands of the sect. The people who broke away from the state churches in England and Scotland in the eighteenth and early nineteenth century some-times suffered political, social, and financial penalties. The state could confiscate their property, exclude them from holding political office or mil-itary rank, and remove their children to have them raised as good Anglicans. How vigorously such powers were used depended on local magistrates. The diaries of George Fox, the founder of the Quaker movement, make his England appear as a bizarre snakes and ladders board. In some villages he was welcomed by the local squire, wined and dined and invited to preach. The following week and only twenty miles away he was thrown into a dungeon and beaten and starved.[35] Overall those charged with applying the laws behaved with more charity and flexibility than those who framed and passed them. None the less religious dissent did incur a loss, if only the loss of social esteem. In so far as they made sacrifices for their beliefs, the founding genera-tion of sectarians invested more than just their hopes in the new faith, and their commitment, thus tested, was all the greater. But the second generation, the children of the sect founders, did not join voluntarily. They were born into it and, even when the greatest effort was put into socializing the children into the sect's ideology, it was inevitable that their commitment would be less than that of their parents.

Told in this way, the high levels of commitment found among the early dissenters seems to fit well Iannaccone's claims for the beneficial effects of sacrifice. However, I would want to tell the story in a way that removes the suggestions of utilitarian manipulation and corrects the causal sequence. Sacrifice does not operate primarily by enhancing the faith of those who make it. Rather, the knowledge that sacrifice will be required selects from the wide pool of potential members those whose belief is strong enough to survive the testing times. The sect is founded by strongly committed people rather than (as the Iannaccone and Kanter formulation would have it) that the commitment mechanisms of the sect make its members strongly committed. The second and subsequent generations have not been selected for the strength of their beliefs; their presence in the sect is an accident of birth. It follows that, unless the sect can successfully socialize them (by, for example, teaching them the glorious history of the sufferings of the founders), their levels of commitment will vary across the full range.

There is thus a natural tendency for the attachment of sectarians to their distinctive beliefs and culture to decline with each generation. This may be exacerbated by the inadvertent consequences of puritanism: increased wealth and upward social mobility. As the Methodists, by working diligently to glorify God and avoiding expensive and wasteful luxuries, became better off, they put their children in a position of heightened temptation. They mixed with others of more elevated status than their parents. They were a little embarrassed at the roughness and lack of sophistication of their place of worship, their uneducated minister, their rough folk hymns and liturgies. They began to press for small adaptations towards a more respectable format, more comparable to that of the established church. Whatever advantage their puritan ethics conferred, the dissenters would have become more prosperous simply because of the steady expansion of the industrializing economies.

The children are a further problem in that they force a revision of the sect's initial firm divide between the saved and the unsaved. Usually the sect is highly critical of the church for accepting children, because it believes that only a conscious, voluntary, informed, and hence adult conversion experience guarantees salvation. But the sect's own children threaten that demarcation. After all, it is a little hard for the sectarians to believe that their own children, raised in the true faith, immersed in the Word since they were babies, and surrounded by examples of pious living, are as fully excluded as the offspring of outsiders. Gradually the very strict membership criteria are relaxed until they are indistinguishable from those of the corrupt church so bitterly denounced at the sect's formation.

There is a further point that the German political scientist Robert Michels elaborated in his studies of change in left-wing political organizations and that concerns the development of organizational structure and the interests of officials.[36] Although most sects began as primitive democracies, with the equality of all believers and little or no formal organization, gradually a professional leadership cadre emerged. Especially after the founding charismatic leader had died, there was a need to educate and train the preachers and teachers who would sustain the movement. There was a need to coordinate the growing organization. There were assets to be safeguarded and books to be published and distributed. With organization came paid officials and such people had a vested interest in reducing the degree of conflict between the sect and the surrounding society. They could also compare themselves to the clergy of other churches and want the same status and levels of education, training, and reward that they enjoyed. We should also recognize the pressures that come from the rest of the society (government agencies in particular). Professionalism and bureaucracy are just how modern societies organize things and many sectarians find themselves obliged by the need to negotiate various forms of recognition from the state (the right to be conscientious objectors, for example) to become more organized.

It is also important to note that, whatever internal pressures to moderate affect the sect, their impact will be related to the expectations of the wider society and its willingness to accept the moderating sectarians. In the case of the Gay Quakers their desire to be accepted by their social peers outside the movement was stimulated by the willingness of those peers to accept the Quakers as social equals. The increasing moderation was thus a product of mutual acceptance. An institutional example can be seen in the history of British universities. As they were excluded by religious tests from Oxford and Cambridge, dissenters established their own colleges. By the middle of the nineteenth century these were widely accepted by British élites as part of the national provision of higher education, and the many theological colleges established in Oxford and Cambridge by dissenting organizations were, in the twentieth century, fully assimilated in the degree-awarding structures of the institutions that had once excluded them.

Even the material basis for the change, the increased affluence of the dissenters, was not solely the result of the internal dynamics of dissenting religion. The social ethics of puritanical religion might explain why the dissenters had the potential to become successful entrepreneurs and the early evidence of that potential was one compelling reason for the state to relax its penal restrictions: rich minorities usually get a better reception than poor ones. But repression could have been maintained. The affluence of the minority could have triggered envious attacks. In the 1980 race riots in California blacks specifically targeted Asian shops and businesses. In Indonesia in the 1990s, the Chinese minority had their businesses and homes looted. That the dissenters in Britain in the early nineteenth century were encouraged to assimilate shows how advanced was the culture of tolerance. 'Toleration had brought with it, as Bunyan feared it might, material benefits which threatened to sap the spiritual zeal of Dissent.'[37]

We need to beware of treating all sects as much of a muchness. As Bryan Wilson has argued in detail, doctrinal differences between sects make them variously susceptible to the sort of accommodation Niebuhr describes. We need not pursue the differences further than noting that sects can organize themselves and their relations with their surrounding society so as to remain sectarian for many generations.[38] To give just one example, the moderating effects of increased prosperity can be blunted if, as is the case with the Seventh Day Adventists, that prosperity is channelled and controlled by the sect itself.[39] The drift towards the denominational compromise is not inevitable. None the less, it happens often enough for us to be confident that it is not an accident and I have tried to explain its major causes.

Finally, I would like to return to an observation that we can easily lose sight of in concentrating on the link between sectarian beliefs, communal structures, and sectarian distinctiveness. Unless the sect follows the path of such communitarians as the Amish, the Hutterites, and the Doukhobors and succeeds in isolating itself entirely from the surrounding environment, its members will be in frequent contact with unbelievers. Sectarians may have various strategies for dismissing as of no consequence such people, but, provided they have frequent and positive and rewarding relationships with outsiders, then the idea that the sectarians possess a monopoly of the truth is bound to become more difficult to sustain. The simple fact of human sociability will cause a gradual reduction of the claims that the sectarians make for their sect.

Sectarian Attacks on Differentiation

Those who believe they have the entire divine truth often try to orient their entire life around it. As Chapter 1 explained, one of the features of modernization is the increasing division of the lifeworld into a variety of relatively separate 'compartments'. In particular, modern societies operate with a significant divide between the public and the private sphere. We are increasingly prevented from exercising our prejudices in the public arena (witness the expanding body of anti-discrimination law) while given ever greater freedom to do and believe what we like in the private leisure world of family and friends. One way of diffusing the potential for social conflict inherent in religious diversity is to prohibit everything in public and permit everything in private, which is what the US constitution, with its prohibition on the state supporting or inhibiting religion, recommends.

Conservative religion is generally opposed to such differentiation on procedural and substantive grounds. First, the very principle of confining the obedience of God to one sector of life is offensive. Secondly, the Godless atheism that fills the public sphere offends. Even if the sectarians could accept such a demarcation, there would be constant battles over where the border lay.

Modern states differ in the extent to which they permit minorities the right to create their own sub-societies and sectarian types of religion differ in the extent to which they will accept that gift from the state. Communitarian sects such as the Amish and the Hutterites became such when they gave up trying to impose God's will on their neighbours and set out for the empty lands of the USA and Canada to build their own Godly societies free from interference. Many of those sectarians who do not go that far in isolating themselves find it difficult to live with the terms of their implied contract with their host society. US fundamentalists have a history of oscillating between pious retreat and theocratic assault. For a while they sit in their rocking chairs on their porches and 'walk with the Lord' while the country goes to the dogs. Periodically (with temperance crusades at the start of the century and anti-communism in the 1950s) they get motivated to fight back against the secularity (and specific vices) of what they believe was once God's own country. In a variety of places I have written extensively about the New Christian Right (NCR) (the term given to a variety of fundamentalist-inspired conservative political movements that started in the late 1970s) and I do not want to repeat a great deal of detail here.[40] I will mention only two general problems.

First, even in the USA, which offers more opportunity for creating distinctive sub-societies than any other modern society, the secular world presses in. They may have their own language, economy, and clearly demarcated physical space, but the Amish meet the tourists who visit their towns and they sometimes visit the big cities. Fundamentalists such as Joe and Jolene are isolated from the wider society only by an act of will.

Secondly, when the minority fights back, it is either defeated or seduced. For all the noise, the NCR has failed to achieve any of its specific goals. It has given some useful backbone to the secular conservative wing of the Republican Party, but it has not succeeded in stopping abortion, reducing the proportion of women in employment, restoring public prayers and other religious ceremonies to state schools, making divorce more difficult, requiring that the teaching of Darwinian evolution be balanced with an equal time for 'creation science', or forcing homosexuals back into the closet. In 1987 Pat Robertson, founder of the Christian Broadcasting Network, televangelist and leader of NCR organization Christian Coalition, ran for the Republican Party nomination for President. Despite having a large cadre of disciplined supporters and spending an unprecedented sum of money, he failed to win a single primary. Where NCR groups have become a powerful force in the Republican Party, they have taken the party too far out of the middle ground. In the 1998 mid-term elections, the Republican Party attacked President Clinton's moral record and promoted a number of NCR-supporting candidates; it lost badly and Newt Gingrich, a strong supporter of the NCR, had to resign his post as Speaker of the House. Even with the hundreds of conservative judges appointed during twelve years of Republican presidents, the courts have signally failed to support the NCR agenda.

Behind all the other elements of a full explanation of the failure of the NCR is the simple fact that most Americans appreciate the value of liberalism and toleration. Some have a conscious commitment to the separation of church and state; others just have a vague sense that preachers should not be telling people what they cannot do. The result is that in 1987 even self-identifying evangelicals and fundamentalists preferred to vote for George Bush than for Pat Robertson. This means that, for NCR organizations and candidates to have any serious chance of success, they cannot make their pitch on their own terms but must accept the logic and parameters of the secular world. They cannot say that Creation should be taught in schools because God requires it. They have to argue that the Genesis account of the origins of the world and species is as consistent with the scientific evidence as any other explanation. They repeatedly fail to persuade the courts. They can present themselves as a legitimate minority that should be treated no worse than any other interest group. For example, a hard line on the separation of church and state led to Christian student groups being banned from campuses or refused university funding where racial, cultural, and political groups were permitted or funded. A series of judgments have overturned such bans but what has not been permitted is any particular privilege for the people of God.

The need to accept the logic of the enemy has its counterpart in the need to form alliances with conservative Catholics, Jews, Liberal Protestants, and atheists. Jerry Falwell called his organization the Moral Majority. Politically involved sectarians might be the first word but they are not the second. Hence the need for coalitions. Successful coalition requires the sectarian to switch between two frames. On a Sunday evening Baptist fundamentalism is the only way to God and the Vatican is the anti-Christ. On a Monday morning the NCR activist sits down with his Catholic colleague to plan a campaign for the state funding of religious schools. That switch is difficult for conservative Protestants, because it requires the very compartmentalization (now I am doing religion; now I am doing politics) that they bitterly oppose. This is the paradox. NCR campaigns to reverse the differentiation of the modern world require activists to accept that differentiation.

The relative openness and diversity of the USA allows sectarians to create distinctive sub-societies and subcultures. These ghettos offer some protection against Godless America but not enough to prevent unpleasant incursions, as with the decision that independent Christian schools that deviate too far from public policy (by being racially exclusive, for example) should lose their tax-deductible status. The subcultures are strong enough to initiate political and social movements but they are not powerful enough to set the terms of engagement with the secular society. To fight back with any chance of success, the sectarians must give up the core of what makes them distinctive.

Conclusion

This chapter has had a number of purposes. First, I have tried to explain the relative success of conservative religion over the twentieth century by showing how it can be readily embedded into an enclosed supporting community. This offers a more plausible explanation than the rational choice approach, which neglects plausibility and social relationships in favour of a thoroughly un-sociological vision of individuals maximizing their returns. I do not think people believe in God because they get a good return on that belief. Most people believe because they are socialized into a culture of belief. A few change, not *in order to* maximize their utility, but *because*, almost invariably as a result of forming a warm relationship with an existing believer, they are persuaded to believe. Persuaded, not bribed. Notions such as price and cost and reward and sacrifice cannot be used in utilitarian calculation (either by the actor or by the analyst) because all of them are rhetorical and persuasive devices, the meaning of which changes depending on the religious beliefs and values of the people whose behaviour we are trying to understand.

Secondly, I have tried to convey a sense of mutation through alternation. The epistemological claim at the heart of the sect strengthens it but also makes it brittle. The belief that there is just one truth permits the features that Kelley attributes to 'strong' religion, but, when augmented by the Protestant notion that all of us can discern that truth, the result is factionalism and schism. The combination at the epistemological level of dogmatism and democracy explains most of the religious pluralism that characterizes the modern world. In that sense, sects have inadvertently been responsible for creating the liberalism and toleration that they despise and fear. While the sect worked hard to preserve itself (and in that it differs from the denomination), a number of internal pressures to moderate combined with such external forces as growing prosperity and pressure to accept liberal public policy to shift most sects in the denominational direction. As they accommodated, new radical sects were formed, but, and this is where I depart from Stark's stable economy assumption, each wave was smaller than the one before. Because the sect recruits primarily from those people who are already deeply religious, each wave of moderation reduces the pool from which the new wave of sectarian religion can recruit. To study the creation, mutation, and decline of sects is not to see the antidote to secularization: it is to see how secularization works.

Finally I introduced the New Christian Right. Some scholars have presented the NCR as proof that the secularization thesis is mistaken. I am struck by quite the opposite conclusion. That the movement exists at all supports my assertion that much of the vitality of American sectarianism derives from its ability to use diffuse pluralistic structures to create local monocultures. That so much effort and money could achieve so little seems strong evidence for the view that modern societies will not permit such monocultures to dominate the public square.

7

Liberal Religion

ONE common response to the argument presented in Chapter 1 and to the details of declining church membership and church attendance scattered throughout this book is to argue that, while religion may have changed its shape, it has not actually declined. What we see in the twentieth century is not secularization but merely the adaptation of religion. This case is commonly made by Christians looking for some reason to be cheerful (some of whom go so far as to suggest that what is left is 'better' religion than that which prevailed in, say, the eighteenth century because it is less entangled with the mundane and hence more pure). It is also made by those scholars who believe that there is something about the human condition that gives us a perpetual need for religion or something very much like it.

My purpose in this chapter is to argue against both of those responses by pressing my case that choice undermines faith. What I will try to show is that the dominant forms of religion in modern industrial societies are not just different but also weaker than those that preceded them. While the mutation of religion from church and sect into denomination and cult types may seem like successful adaptation to increasing cultural diversity and individual autonomy, it is unlikely to retard secularization. Finally, I will consider the case for proposition that the spiritual quest is an essential part of the human constitution.

Before I begin detailed consideration of the precariousness of what, for brevity, I will call liberal religion, I want to make it clear that nothing in what follows implies any judgements about 'true' or 'real' religion. No doubt conservative Catholics and Protestants could (and do) offer a partisan version of my argument for their own purposes, but their purposes are not mine. If it is possible to describe belief systems without taking sides, it should also be possible to frame testable propositions about the organizational and behavioural consequences of beliefs. What I argue may well be wrong, but it need not be partisan. We can see a parallel in political ideologies. To argue that anarcho-syndicalism is difficult to organize and hence that the failure of anarchists to create enduring political movements is not an accident but results from

properties of the belief system is not to say that anarchism is not 'real' politics. If we can investigate the links between political ideas and organizations in
a neutral spirit of social-scientific enquiry, I do not see why we cannot do the
same for religious ideas.

To recap the definitions offered in Chapter 1, the denominational and cultic
forms of religion differ from the church and sect in that they do not claim a
unique grasp of the salvational truth. They accept that there is more than one
way to God. Hence they tend to be inclusive and tolerant. They are also epistemologically individualistic and egalitarian. Most denominations have
hierarchically organized professional clergy and a considerable respect for tradition and learning, but these are only conventions; they are not rooted in
core beliefs and act as no barrier to the individual making his or her own decisions about what to believe. Hence they have what Wallis and I have called
diffuse belief systems. The primary difference between the cult and the denomination is that the latter is large and respectable while the former is small and
deviant. Or at least that was the case in the early 1970s when Wallis formu-
lated his distinctions. It follows from the argument advanced here that this
distinction is gradually being reduced in importance. As the Christian denominations shrink, so their power to stigmatize alternatives also declines, so that
what were once seen as dangerous and threatening are now often treated as
merely exotic or silly.

As much of what follows applies equally to the denomination and the cult,
I will often treat the two together and draw attention to differences only when
they are significant for my presentation, and, because it is more obviously
symptomatic of the underlying social changes to which I wish to draw attention, I will begin with the cultic form of religion.

Two further points about the general approach of this chapter: except where
there are important points of difference, I will elide the more cultic of the new
religious movements of the 1960s and the more general phenomenon known
as New Age spirituality. There is historical continuity: many of the key ideas
and therapies of the New Age first came to prominence in the West through
the new religions of the 1960s (and many 1960s organizations remain major
operators in the cultic milieu of the New Age). And, in structure, popularity,
and social impact, the divide between sectarian and cultic movements seems
more significant than anything that follows from their founding date.

A second general point about the scope of this chapter is that I will include
in my discussion a variety of 'human potential' movements that might want
to distinguish themselves from more obviously spiritual belief systems and
organizations. Again there are two justifications for this. First, though many
would initially avoid the religious tag, most human potential organizations
do have at their core explicitly religious propositions. Heelas calls them 'self-

religions' because, if nothing else, their claim that the self is perfectible is a religious one.[1] Insight, for example, claimed that 'each person starts life perfect and unlimited' and can, with Insight training, return to that condition.[2] Secondly, many of what could be secular therapies are treated by their consumers as aids to spiritual development.

The World of Cultic Religion

We cannot infer the extent of public interest in some phenomenon directly from the sales figures for books. If we could, the popularity of Stephen Hawking's *A Brief History of Time* would make the Britain of the 1990s a nation of theoretical physicists. None the less, we can draw some conclusion from the fate of an entire genre and what we see in most Western countries is that, although religious titles have declined as a proportion of all books published and bought, within the category of religion New Age spirituality broadly defined has displaced Christianity.[3] The leading bookshop in Oslo in 1998 gave 60 metres of shelf space to 'Mind, Body and Spirit' titles; conventional Christianity got less than a metre.

But, striking though it is, the growth of the New Age should not be exaggerated. A major Canadian survey asked people if they were familiar with New Age ideas.[4] About 30 per cent said they were. But only 3 per cent said they were 'highly interested' and only a further 8 per cent were 'somewhat interested'. Or, to describe responses from the other end of the scale, 89 per cent said they were not interested in the New Age. Only 3 per cent of the sample said they had any kind of involvement in New Age activities. What Bibby finds particularly intriguing is that the vast majority of that small number of people do not see New Age ideas as an alternative, but as an addition to their conventional religious identities as Protestants and Catholics. Less than 1 per cent of the sample were *exclusively* involved in New Age religion.

Equally revealing is an open-ended study of the sources of significance for young people in England. Sylvie Collins reports that, in talking about what mattered to them and what gave their lives meaning, not one of the young people she interviewed mentioned New Age ideas.[5]

The New Age is not large and powerful but it represents an interesting attempt to 're-sacralize modernity' (in Heelas's phrase). By understanding the new forms of spirituality we can come better to appreciate the difficulties that religion faces in increasingly secular societies and thus avoid the seductive trap of supposing that new religions can simply replace the old ones and keep the religious economy in a steady state. I will begin by trying to capture the essence of modern cultic or New Age religion and then make some general points about the social power and hence likely influence of this sort of religion.

First, there is the belief that the self is divine. Christianity always assumed a division between God the Creator and the people he created. God was good; people were bad. People became good only by subjecting themselves to God's will and God's commandments. Religion provided rituals, therapies, and dogmas to allow us to control the self and shape it into a valuable object. The New Age does not have that division of God and his creation. Instead it supposes that we have within us the essence of holiness. The human self is essentially good because it is essentially God. If it is bad, that is a result of our environment and circumstances. The aim of many New Age belief systems and therapies is to strip away the accumulated residues of our bad experiences and free our human potential. The point of the spiritual journey is to free the God within, to get in touch with our true centre.

Secondly, in the New Age there is no authority higher than the individual self. How could there be if we all possess the essence of divinity? Of course we can learn by reading books and listening to great teachers, and many New Agers have an unfortunate fondness for gurus who turn out to have, not just feet, but entire bodies of clay, but the final arbiter of truth is the individual. As a Neo-Pagan small shopkeeper tried to explain to an American researcher:

Gnosis, direct knowledge. Uh, books can give you hints and directions to where you might look, but you gotta do it. . . . I have a hard time believing anything without some form of personal proof, it—now it doesn't have to be objective, it can be subjective, for me, but if I've experienced it, then to me, it—it—I can accept is as true, but if I don't experience it, I can't—I have a very hard time accepting it. I have to check it out myself.[6]

Thirdly, individual autonomy brings eclecticism. As we differ in class, in gender, in age, in regional background, in culture, we will all have different notions of what works for us and this is reflected in the enormous cafeteria of cultural products from which New Agers can select. A simple way of illustrating that range is to consider the subjects covered in a very popular series of books called 'the Elements of . . .'. The nouns that follow that opening phrase include: Aborigine Tradition, Alchemy, Astronomy, Buddhism, Chakras, Christina Symbolism, Creation Myth, Crystal Healing, Dreamwork, Earth Mysteries, Feng Shui, Goddess Myths, the Grail Tradition, Herbalism, Human Potential, Meditation, Mysticism, Natural Magic, Pendulum Dowsing, Prophecy, Psychosynthesis, Qabalah, Shamanism, Sufism, Taoism, Visualization, and Zen.

I do follow by a lot of different spiritual paths. I don't consider myself—I call myself a witch but I'm not Wiccan. I study tantric techniques but I'm not a tantric Buddhist. Uh, I do dream work techniques, but I don't really follow that original path. Um, I look into Native American studies and at what they have, but I don't consider that my path. I'm very eclectic—I like this idea of pulling from all different sources to find what works for me . . . diversity is the key.[7]

This is the simultaneous sampling of one person. There is also a great deal of sequential sampling. Even many of the new religious movements of the 1970s such as Scientology and Transcendental Meditation that would like to be sects, whose cadres privately believe that they have the truth and everyone else is plain wrong, have been forced by market pressures to accept the eclecticism of the New Age milieu. Instead of recruiting loyal followers, they market their services to people who will take some course, attend some events, acquire the important knowledge, and then move on to some other revelation or therapy. As a consequence, the milieu is rich in its diversity. At the annual 'Mind, Body and Spirit' conventions in London hundreds of individuals and organizations set out their stalls under one roof.

Fourthly, eclecticism requires an appropriate epistemology. Though they rarely pay much attention to the inherent difficulties in accepting apparently incompatible revelations, New Agers are relativists; they simply sample a range of ideologies and therapies without noticing incompatible assumptions and truth claims. If forced to attend to tensions, they find philosophical reconciliation in the Eastern notion of a fundamental unity behind apparent diversity. It is all really cosmic consciousness.

A final central feature of New Age spirituality is its focus of attention or manifest purpose. All the major world religions have claimed that, if we follow their teachings, we may be happier and healthier people, but those therapeutic benefits have been secondary and by no means assured. Medieval Christians followed the instructions of the Church because that is what God required. While they might have hoped for a good life, it was always possible that God's inscrutable providence destined otherwise. In this scheme of things, suffering could be given spiritual significance. In the New Age therapy is the primary, not the secondary, function. This leads to one of the features of the New Age that outsiders find most objectionable. As the self is divine, and New Age therapy offers a way of freeing that divine essence from its socially acquired constraints, the best explanation for failure is a lack of will. If you can (and should) take command of your own fate, then it is your fault if the cancer kills you.

The Denominational Echoes

The characteristics just listed can be found in a minor key in the mainstream Christian denominations (and increasingly among conservative evangelicals).

The twentieth century has seen an increasingly positive evaluation of the human self and a corresponding decline in the notion of God the all-powerful creator. The modern Christian self may not yet be divine but it is a pretty splendid thing. The idea that most people are going to hell has completely disappeared. Indeed, hell itself has vanished from all but the smallest and most conservative Protestant sects.

Above all, the modern Christian decides what he or she will believe. Even regular churchgoers are reluctant to do what their churches tell them to do. British Catholics may admire the Pope but very few follow his instructions on abortion, contraception, or divorce.

That egalitarian attitude to authority is mirrored in an inclusive attitude to salvation. A example was provided for me by an acquaintance who took an Alpha course with a rural Church of Scotland congregation. Seven new Christians spent ten weeks learning what a fairly conservative group of Anglican evangelicals think are the essentials of the faith. At the final discussion group, one chap said that he had really enjoyed the course and now felt much better educated about his faith and better able to explain it to others. None the less, he still felt that God was so good that He would surely save everyone in the end! And no one disagreed with him. What a century ago was the preserve of the small movement of Unitarian–Universalist churches has now become the dominant ethos of a religion that used to draw a clear divide between the saved and the unregenerate, those who pleased God and those who sinned.

There has also been a major shift in the primary purpose of Christianity. Personal healing and therapy has gone from being a hoped-for (but not demanded) by-product of pleasing God to being the main reason for religious belief and behaviour. In the 1950s American Presbyterian clergyman and best-seller author Norman Vincent Peale reconstructed the gospel as *The Power of Positive Thinking*. The extremely popular American television preacher Robert Schuler signals this with (I suspect) unintended humour when he calls his statement of faith *The Be-Happy Attitudes*.[8] The turn inwards, from the social to the personal and from glorifying God to improving the self, can be seen very clearly in the relative fortunes of tendencies within Christianity. Simply to compare conservative and liberal forms of Protestantism (as I did in the previous chapter) misses an important change within conservative Protestantism. The organizations that have been most successful in the last twenty years of the twentieth century have often been those Pentecostal and charismatic churches that have either balanced the previous requirement for asceticism with therapeutic benefits or given the latter pride of place. God the Father has become God the psychotherapist.

In a general summary of the nature of US religious life at the end of the twentieth century, Wade Clark Roof offered a summary that is valid for the whole industrial world: 'the religious stance today is more internal than external, more individual than institutional, more experiential than cerebral, more private than public.'[9]

The Advantages of Liberal Religion

It follows from my explanation of the rise of denominational and cultic forms of religion that they must be better adapted to those parts of the modern world in which they thrive (that is, outside self-created sectarian ghettos and areas of enduring religio-ethnic conflict) than the church and the sect. The advantages have been spelt out at various places in the book but I will summarize them.

One of the major virtues of liberal religion is that its epistemology solves the problem of cultural pluralism. If everyone believes the same thing and sees the world the same way, then it is possible for a society to believe that there is one God, one truth, one way of being in the world. However, when that single culture fragments into a series of competing visions, we have the possibility of endless argument and conflict. One resolution is to change the basic idea of knowledge so that we become relativists. We suppose that there is no longer one single truth, one single way to God, but a whole variety of equally good ways.

Relativism also accords well with our egalitarian culture in that it is a thoroughly democratic theory of knowledge. We can picture the 'new science' and 'new medicine' of the New Age as the third phase of a progressive loss of faith in external authority. Once culture was defined by experts. Now we accept the freedom of personal taste: I may not know much about music or art but I know what I like. In the late 1960s this assertion became increasingly common for an increasing range of matters of personal behaviour: I may not know much about ethics and morals but I know what I like to do and I claim my right to do it. We now find such an attitude displayed in relation to many fields of expert knowledge: I may not know much about the nervous system but I know what I like to believe in and I believe in Chakras and Shiatsu massage and acupuncture.

But such individualism would bring social conflict if it were framed within the traditional notion that there is one true version of reality: hence the need for relativism. Though the term 'hermeneutic' is still foreign to most people, the general notion that different sorts of people will see the world in different ways has become deeply embedded in our culture, as has the related proposition that no one person's view is better than any other's.

There is no space here to explain fully the rise of relativism, but I suspect that our increasing unwillingness to accept the authority of professionals and experts is part of a general decline, not in objective class differences (for they persist), but in subjectively appreciated class differences and in the deference that used to accompany status. In the early 1960s sociologists used to distinguish professions from other occupations by accepting at face value the claim made by professionals that they were motivated not by a desire for money and power but by a commitment to serve fundamental social values. Professional autonomy (including the power to maintain lucrative closed shops) was defended as essential to preserving some social good (justice or health, for example). Sociologists are now much more sceptical, as is the general public. Interests are now imputed to any group of people with a casual 'They would say that, wouldn't they!'.

Claims to professional expertise have also been undermined by the very success of the natural sciences. When scientific knowledge was not extensive and relatively undifferentiated, it was possible to have widespread social respect for those who carried it. The 'professor', the man in the white coat who saved the planet from space invaders in those early 1950s science-fiction films, was just a 'scientist'. Now biology, physics, and chemistry are subdivided into hundreds of highly specialized subfields. The number of practitioners has vastly expanded and their social status has been reduced. What they do is too esoteric for us to admire and they are too ordinary to command respect.

Combined with increasingly widespread scepticism about experts is increasing arrogance about ourselves. Even if graduates are now less well educated than was the case between the wars, there are an awful lot more of them. Misplaced it may be (and, given the huge increases in highly specialized knowledge, misplaced it must be), but these graduates have sufficient confidence to reject conventionally defined expertise. In truth, the gulf between the expert archaeologist and the well-educated lay person who has read three paperbacks about ley lines is vastly greater than it would have been in the 1930s. But the well-educated lay person now has a university degree and is not easily cowed.

These observations deserve to be explored further, but it is enough to note here that the high place accorded to the self in the New Age fits well with the class background of most New Agers. The principal denizens of the New Age milieu are graduates with degrees in the arts, humanities, and social sciences. They work in the social services, education, the media, and the arts. They are not natural scientists and they do not work in manufacturing industry. The spiritual questing of the New Age is a firmly bourgeois pursuit. Because none of its forms are sufficiently well rooted to provide widely shared communal services to gloss rights of passage and major social events, the influence of New Age religion has not spread beyond the middle classes.[10]

The assumptions of the New Age also fit well with a society that is short on authority and long on consumer rights. In the free market for consumer durables, the autonomous individual maximizes his or her returns by exercising free choice. In the free market for ideas, the individual New Ager exercises free choice and synthesizes his or her best combination of preferences.

The Precariousness of Liberal Religion: Consensus

The individualized religion of the denomination and cult type is precarious because it is difficult to structure and organize. A diffuse belief system is difficult to embody, sustain, and transmit because lack of obedience to a central authority (be that an organization, a charismatic leader, or a text) makes it hard to develop consensus, to generate high levels of individual commitment, or to preserve the tradition from mutation, and removes the motivation to evangelize.

Getting people to agree (especially about making sacrifices) is always difficult. Consensus is not the default position, even for people who inhabit similar social circumstances. It must be engineered. For any belief system to survive intact there must be control mechanisms. These may be formal and bureaucratic, as they are in the Catholic Church, where officials deliberate slowly before announcing the Church's position. They may be informal and 'charismatic', as they are in many branches of Protestantism: the minister who preaches a message unacceptable to the audience finds himself without an audience. To put it starkly, *consensus requires coercion*. In the church and sect types of religion, coercion is possible. It is legitimated by the claim to have unique access to the will of God. As the denomination and the cult do not claim a monopoly of salvational knowledge, they are severely constrained in what they can do to maintain discipline. Indeed, they often relish their freedom from such oppressive notions.

Of course New Agers share much in common. However, the consensus is greater the more abstract or procedural the proposition. Thus there is near unanimity on the principle of individual autonomy. There is considerable agreement in theory on a variety of inclusive social principles: racism is bad, sexism is bad, environmental concern is good, egalitarianism is good, everyone should be treated with dignity, no one has a right to 'put anyone else down'. However, when we get to specifics we find little agreement, precisely because the things on which we do agree encourage autonomy and diversity and there is no widely accepted system for settling disputes authoritatively. One of Bloch's New Age interviewees put it brutally but succinctly: 'I have a problem with a lot of mainstream religion, because they're fucking with other people's business.'[11] It is characteristic of New Age communication that one does not argue. At Findhorn, one of the oldest New Age sites, there is a general rule that people must always make 'I statements'. They should speak from personal experience. That very simply prevents argument, because the speaker clearly has privileged access to his or her personal experience. There are no good reasons to argue. If someone says something, well that is how it seems to them and there is no good warrant for 'fucking with other people's business'. Another of Bloch's interviewees said: 'I haven't met anybody that I could agree with everything on, but I've met with people that will say "It's okay if you do that over there, just don't pollute where I'm at, and keep it in your space".'[12]

The problem that such a practical attitude engenders for any belief system should be obvious. If everything can be accepted, and nothing denounced or shunned, then nothing in particular can be shared.[13] Or, to put it in biographical terms, on becoming evangelical, novices are socialized into a culture that makes them more alike than they were previously. Liberals remain as they were or change in a variety of directions, so that whatever cohesion they have derives solely from their social background, pre-liberal religion, and is not enhanced.

Individual autonomy, the freedom to choose, competes with the power of the community. It used to be conventional for sociologists to distinguish religion and magic by the importance of the group. Religion was a shared, communal activity, but magic 'is an entirely different matter. Granted, magic beliefs . . . are often widespread among broad strata of the population . . . But they do not bind them who believe in them to one another and unite them into the same group, living the same life. . . . there are no durable ties that make them members of a single moral body.'[14] Magic can be done in groups but at its core is the individual seeking to change something specific in his or her circumstances.

This distinction highlights the paradox at the heart of much of the New Age. Most alternative spirituality is magical rather than religious (and deliberately disavows the label of religion because of its suggestions of order, dogma, creed). It is thoroughly individualized. Bloch thinks that only about 10 per cent of those who might be called 'neo-Pagan' actually belong to an organized group.[15] Yet New Agers like to see themselves as belonging to some shared entity. In practice, by positing all of the natural world (or Gaia) and all of the supernatural world as the thing to which they belong, they avoid recognizing their failure to create actual communities.

This attempt to mask hyper-individualism by claiming the existence of a 'virtual' community is rather surprisingly endorsed by Bloch, who says that 'explicit flight away from rigid organization and dogma provides common-

alty and social solidarity amongst counterculture spiritualists'. His New Agers
are characterized by 'Strong individual self-autonomy, avoidance of ties to any
one organized group, and yet—possibly—an overriding sense of community
based on other kinds of shared values'.[16] He is wrong, and understanding why
will give us additional insight into the New Age.

Bloch mistakes coincidence for community. 'Technically, *Green Egg's* readers
may not share the same affiliations, but presumably there is something per-
taining to spirituality that the people who read it share in common.'[17] Well,
yes and no. The members of the British Consumers' Association magazine
each month simultaneously read *Which* magazine's surveys of the ten best
food mixers and Top Tips for Freezer Maintenance, but that does not mean
they form any sort of community, any more than the thousands who attend
the Ideal Home exhibition share anything in common other than an interest
in home decorating and outfitting.

The three reasons Bloch offers for talking about his alternative spiritualists
as forming some sort of community are that they agree about individual
autonomy, they talk positively about groups, and they all refer to some
significant group experience. The first of these is, of course, the problem. Individualism undermines community. The second may be no more than sugary
words. Community is one of the unquestionably good things. Politicians in
Northern Ireland almost invariably talk about 'the community' when they
mean two populations so divided that they have spent thirty years in a low-
level civil war and, when they are not fighting, boycott each other's businesses.
The third is the interesting point.

Not all groups are communities. In the social sciences the term has a well-
understood and long-standing usage as part of a contrast with 'association'.
The archetype of 'community' is the closed feudal village in which social relationships are largely non-negotiable. Social ties last over years and generations
and are characterized more by mutual obligation than by choice. Furthermore, relationships are multi-stranded. People work, play, worship, and live
together. Their bonds are rarely confined to some simple task in hand or to a
single role. There is a large degree of inevitability about social relationships.
The contrast is with the voluntary association of people who come together,
of their own free will, for a specific purpose, and who may, if they wish, have
no further communication outside that setting. Much modern interaction is
governed, not by diffuse, reciprocal, and enduring obligation but by specific
contract. When I want my roof repaired, I can go to the *Yellow Pages* and hire
a roofer to perform a specific task for a specific reward. I do not have to live
with him, drink his wine, or marry his daughter. I do not even need to employ
him next time I need a roofer. Not to renew the bond does not endanger my
livelihood, my marriage prospects, or my hopes of ever having another friend

in the village. For a medieval peasant to break ties with his fellows would often have had all of those consequences.

Of course many forms of voluntary association do engender a sense of obligation. I have often turned out for my Badminton Club on a wet Monday night when I would rather sit by the fire because I know that the Club would cease to function if most of us went only when we really wanted to. But the weakness of that obligation can be seen when I recall how easy it is to leave the Club. Over the years I have belonged, many people have come and gone. All that is required to quit without leaving ill-feeling is some story of a new competing obligation.

The crucial point about liberal religion (of the denominational or the cultic variety) is that it is much closer to the archetype of 'association' than to that of 'community' in that it engenders only very weak ties of obligation. Any ethnographic study of cultic religions shows the ease with which people can come and go. Shaw's excellent account of joining the Emin makes it clear just how little ex-members felt bad about leaving.[18] And why should they? If the individual is the final arbiter of what works for him or her, then there is no reason to feel obliged.

At best Bloch's countercultural spiritualists form an association rather than a community, but, as Bloch's own evidence shows, they do not associate much or often. They are so thoroughly individualistic that they do not have the sorts of enduring relationships with the like-minded one would find in a voluntary association such as a Badminton Club or the Church of Scotland's Women's Guild; those at least meet regularly and people stay involved for years rather than months.

Not surprisingly very few of even the most cultic religions are happy with the weak attachment implied in such bonding. Transcendental Meditation (TM) tries to keep the loyalty of its followers by asserting that its product works only in its pure form: 'If anything extraneous is introduced then it is no longer Transcendental Meditation and the good benefits of Transcendental Meditation are longer found.'[19] It also tries to retain those initiated beyond the stage of learning basic meditation techniques by offering a progressive career. It has introduced the Siddhis programme that promises additional benefits (including yogic flying) to those adepts who have moved on to the higher level. L. Ron Hubbard responded to people developing their own version of his Dianetics by replacing it with Scientology, which had a very clear progressive career structure built into the delivery of its revelation.

The lack of strong bonds is only to be expected given the diffuseness of the New Age milieu. For most of those in some way involved, their participation is confined to reading books and magazines, attending lectures, and buying products (such as tarot cards, horoscopes, and healing crystals). Those people whose interest is deep enough for them regularly to attend workshops and courses or belong to a Wicca coven are very rare. But the point I want to stress is that, even for those who have enduring relationships with other New Agers, the consequence of the epistemological base of New Age ideas is that such relationships can be readily terminated. So long as the key principle is 'To your own self be true', the residents of a New Age community such as the Findhorn Foundation can pack up and leave anytime they find the company of their fellows uncongenial and their wills thwarted, or simply decide that they have got out of this particular revelation or tradition all it offers them and it is time to move on to something else.

My stress on the debilitating effects for solidarity of individualism could be criticized for taking too rational a view of religion by reducing it to dogma and doctrine. It is certainly the case that conservative and liberal religion can be distinguished by the habit (and ability) of the former to list what its adherents must believe. But I do not think my observations are confined to doctrine and hence misunderstand the nature of religion. Even if a group is to be identified only by shared ritual or architectural preferences or dress codes, it can be so identified only if there is a degree of consensus about where the boundaries of the group lie. For any entity to endure it must have some identity and that requires some consensus and that in turn requires coercion and that in turn requires a belief system that permits the individual to be overruled.

The Precariousness of Liberal Religion: Ethics

One obvious illustration of a lack of consensus in liberal religion is the lack of a strong ethical or behavioural code. The New Age language of discovering yourself and getting in touch with the God within can be and is used to justify any sort of behaviour. To give the most obvious example, for all the talk of radicalism, many male New Age gurus have a thoroughly patriarchal and exploitative relationship with their female followers. If my wife and my best friend decide that they can discover the divine within by taking each other's clothes off, there is no authoritative standpoint from which I can denounce such behaviour. Consider the personal lives of Peter and Eileen Caddy, two of the three founders of the Findhorn Community and leading figures in the British New Age movement. Peter Caddy left his first wife Sheena, seduced Eileen, a married woman with five children, and persuaded her to leave her family. In his search to find himself, Peter periodically abandoned Eileen to the malign influence of Sheena, who abused and dominated Eileen and even abducted Eileen's first child by Peter. Peter, a handsome, glamorous, and powerful figure, was attractive to many of the young idealistic women who visited the Findhorn Community. He had affairs with some and in 1979 he left his wife for a younger more glamorous Californian. In all he married five times. One obituarist tried to find a silver lining in what might reasonably be viewed as a history of failure by noting that each change of partner 'coincided with a major change of direction'.[20]

It may be that Eileen has had as exciting and fulfilling a love life as her husband, but her biography gives no hint of it.[21] Rather it suggests the traditional double standard of a powerful man frequently trading in his partner for a younger model, while his middle-aged wife remains single, loved by everyone in general and no one in particular.

Judith Boice's fascinating and frank account of her sojourns at various Gaian communities (including Findhorn) describes many difficult personal encounters. It begins with her stay with the Bear Tribe, a Native American Medicine Society, outside Spokane, Washington State. Within weeks of her arrival she was having an affair with Carl, her instructor, and was pregnant. Her instructor made it clear, in a nice New Agey way, that he was not ready to be a father. She was not ready to be a mother because she had not yet discovered herself, so, after consulting the runes, visualizing, and performing a number of cod Indian rituals, she had an abortion.

Boice notices that sexual exploitation plays a large part in the interests of the Tribe's leader:

I watched this morning as Sun Bear began his usual approach that signals his interest in a woman. First and foremost is the 'Medicine Man Hug', a close bear hug with hands held firmly, to the point of trembling, on the behind. Innocent talk and questions follow, with a lot of wandering gazes. Most women who come to the Tribe are both flattered and embarrassed by the attention, flustered by sexual advances when they expected a 'spiritual' man. For Sun Bear, though, sexuality is not separated from spirituality.[22]

Some seekers after enlightenment did not need the advances.

The members warn the new arrivals but the women continue to flock. Some even offer themselves without solicitation. . . . They revel in strutting from Sun Bear's room in the morning and smile knowingly when people ask how they slept. . . . They seem to love the status brought by being in close quarters with a man of power more than they actually love the man himself.[23]

The male spiritual leader sexually exploiting his female acolytes was a feature of three of the four communities that Boice visited. Sun Bear and Peter Caddy have already been mentioned. When she joined an aboriginal 'Dreaming Camp' in Australia, Gubboo, the spiritual guide, invited her to sleep with him.

He so frequently forced himself on the Western women who sought his wisdom that a group of women publicly challenged his behaviour.[24]

Not only are the facts of the sexual relationships in these Gaian communities rather unappealing, but there is also something rather distasteful in the way in which the satisfaction of personal desires is legitimated by an implied reference to inevitability and the cosmic order. The week before Boice was due to leave the Bear Tribe and travel to Findhorn, she found Carl already lining up a replacement lover by making up to a new visitor to the community, Heike. When she got to the Findhorn Foundation, Boice dreamt that Carl was sleeping with Heike. She decided to phone him to confirm her dream.

Carl does answer the phone. 'Hey, Jude, how are you?' he asks. I tell him a bit about my travels and my impressions of the Foundation. 'And I had this dream, Carl'. I am uncertain of how to approach the emotions broiling inside me. 'It was about . . . well . . .'. 'Yeah, I know. I had a dream, too, and I knew how you would respond.'

'What did you dream?' I ask, shoulders clenched, bracing myself for the response.

'I dreamt I met you and Hilary in a roadside cafeteria, like a rest stop. We sat at a table, and I told you about Heike and me. I told you I was afraid someone else would tell you about us before I could, that they would talk shit about me. I wanted to be the first to tell you.'

'And what did I say?' I ask quietly.

'You said you already knew, and it was all right.'

Tears sting my eyes. 'It's true. I dreamt about you being together. Are you happy?'

'Yeah, Heike and I have a real strong connection. It's good.'

'Then I'm happy for you.' . . .

My heart aches. I feel hollow and lonely in the centre of my being. Our plans to meet in January and possibly move to Portland, Oregon, together, where I would study naturopathic medicine, dissolve in that moment.[25]

The full account demonstrates it, but even this brief extract shows the way in which the rhetoric of loving, and openness, and cosmic consciousness can be used by a cad to justify his promiscuity and to manœuvre his jilted lover into giving her approval of being cheated. That Boice suspected she would be betrayed is used by Carl to present the betrayal as no such thing. But Boice was hardly a model of constancy herself. At the very first meeting of her Findhorn induction group, she had become attracted to Alan, the 'focalizer' of the group.

Our courtship begins with a walk in the woods and an evening of conversation with many silent spaces. I am tongue-tied and giddy as a 15-year-old in Alan's presence. . . . Alan immediately tells me that he is in love with a woman who was in an Experience Week he focalised two weeks before mine. Although she is not interested in pursuing a sexual romantic relationship, Alan describes the deep heart connection he felt with her.[26]

This does not stop him sleeping with Boice and she begins another turbulent relationship. At one point she is worried that Alan will have an affair, but 'my worries about Patricia were unfounded—within a week of arriving in the community she fell in love with one man and by the end of the summer she left to marry another'.[27]

Of course it might be that the Caddys and Boice (and those she describes) are unrepresentative, but the Caddys were doyens of the New Age and Boice's book is published by the Findhorn Foundation, which gives it something of an official imprimatur. At the very least, we can be confident that a large number of 'professional' New Agers think the Caddys and Boice are an advertisement for their world.

One good reason to suppose that the prevalence of what looks very much like sexual exploitation in New Age circles is not an accident is that the purveyors of enlightenment often see such bonds as monogamy as an obstacle to the liberation of the divine within. A good example of this is provided by a disciple of Da Free John (a.k.a. Da Love-Ananda), a US guru popular in the 1970s, whose account is worth quoting at length:

I had been a formal student for only a few months when, one night, my wife and I were invited over to Da Love-Ananda's home. Both of us felt an inner need to make personal contact with him, since we had only seen him in quite formal situations. So we were understandably very excited about the invitation but also a bit terrified, because we knew our teacher was a 'difficult man' and we could expect to be tested by him. I found my spiritual hero sitting on his big bed, holding a glass of beer in one hand and a cigarette in the other . . . No sooner had we sat down before him than I was handed a can of beer. I politely refused. I had done without alcohol for years, and I figured I wouldn't start drinking beer now. Da Love-Ananda playfully teased me about it. I noticed myself getting uptight and in an instant saw that my refusal was simply an egoic program. So, I chucked my resistance and had a beer. And another. And another. His conversation got increasingly animated, amusing, but also barbed. He had his talons in me. I knew this to be 'my' evening. I answered his various questions respectfully but guardedly [and] listened to his barrage of good-natured criticism.

Once everyone was drunk, they started dancing.

The psychic energy in the room was phenomenal. It seemed to increase whenever he raised his arms. I began to feel an incredible wildness inside me, which was scary. . . . He wanted to break down my walls, I badly wanted them up. Yet, there was something deep within me, a still observer, perhaps, that wanted to see them crumble as well.

In our earlier conversation, he had asked me many times what it was I was after and I had repeatedly told him I wanted to attain enlightenment. His response had been to call me a benighted individual and to remind me of the rareness of such an eventuality. But I had persisted. Now that I had made my choice, he felt free to teach me a lesson.

In front of me, my wife was being sexually prepared for the guru. I coped with my violently irrational feelings by going into emotional numbness. Happily I did not have to witness my teacher bedding my wife. We were all asked to leave the room. I was sent to a different building where I sat for several hours in the dark, dealing with the emotional hurricane that had been unleashed in me. Finally, I got a handle on my feelings. I realized that one of my greatest attachments was to my wife, and that the guru was doing radical surgery on me for that. I had asked him, indirectly but loudly and clearly, to help me in my struggle for enlightenment. That night he was doing just that.[28]

The reader might wonder why the author does not say more about his wife's feelings about being used as a device to help her husband free himself from worldly attachments. The cynic might point out that, stripped of the rhetoric, this story amounts to one man getting another drunk and having sex with his wife. I cite the story (and I could have chosen examples from the early history of Moses David and the Children of God or the Rajneesh movement) only to make the point that, when the only fixed points of a belief system are that the self is divine and that social conventions are obstacles to self-discovery, anything goes.[29] With no comprehensive and binding ethical code, in the New Age there is always the danger that pursuing self-growth actually means pursuing self-interest.

The Precariousness of Liberal Religion: Commitment and Conformity

The increasing power given to the individual in liberal religion has important social psychological consequences. It is unlikely that such a religion will attract the high levels of commitment found in other forms of religion. Sectarian Protestants often give a tenth or more of their income to religious activities. Liberal Protestants give very little. Perfectly typical are these Canadian figures. While the mainstream Presbyterian, Anglican, Lutheran, and United churches received on average under $400 from each member in 1990, the Christian and Missionary Alliance got over $2,000 and a range of Baptist, Adventist, and Pentecostal churches got over a $1,000 per member.[30] New Agers determine for themselves the extent of their involvement. And for most that is very slight. We see this reflected in the careers of the new religious movements post-1960 and the various New Age providers. It is those that are least demanding that have attracted the greatest number of recruits and consumers: TM (which in its adverts says that 'no change of belief is required') has attracted hundreds of thousands of mediators. Krishna Consciousness has attracted only small thousands.

One of the consequences of having the believers determine what it is they will believe is that there will be insufficient momentum to oppose the demands of mundane everyday life. They cannot band together to form a counter-community with its own values and principles, nor can they, as the English evangelicals of the eighteenth and early nineteenth centuries did, generate the momentum needed to change profoundly a society. Between them a few hundred leading Quakers, Methodists, and evangelical Anglicans mobilized millions to support campaigns to end slavery, curtail child labour, end the use of women and children in coal mines, prevent companies paying wages in tokens that could be redeemed only in company shops, and end the payment of wages in gin shops.[31] It is no great exaggeration to say that the civilization of industrial capitalism resulted largely from campaigns led by the religiously inspired.

That the New Age is a far more diffuse movement makes it harder to assess its contribution to social reform, but it is enough to note that the Aquarians are having little visible effect on their wider societies, and little is claimed, even by sympathetic outsiders. Heelas notes:

there are fewer New Age schools than one might expect; fewer New Age businesses or farms and smallholdings; fewer communes of the Findhorn variety, attempting to find better ways of living daily life . . . With notable exceptions, New Agers do not often go out into the community, working with the poor, the elderly, or the violent. There is less *engagement* with the realities or consequences of modernity than might be expected.[32]

One of the few things that Bloch can find in common among his alternative spiritualists is 'their flight away from mainstream social controls', but he actually offers no evidence for this feature.[33] My impression from personal experience and from such well-informed sources as Luhrmann[34] and Heelas is that most New Agers are perfectly conventional in their public lives; they hold down middle-class professional jobs and they pay their taxes. Apart from a private interest in alternative religion (which may have no outward appearance whatsoever) and a slightly strange dress sense, there is often nothing remarkable about such people.

Some elements of the New Age (those closest to the secular human potential movement) do not aspire to radical social change. Exegesis and est courses did not turn stock traders and bankers into trade-union activists, community workers, or subsistence farmers; they just made them happier and more effective stock traders and bankers. However, even those therapies that claim to be alternative, countercultural, and life-transforming often do more to reconcile people to their place in the world than to change either the world or their position in it. What is advertised as personal transformation is actually the acquiring of a new vocabulary to describe an unchanged reality. At its most banal, it is simply the adoption of the insistence of Voltaire's Dr Pangloss that everything is for the best in this best of all possible worlds. What the Brahma Kumaris advertise as a way of taking control of one's destiny turns out to be more a way of accepting one's fate.

We can see how transformation can become acceptance if we consider the way that Zen Buddhism has been adapted in New Age circles. In some schools of Zen, the highest point of spiritual enlightenment is not to think of God while peeling the potatoes but simply to peel the potatoes. The process of enlightenment involves the development of a rigorous spiritual discipline that frees the monk from worldly attachments. In the initial stages, it is the material world that must be abandoned, but even the search for enlightenment is a goal of the ego that must be transcended. Thus the highest stages are signalled by going beyond cultivating the appearance of saintliness. The one who has attained enlightenment is so thoroughly detached from this world that he can re-engage in mundane roles and tasks without becoming tainted by them. Indeed, the proof of enlightenment is this facility. In some shallow Western interpretations of this principle, the difficult middle bit is dispensed with and the supposedly enlightened person merely carries on much as before but claims a detached and spiritual *attitude* to a life that is, to all external appearances, exactly what it was before the voyage of spiritual discovery. What is advertised as 'personal transformation' looks very much to the outsider like 'no change'.

This should not be scorned. There is doubtless much to be said for accepting one's self and circumstances. However, transformations of the personality that do not much change behaviour should not be confused with those that do. Methodism profoundly changed those people who adopted it and it profoundly changed the society. The New Age has not, and I would argue that its failure to do so is not an accident but follows directly from the diffuse nature of the core beliefs.

One way of both summarizing and restating the problem of liberal religion is to bring together two typologies developed by Roy Wallis. In the system I have been using throughout this book, a wide variety of types of religion are grouped by the supposed nature of their original ideological basis. The church and the sect are 'epistemologically authoritarian' in that they believe that there is only one truth to which they have a unique or at the very least highly privileged access. In contrast, the denomination and the cult are 'epistemologically individualistic' and democratic. A decade after this typology had been published, Wallis argued, in a major essay on new religious movements, that, 'despite their apparent diversity in origins, aims of style, certain basic similarities can be discerned in the new religions by construing them as ranged along a continuum marked at its poles by two types: (1) the world-rejecting religion, and (2) the world-affirming religion'.[35] The Divine Light Mission, the Children of God, and the Moonies rejected the materialism of the prevailing order, especially its stress on individual success as measured by wealth and consumption patterns, and advocated a simpler, more loving, more human and more spiritual order. They sought to take the faithful out of the world. In contrast, movements such as Scientology, Soka Gakkai, and est offered to make their adherents more effective in the world. The Wallis distinction followed a similar contrast offered by David Martin. As Martin put it, one sort of religion is

largely concerned with enabling the individual to fulfil the norms of his particular environment, by making him more self-assured, by increasing his intellectual power and by equipping him with manipulative techniques . . . whether the main emphasis is on social manipulation or on psychological and bodily health, no norms will be generated which set the member in conflict with society.[36]

But there is another type of religion that is concerned with 'a programme of self-mastery and cultivation in terms of a condition of personal grace which may differ radically from the ideal of the wider society'.[37]

We can see what interests me if, as in Fig 7.1, we put the 'deviant' part of Wallis's first typology—the sect and the cult—together with his later 'orientation to the world' principle and try to add some examples. Though there is no problem finding examples for three of the combinations of characteristics, one box remains empty. World-affirming movements may be sectarian or cultic but I can think of no obvious examples of world-rejecting movements that are cultic rather than sectarian. Or, to put it the other way, the claims of adherents of the cultic type of religious innovation to be world-rejecting seem rather thin and I have above contested them. For all its pretensions, much of the New Age seems thoroughly at ease with the world. Spiritual questing has been slotted into weekends and summer holidays. Mary-Margaret Moore channels revelations from a supernatural source she calls 'Bartholomew' 'in a variety of locations around the globe that Bartholomew considers to have transformative powers. Fans of Bartholomew travel to these places as a group, under the auspices of Inward Bound Tours.'[38]

The Precariousness of Liberal Religion: Transmission

Having discussed consensus and commitment, I would like now to turn to what is a vital issue for any ideology: reproduction. As I showed in the

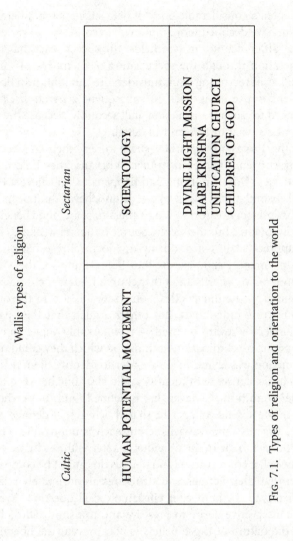

Fig. 7.1. Types of religion and orientation to the world

previous chapter, a considerable body of data suggests that liberal versions of Protestantism have declined more rapidly than conservative varieties and that much of the difference lies in two fields: the success each has in recruiting its next generation through the socialization of members' offspring and the success each has in recruiting adult outsiders. To put it bluntly, liberal religion has a problem transmitting itself to subsequent generations, first, because there is no need for such transmission and, secondly, because there is no basis for agreement on what to transmit in detail.

Conservative Protestant sectarians strive to raise their children in the faith (and to convert friends and even strangers) because they hold that unbelievers will go to hell. But, if nothing bad happens to unbelievers (or, as in the most liberal formulations, the category of unbeliever disappears altogether), then the most pressing reason to want others to share one's beliefs is missing. That much is obvious. But the second source of liberal weakness is as important. I first appreciated it when, during my doctoral research on the Student Christian Movement, I came across the 1955 minutes of the Mission Committee. Various SCM officials and other church leaders met to discuss an ecumenical mission to the universities. Some saw mission in the old-fashioned sense of converting individuals. But others argued that the mission should make 'the university aware of itself'—a remarkably vague intention. After much discussion and elimination of things on which they could not agree, the plan for a mission was abandoned. In order to identify the target for change, there has to be a clear sense of identity and a clear line between those already in the proper condition (however that is defined) and those who need to be persuaded. In the absence of specific shared beliefs that defined an appropriate audience for mission, evangelistic outreach is impossible. This brings us back to the point I made in the previous chapter with regard to 'commitment mechanisms'. What conservatives and liberals do cannot be compared without appreciating that their actions and structures are intimately related to their specific beliefs and to the deeper epistemological question. Even if liberals shared the conservative desire to preserve and transmit their beliefs, the differences in the nature of those beliefs would prevent the liberals emulating conservative methods or success rate.

The Narrow and Limited Appeal of Liberation

This is not to say that liberal religion is so amorphous as to defy identification. It is to say that liberalism is defined primarily by a vague ethos, by agreement on procedural rather than substantive propositions, and by not being conservative. It is important for understanding the future of liberal Christianity to appreciate the extent to which it is parasitic on a more conservative or orthodox past. This assertion exaggerates but only slightly: liberal Christianity appeals primarily to conservatives. For those people raised in a rigid and orthodox religious culture, freedom from some constraints, the novelty of choosing what to believe rather than simply inheriting a tradition, and the experience of meeting as brethren people who would previously have been shunned are exciting. But a movement that is defined by relaxing the specific requirements of a religious orthodoxy, by challenging its doctrines, and by increasing the autonomy of the individual has little appeal to those outside that culture. People who have never believed that the Bible is the revealed Word of God or that Christ's death was an atoning sacrifice are hardly likely to become liberal Christians just because liberals have given up those beliefs. The open prison may be attractive to the high-security prisoner, but it will not attract the free.

Within the broad range of what I am terming liberal religion, there is a clear difference between the denomination and the cult. The denomination has a past that gives it an enduring presence. Its history has nostalgic appeal and the funds gathered during a more religious era allow it to sustain itself despite low present levels of interest. That there was once a sectarian core, with a clear body of doctrine, shared beliefs, and a common liturgy, means that today's Methodists, for example, can still have something in common. We see this clearly in the biographies of early ecumenical activists such as leaders of the SCM. They could not anticipate that the long-term effect of giving up detailed statements of agreed doctrine would be the abandonment of what they held to be true. Because their orthodox upbringing had given them limits to their innovation, they failed to see that the next and subsequent generations would have ever less in common.

The cohesion that its past gives to the contemporary denomination (like its invested capital) is a wasting asset. While conservatives can continue to be attracted by the liberating power of liberal religion, the children and grandchildren of liberals become secular.

The cultic milieu gains no cohesion from a common tradition. Precisely because there are innovations (and diffuse innovations at that), most elements of New Age spirituality have little momentum from a more solid past. We should not be deflected from that observation by the frequency with which New Age ideas and therapies are presented as 'ancient' and 'traditional'. Most modern witchcraft, for example, goes no further back than *Witchcraft Today*, published in 1954 by retired English civil servant Gerald Gardner.[39] Even when New Age ideas are traditional, they are someone else's tradition, from some other place. Plucked out of context, what were powerful cultural constructs can be reduced to glossy magazine trivia: Chinese geomancy becomes just another interior decor style.

To summarize, the decline of Christianity has removed much of the stigma from cultic religion, but the result has not been the rise of powerful new religions to fill the gaps left by the demise of the old. Rather, it has been a small number of left-leaning university-educated middle-class people primarily employed in the arts and caring professions constructing their own idiosyncratic and low-salience spiritualities from a global cafeteria.

Thus far I have tried to show the considerable differences between conservative and liberal religion. The epistemological proposition at the heart of liberalism makes it a diffuse belief system that is difficult to sustain. Although liberalism offered a successful adaptation to the rise of individual autonomy, it could provide only a temporary holding operation and not a long-term solution to secularizing forces. If we combine that observation with the argument in the previous chapter about the common evolution of sects into denominations, we end up with a cyclical theory of religious change but one that results, not in Stark's equilibrium, but in decline. Orthodoxy, when it cannot be preserved either by ethnic conflict or ghetto-building, produces liberalism. Liberalism fails to reproduce itself and leaks adherents to the secular world. A new wave of orthodoxy, smaller than the previous one, in turn produces liberalism and so on. To switch metaphors, the Stark–Bainbridge view is of a wheel turning. Mine, which better fits the overwhelming evidence of secularization, is of a declining spiral.

The Possibilities for Religious Revival

I would like to draw together the themes of this chapter to consider the possibility of religious revival. It is increasingly common for some of those scholars who like the language of postmodernism to speculate that the death of tradition ironically opens the way for people to discover and develop new traditions.[40] There are a number of ways of coming to this conclusion. One is to suppose that secularization has been brought about by committed secularists who share a specific ideological 'project' of promoting rationality and modernization. This project backfires because the relativizing tendency of modern thought undermines rationality. Thus what appears to be a very firmly irreligious culture is actually a fragile ideological construct that can be blown away by a new religious ideology. As I hope is clear from Chapter 1, it is no part of my explanation of secularization that it was brought about by committed ideologues. On the contrary, my explanation rests almost entirely on the notion of unintended consequences. I do not think there is much about our world that is as it is because people wanted it like that.

What might drive a revival of religious interest is the poverty of contemporary life. It is easy to point to many unpleasant aspects of the modern world, attribute these to the malign influence of individualism, and suppose that a deep yearning for a better life will bring people to appreciate the error of their ways. Most ideologies can produce their own version of that argument to hope that there will be an evangelical revival, a resurgence of socialism, or a return to the guilds of medieval Catholicism. Underpinning much of this hope for a return to shared spiritual values is the belief that informs the Stark–Bainbridge theory of religion: that, because there is something about the human condition that will prevent us being satisfied with a secular world, we will always ask ultimate questions and thus generate religious answers.

That view is intuitively attractive because it fits with the observation that, with very rare exceptions, all the peoples of the past have been religious. But that does not preclude the possibility that previous societies have been religious because they have succeeded in maintaining a religious culture, which in turn shapes individual world views, rather than that biological necessity creates culture. My own preference (and it has some bearing on this argument but fortunately does not preclude any option) is that whatever we gain from our biologies is so slight, compared to the instinctual constraints of most other species, that for most practical purposes we can view the human consciousness as a blank sheet on which culture can write almost anything. While we undoubtedly have some instinctual drives, the shapes in which they can be expressed are shown by the anthropological record to be so many and varied that we are probably wisest to assume that little about us is inevitable. But I suspect that my own preference for viewing culture as primary makes little difference to the following argument.

I will begin by stipulating that a considerable body of contemporary survey data shows that many of those who have no strong attachment to any particular religion none the less claim an interest in matters spiritual. Are we to take this as evidence of an enduring need for religion? The WVS asks 'How often, if at all, do you think about the meaning and purpose of life?' Inglehart notes that in eighteen of the twenty-one societies for which he analyses data, a growing part of the population claims to think often about the meaning of life.[41] He sets this against the decline of conventional religion to imply a steady state of religious questing.

Before we make anything of Inglehart's data, we must consider a number of questions about their significance. First, we need to appreciate that the very fact of a survey asking about an attitude or belief may generate a false appearance of interest. Political pollsters have long understood that people's willingness to cooperate in research may lead them to express beliefs and sentiments that have little salience in their lives. Secondly, we need to beware of the implied moral connotations of certain terms. Hoggart's wonderful account of working-class life in northern England in the 1940s and 1950s (it would now be called 'ethnography') explores how the term 'Christian' was used to mean 'ethical' or 'moral'. If asked, anyone who saw themselves as a decent person, trying to do the best they could in the circumstances, would describe themselves as 'Christian', largely because it was taken to be part of an explicit and invidious contrast pair of which the other term was 'heathen'. If you were not a Christian, then you were a savage. I suspect something similar is going on with responses to words that suggest spirituality. What sort of person would say out loud 'I am not spiritual'? Who would confess to an entirely mundane life?

There is a further problem that an increase in unorthodox spiritual questing is in the first place a purely statistical artefact that tells us only that conventional religion has declined. If one way of doing something becomes unpopular, then other ways of doing something like that must become relatively more popular. Let us suppose that the number of homosexuals living together remained stable while the number of heterosexuals maintaining joint residences declined. Then same-sex cohabitation would appear to be on the increase.

Even if same-sex cohabitation showed a real net increase, this might simply reflect the increasing freedom felt by people who had always wanted to do that but had been discouraged by the greater weight of the orthodox social institution: the decline of heterosexual cohabitation reduces the stigma attached to homosexuals living together. The crucial question for interpreting Inglehart's data is not whether alternative ways of posing spiritual questions become more popular with the decline of conventional religion (we would expect exactly that). What matters is the scale of the alternative. Is there enough innovative spiritual questing to come close to balancing the decline in the conventional methods of answering spiritual questions?

We also need to appreciate an element of sleight of hand in the way that the argument that people are enduringly religious is made. For example, Bibby says: 'it's not just religious folk who are trying to work out theological details . . . Concern about resolving the question of life's purpose is higher among those Canadians who do not place a high value on religion than those who do.'[42] Of course it is. Those people who are firmly fixed in a conventional religion do not need to be concerned about the purpose of life because they know what it is. The trick in the Bibby statement is the use of the term 'theological' to describe 'questioning the purpose of life'. Without any further justification he rules out two crucial possibilities: first, that people can question the purpose of life and conclude that the question is unanswerable, and, secondly, that life can have secular purposes. That, until the nineteenth century, organized religions had a near monopoly of defining the purpose of life does not give either sociologists or religious officials a warrant for claiming all interest in large abstract questions as proof of the primacy of religion.

So my first response to the assertion that people are enduringly religious is that the evidence currently offered for that case is, to put it no stronger, not overwhelming. But let us suppose for a moment that there is something about the human condition that causes us to consider that there is more to life than meets the eye. I still do not expect any major return to religion because I can see nothing that would reverse the two master trends of modernization that prevent us giving a common answer: cultural diversity and individual autonomy. The very fact of cultural diversity is proof that, even if existential questions are biological givens, 'hard-wired' into our psyches, the answers to those questions are not. So, even if, in staring at the stars or contemplating the death of a loved one, we all feel the same smallness or loss, it does not follow that we will elaborate or conceptualize our concerns in similar terms. So long as we insist on our right to determine what it is we will believe, then, even if we are all troubled by such abstract questions as 'What is the meaning of life', we will not be able to agree on more detailed formulations of those questions or on what would count as acceptable answers.

I would offer a similar rejoinder to those who base their hope for religious revival on common unease about any social ill. Even if we could all agree that the world would be a better place if we shared a set of common values, legitimated by divine authority, we would not be able to agree on what those values should be nor on the shape of the divinity that gave them power. Even on the much more mundane matter of promoting ethical codes, we prove signally incapable of giving up our freedom. I offer this example not to show hypocrisy but to illustrate the difficulty of resisting personal choice. The 'culture wars' promoted in the USA by the New Christian Right, on the one side, and, on the other, various organizations pressing for gender equality and gay rights have forced all American politicians to take very public stands on socio-moral issues. On the right many political leaders have committed themselves to a conservative agenda. Yet on close inspection many of the same people turn out to be divorced, to have had extramarital affairs, to have fathered children out of wedlock, to be homosexual, or, in one case revealed during the impeachment trial of President Clinton, to have paid for his ex-wife to have an abortion.[43] If even people who have an articulate commitment to a particular socio-moral position cannot themselves adhere to it, what chance is there of persuading any larger constituency to forego personal choice?

In the end I go back to the notion of the organic community. The fondness of politicians, social workers, and countercultural spiritualists for talking about community should not blind us to the fact that modernization has destroyed it. A collection of individuals voluntarily associating is not a community. The sovereign consumer of late capitalism is too self-regarding, too knowing, to step back into a condition of sublimation to an organic whole. Even when we consume the religious ideas and rituals of what was, in some other society or some other time, a powerful tradition, we cannot forget that it is we who choose the tradition rather than the tradition that has created us. This is the problem that is neglected by those who hope that, by showing the social virtues of shared beliefs and values, convergence can be created. That we can all consciously desire the secondary benefits of some shared belief system is not itself enough to make that belief system plausible. Indeed, such a knowing attention to the secondary benefits, such conscious instrumentalism, prevents belief. A God who can be adopted because His injunctions will serve our purposes is not sufficiently powerful to override our individual preferences and coerce conformity.

This is the cancer of choice. To the extent that we are free to choose our religion, religion cannot have the power and authority necessary to make it any more than a private leisure activity. Far from creating a world in which religion can thrive, diversity and competition undermine the plausibility of religion. The crucial question for the possibility of religious revival is this: can we forget our individual autonomy? I do not think so. We have been expelled from that particular Garden of Eden and there is no possibility of return.

NOTES

Chapter 1. Choice: Origins and Consequences

1. Henry Kamen, *The Rise of Toleration* (London: Weidenfeld & Nicolson, 1967), 14.
2. Ibid. 30.
3. Tissington Tatlow, *The Story of the Student Christian Movement* (London: SCM Press, 1933), 400.
4. Quoted in Paul Greer, 'The Aquarian Confusion: Conflicting Theories of the New Age', *Journal of Contemporary Religion*, 10 (1995), 159.
5. Ernest Troeltsch, *The Social Teaching of the Christian Churches* (Chicago: University of Chicago Press, 1976), ii. 729–805; Roland Robertson, *The Sociological Interpretation of Religion* (Oxford: Basil Blackwell, 1970); Bryan Wilson, 'An Analysis of Sect Development', *American Sociological Review*, 24 (1959), 3–15; Benton Johnson, 'A Critical Appraisal of the Church–Sect Typology', *American Sociological Review*, 22 (1957), 88–92.
6. Ernest Gellner, *Plough, Sword and Book: The Structure of Human History* (London: Paladin, 1991).
7. David Martin, *The Dilemmas of Contemporary Religion* (Oxford: Basil Blackwell, 1978), 1.
8. A theory of factionalism and schism is advanced in Roy Wallis, *Salvation and Protest: Studies of Social and Religious Movements* (London: Frances Pinter, 1979), and Steve Bruce, *A House Divided: Protestantism, Schism and Secularization* (London: Routledge, 1990), 37–47.
9. Bryan Wilson, *Religion in Sociological Perspective* (Oxford: Oxford University Press, 1982), 154.
10. Ernest Gellner, *Nations and Nationalism* (Oxford: Basil Blackwell, 1983); 'Nations, States and Religions', in Richard English and Charles Townsend (eds.), *The State: Historical and Political Dimensions* (London: Routledge, 1998), 235–47.
11. Peter L. Berger, *The Social Reality of Religion* (London: Faber & Faber, 1969), 115.
12. Robert K. Merton, *Science, Technology and Society in the 17th Century* (New York: Fettig, 1970).
13. David Martin, *The Religious and the Secular* (Oxford: Basil Blackwell, 1969), 116.
14. Peter L. Berger, Brigitte Berger, and Hansfried Kellner, *The Homeless Mind* (Harmondsworth: Penguin, 1974).
15. Ernest Gellner, 'From Kinship to Ethnicity', in his *Encounters with Nationalism* (Oxford: Basil Blackwell, 1994), 34–46.
16. Of itself, I would not describe religion's loss of social functions (or change

societal to personal functions such as providing psychic stability) as 'seculariza-tion'. My point is the causal one that such a change caused secularization by reducing the relevance and salience and presence of religion.

17. Peter L. Berger, *The Heretical Imperative: Contemporary Possibilities of Religious Affirmation* (London: Collins, 1980).

18. This is a simplified version of the patterns identified in David Martin, *A General Theory of Secularization* (Oxford: Basil Blackwell, 1978).

19. Bryan Wilson, 'Religion and the Churches in Contemporary America', in William G. McLoughlin and Robert N. Bellah (eds.), *Religion in America* (Boston: Houghton Mifflin, 1968), 73–110.

20. Will Herberg, *Protestant–Catholic–Jew: An Essay in American Religious Sociology* (Chicago: University of Chicago Press, 1983).

21. This case is well made in Callum Brown, 'A Revisionist Approach to Religious Change', in Steve Bruce (ed.), *Religion and Modernization: Sociologists and Historians Debate the Secularization Thesis* (Oxford: Oxford University Press, 1992), 31–58, and *The Social History of Religion in Scotland since 1730* (London: Methuen, 1987). Where he is wrong is in presenting his observation about the civilizing role of religion as a counter to the secularization thesis. Wallis made the same points to me when I was an undergraduate in 1972.

22. Bob King, 'White Witch to Sue Minister', *Press and Journal*, 10 Feb. 1998.

Chapter 2. Rational Choice Theory

1. Rodney Stark, 'Must All Religions be Supernatural?', in Bryan Wilson (ed.), *The Social Impact of New Religious Movements* (New York: Rose of Sharon Press, 1981), 161.

2. William Sims Bainbridge and Rodney Stark, 'Cult Formation: Three Compatible Models', *Sociological Analysis*, 40 (1979), 284.

3. Ibid.

4. Stark, 'Must All Religions', 162.

5. Ibid. 165.

6. Ibid. 170.

7. Ibid. 173.

8. William Sims Bainbridge and D. H. Jackson, 'The Rise and Decline of Transcendental Meditation', in Wilson (ed.), *The Social Impact of New Religious Movements*, 135–58.

9. Rodney Stark and William Sims Bainbridge, 'Toward a Theory of Religion: Religious Commitment', *Journal for the Scientific Study of Religion*, 19 (1980), 117.

10. Ibid. 124.

11. Ibid. 122.

12. Moreover, contemporary philosophy of science assures us that no explanation is

conclusively verifiable, in part because of the problem of induction, but also because all singular explanations rest on an implicit claim that, given the same circumstances, the same outcome would occur, and thus they rest on tacit generalizations that themselves fall prey to the problem of induction; see Karl Popper, *The Logic of Scientific Discovery* (London: Hutchinson, 1959), and *Conjectures and Refutations* (New York: Basic Books, 1962). For precisely the same reason, however, no explanation is conclusively falsifiable either, since any singular falsification itself rests on precisely the same sort of background of tacit generalizations that are susceptible to the problem of induction. This does not mean that science and metaphysics are the same, nor undermine the empirical and testable character of science, but it does mean that there is no verifiable knowledge of the kind Stark and Bainbridge rely upon for their argument.

13. Stark, 'Must All Religions', 161.
14. For a comprehensive discussion and critique of this approach to moral crusades, see Roy Wallis, *Salvation and Protest: Studies of Social and Religious Movements* (London: Frances Pinter, 1979).
15. Stark, 'Must All Religions', 163–70.
16. Laurence Iannaccone, 'Religious Practice: A Human Capital Approach', *Journal for the Scientific Study of Religion*, 29 (1990), 297–314.
17. Eileen Barker, 'Who'd be a Moonie?', in Wilson (ed.), *The Social Impact of New Religious Movements*, 64.
18. Reginald Bibby, *Unknown Gods: The Ongoing Story of Religion in Canada* (Toronto: Stoddard, 1993), 58.
19. On Scientology, see Roy Wallis, *The Road to Total Freedom: A Sociological Analysis of Scientology* (London: Heinemann, 1976); on The Process, see William Sims Bainbridge, *Satan's Power: A Deviant Psychotherapy Cult* (Berkeley and Los Angeles: University of California Press, 1978).
20. Wallis, *The Road to Total Freedom*.
21. Something similar could be said of the case of Synanon. Stark says that Synanon's record of drug-addict rehabilitation was poor, which is true. But the transition of Synanon cannot be explained by that failure. The declaration of Synanon as a religion did come after a fall in resident population but in a year in which numbers were again rising (1974/5). This was not the first such fall; there had been one in 1969/70. Moreover, although resident population had fallen, income was rising dramatically (1974/5: gross income $5.6 m. 1975/6: $8.7 m.). There is no evidence that Synanon's founder Church Dederich regarded the non-rehabilitation of addicts to the world as a failure; rather, after at least 1971, Dederich was explicit that rehabilitation and return to the world had not been his intention for his followers at all. Equally, there is no evidence that he regarded the reduction in population as a failure; rather all the evidence indicates that he *wished* this to occur. Indeed, at the time of the declaration of Synanon as a religion, Dederich was actively pursuing a policy designed to bring down the population and increase standards of living to produce a more luxurious way of life for fewer people. Ofshe argues that the purpose of the various changes introduced by Dederich was

precisely to reduce numbers by eliminating 'those least willing to be deployed by management'. Finally, although Dederich declared Synanon a religion in 1974, the transition had, in fact, been a gradual one. The Ouija board had been introduced into 'Dissipations' some years previously, for example. It is hard to see how any of this can provide effective support for the Stark–Bainbridge theory. For details of Synanon, see Richard Ofshe, 'The Social Development of the Synanon Cult', *Sociological Analysis*, 41 (1980), 109–27.

22. Roy Wallis, 'Ideology, Authority and the Development of Cultic Movements', *Social Research*, 41 (1974), 299–327.

23. Gary Becker, 'The Economic Approach to Human Behavior', in Jon Elster (ed.), *Rational Choice* (Oxford: Basil Blackwell, 1985), 112, 114.

24. Ibid. 110–11.

25. Roger Finke, 'Religious De-Regulation: Origins and Consequences', *Journal of Church and State*, 32 (1990), 622.

26. Alexis de Toqueville, *Democracy in America* (New York: Vintage, 1969). See also his *Travels to England and Ireland* (New Brunswick: Transaction, 1988).

27. Daniel V. A. Olson ('Religious Pluralism and US Church Membership: A Reassessment', *Sociology of Religion*, forthcoming) makes this clear. My first published critique of rational choice theory ('Pluralism and Religious Vitality', in Steve Bruce (ed.), *Religion and Modernization: Sociologists and Historians Debate the Secularization Thesis* (Oxford: Oxford University Press, 1992), 170–94) only hinted at this problem.

28. Roger Finke and Rodney Stark, 'Religious Economies and Sacred Canopies: Religious Mobilization in American Cities, 1906', *American Sociological Review*, 53 (1988), 41–9; Finke, 'Religious De-Regulation . . .', and 'An Unsecular America', in Bruce (ed.), *Religion and Modernization*, 145–69.

29. Finke and Stark, 'Religious Economies'; Rodney Stark, 'Do Catholic Societies Really Exist?', *Rationality and Society*, 4 (1992), 261–71; Rodney Stark and Laurence Iannaccone, 'Recent Religious Declines in Quebec, Poland and the Netherlands: A Theory Vindicated', *Journal for the Scientific Study of Religion*, 35 (1996), 265–71.

30. Rodney Stark and William Sims Bainbridge, *The Future of Religion: Secularization, Revival and Cult Formation* (Berkeley and Los Angeles: University of California Press, 1985) and *A Theory of Religion* (New York: Peter Lang, 1987); Finke and Stark, 'Religious Economies . . .'; Laurence Iannaccone, 'The Consequences of Religious Market Structure', *Rationality and Society*, 3 (1991), 156–77.

31. Theodore Caplow, 'Contrasting Trends in European and American Religion', *Sociological Analysis*, 46 (1985), 105.

32. Finke's misunderstanding of British religion is all the more surprising given that almost all of the 'upstart sects', the American success of which he documents, originated in Britain (Roger Finke and Rodney Stark, *The Churching of America 1776–1990: Winners and Losers in our Religious Economy* (New Brunswick: Rutgers University Press, 1992)).

33. David Martin, *The Religious and the Secular* (Oxford: Basil Blackwell, 1969), 122.

34. Iannaccone, 'Consequences of Religious Market Structure', 161.
35. George H. Gallup Jr. and Sarah Jones, *101 Questions and Answers: Religion in America* (Princeton: Princeton Religious Research Centre, 1989); Paavo Seppanen, 'Finland', in Hans Mol (ed.), *Western Religion* (The Hague: Mouton, 1972), 154.
36. 'Layman', *Hand-Book for the Study and Discussion of Popery with Special Reference to its Political Relations* (Edinburgh: George McGibbon, 1868).
37. Philip Hughes, 'Clergy: A Major Part of the Church's Workforce', *Pointers: Bulletin of the Christian Research Association*, 8 (Mar. 1998), 4.
38. Robin Gill, *The Myth of the Empty Church* (London: SPCK, 1993).
39. Iannaccone, 'Consequences of Religious Market Structure', 169.
40. Iannaccone, 'Religious Practice', 297.
41. Ibid. 298.
42. The same point is made by Chaves in a serious of criticisms that have much in common with what I say here and in Chapter 6; see Mark Chaves, 'On the Rational Choice Approach to Religion', *Journal for the Scientific Study of Religion*, 34 (1995), 98–104.
43. Iannaccone, 'Religious Practice', 301.
44. Ibid. 303.

Chapter 3. Pluralism and Religion: Britain, USA, and Australia

1. Alexis de Toqueville, *Democracy in America* (New York: Vintage 1969).
2. Edwin Gaustad, *Historical Atlas of Religion in America* (New York: Harper & Row, 1962), 159.
3. Roger Finke and Rodney Stark, 'Religious Economies and Sacred Canopies: Religious Mobilization in American Cities, 1906', *American Sociological Review*, 53 (1988), 41–9.
4. The problem of multi-collinearity in the work of Stark and his associates is fully examined by Daniel V. A. Olson, 'Religious Pluralism and US Church Membership: A Reassessment', *Sociology of Religion*, forthcoming.
5. Kenneth C. Land, Glenn Deane, and Judith R. Blau, 'Religious Pluralism and Church Membership', *American Sociological Review*, 56 (1991), 237–49.
6. Judith R. Blau, Kenneth C. Land, and Kent Rudding, 'The Expansion of Religious Affiliation: An Explanation of the Growth of Church Participation in the United States, 1850–1930', *Social Science Research*, 21 (1991), 329.
7. Kevin D. Breault, 'New Evidence on Religious Pluralism, Urbanism and Religious Participation', *American Sociological Review*, 54 (1989), 1048–53, and 'A Re-Examination of the Relationship between Religious Diversity and Religious Adherents: Reply to Finke and Stark', *American Sociological Review*, 54 (1989), 1056–9.
8. Finke and Stark offered a typically rude response, in which they claimed that Iannaccone had tried to replicate Breault's research and come to quite the

opposite conclusion: that there was a strong positive connection between diversity and religious vitality. When Olson tried to reconcile the two competing interpretations, he discovered that the statistical package used by Iannaccone contained a simple but fatal mistake. In calculating the Herfindahl Index, it failed to subtract the final calculated value from 1. It thus produced inverted results. What the supply-siders reported as a strong positive correlation was actually a strong negative connection; Breault was right! See Roger Finke and Rodney Stark, 'Evaluating the Evidence: Religious Economies and Sacred Canopies', *American Sociological Review*, 54 (1988), 1054–6, and Daniel V. A. Olson, 'Religious Pluralism in Contemporary US Counties', *American Sociological Review*, 63 (1998), 757–61. When Olson published that finding and made further criticisms of their handling of the collinearity problems, Finke and Stark reacted in their customary way by ignoring the criticisms, again claiming that every other bit of research supported them, and restating their hypotheses (Roger Finke and Rodney Stark, 'Religious Choice and Competition', *American Sociological Review*, 63 (1998), 761–6).

9. Peter Beyer, 'Religious Vitality in Canada', *Journal for the Scientific Study of Religion*, 36 (1997), 272–88.

10. Daniel V. A. Olson and C. Kirk Hadaway, 'Religious Pluralism and Affiliation among Canadian Counties and Cities', *Journal for the Scientific Study of Religion*, forthcoming.

11. Laurence Iannaccone, 'The Consequences of Religious Market Structure', *Rationality and Society*, 3 (1991), 169.

12. Mark Chaves and David E. Cann, 'Regulation, Pluralism and Religious Market Structure', *Rationality and Society*, 4 (1992). It is worth adding, because it shows their general attitude to their critics, that Stark and Iannaccone ('A Supply-Side Interpretation of the "Secularization" of Europe', *Journal for the Scientific Study of Religion*, 33 (1994), 230–52) take a cheap shot at Chaves and Cann when they criticize them for counting the Republic of Ireland as a country with no state regulation of religion. Stark and Iannaccone point out with relish that Ireland should really be counted as an example of state-supported religion because, until its revision in 1972, the constitution accorded a special status to the Catholic Church. This is true, but what Stark and Iannaccone do not say is that state support for the Church was itself relatively recent and dated only from de Valera's 1937 constitution. Until the separation of the Irish Free States from the UK in 1921, in so far as it interfered with Irish religion, the British state was usually anti-Catholic Church.

13. Robert A. Campbell and James E. Curtis, 'Religious Involvement across Societies: Analyses for Alternative Measures in National Surveys', *Journal for the Scientific Study of Religion*, 33 (1994), 215–29; Peter Kaldor, *Who Goes Where? Who Doesn't Care?* (Homebush, NSW: Lancer, 1987); Don Aitken, 'The Two Faces of Religion', in his *Stability and Change in Australian Politics* (Canberra: Australian National University Press, 1977), 161–79; Hilary Carey, *Believing in Australia: A Cultural History of Religions* (St Leonards, NSW: Allen and Unwin, 1996). See also Tables A6.1–A6.3 in the Appendix.

14. Callum Brown, *The Social History of Religion in Scotland since 1730* (London: Methuen,1987).
15. Robin Gill, *The Myth of the Empty Church* (London: SPCK, 1993).
16. Edward Bailey, 'The Implicit Religion of Contemporary Society: An Orientation and a Plea for its Study', *Religion*, 13 (1983), 69–83.
17. Stark and Iannaccone, 'Supply-Side Interpretation', 241.
18. Margaret Spufford, 'Can we Count the "Godly" and the "Comformable" in the Seventeenth Century?', *Journal of Ecclesiastical History*, 36 (1985), 428–38.
19. Keith Thomas, *Religion and the Decline of Magic* (Harmondsworth: Penguin, 1973), 32–3.
20. Rosalind Hill, 'From the Conquest to the Black Death', in Sheridan Gilley and W. J. Sheils (eds.), *A History of Religion in Britain: Practice and Belief from Pre-Roman Times to the Present* (Oxford: Basil Blackwell, 1994), 58.
21. Bernard Hamilton, *Religion in the Medieval West* (London: Edward Arnold, 1986), 105–7. It is also worth noting the vast sums spent by people of all stations on buying Masses. The rich established chantries; the poor paid for just one or two Masses for their souls. Funding Masses for members (either living or dead) was one of the main functions of the guilds (the forerunners of our trade unions and insurance companies). Unions and insurance companies no longer serve that purpose; see Maurice Keen, *English Society in the Later Middle Ages* (Harmondsworth: Penguin, 1990), 274–5.
22. Hamilton, *Religion*, 118.
23. Stark and Iannaccone, 'Supply-Side Interpretation', 243.
24. Peter Laslett, *The World We Have Lost* (London: Methuen, 1983), 70–1. It is worth noting that Laslett removed the word 'Christian' from his description of 'All our ancestors . . .', which in early versions read 'literal Christian believers', presumably to avoid the suggestion that they were the equivalent of the modern pious evangelical. But that does not change the basic point, which is well attested by other historians who are not cited by the supply-siders. See e.g. Sheldon Watts, *A Social History of Western Europe 1450–1720* (London: Hutchinson, 1984).
25. David Martin, *A General Theory of Secularization* (Oxford: Basil Blackwell, 1978), 84–5. In addition to Keen, Watts, Spufford, and Hill cited here, see also Peter Collinson, *The Religion of Protestants: The Church in English Society 1559–1625* (Oxford: Oxford University Press, 1982); Michael R. Watts, *The Dissenters*, i. *From the Reformation to the French Revolution* (Oxford: Oxford University Press, 1978); Robert Whiting, *The Blind Devotion of the People: Popular Religion in the English Reformation* (Cambridge: Cambridge University Press, 1989); and Christopher Harper-Bill, *The Pre-Reformation Church in England 1400–1530* (London: Longman, 1996).
26. Robert Currie, Alan D. Gilbert, and Lee Horsley, *Churches and Churchgoers: Patterns of Church Growth in the British Isles since 1700* (Oxford: Oxford University Press, 1977), table 2.3.
27. Peter Brierley, *UK Christian Handbook Religious Trends 1998/99 No. 1* (London: Christian Research Association, 1997), table 2.2.72.

28. Peter Brierley, *A Century of British Christianity: Historical Statistics 1900–1985 with Projections to 2000* (Research Monograph 14; London: MARC Europe, 1989), 26.
29. Stark and Iannaccone, 'Supply-Side Interpretation', 243.
30. Diana Gregory, *A Social Survey of the Presbyterian Church in Wales: The Churches* (Cardiff: Open University in Wales, 1997); Douglas Davies, Caroline Pack, Susanne Seymour, Christopher Short, Charles Watkins, and Michael Winter, *The Views of Rural Parishioners: Rural Church Project Vol. IV* (Cirencester and Nottingham: Royal Agricultural College and University of Nottingham, 1990), 50–60. Of the general population sample, 66% never attended church and a further 11% had attended fewer than three times a year.
31. See e.g. K. S. Inglis, 'Patterns of Religious Worship in 1851', *Journal of Ecclesiastical History*, 11 (1960), 74–87, or Donald J. Withrington, 'The 1851 Census of Religious Worship and Education: With a Note on Church Accommodation in Mid-19th Century Scotland', *Records of the Scottish Church History Society*, 18 (1974), 133–48.
32. Brown, *Social History of Religion*, 19.
33. Callum Brown, *The People in the Pews: Religion and Society in Scotland since 1780* (Glasgow: Economic and Social History Society of Scotland, 1993), 7.
34. Alasdair Crockett, 'A Secularising Geography? Patterns and Processes of Religious Changes in England and Wales, 1676–1851', unpublished Ph.D. thesis, University of Leicester, 1998, 131.
35. Gill, *Empty Church*, 37–8.
36. Robin Gill, 'Secularization and Census Data', in Steve Bruce (ed.), *Religion and Modernization: Sociologists and Historians Debate the Secularization Thesis* (Oxford: Oxford University Press, 1992), 109.
37. David Gerard, 'Religious Attitudes and Values', in Mark Abrams, David Gerard, and Noel Timms (eds.), *Values and Social Change in Britain* (London: Macmillan, 1985), 50.
38. I am grateful to the ESRC's Data Archive at the University of Essex for providing me with the original BSA data. I am also grateful to Dr Fiona Alderdice, then of the Department of Social Studies, The Queen's University of Belfast, and Dr Sam McIsaac, then of the Department of Sociology, University of Aberdeen, for technical assistance with the analysis. One of my reasons for being confident about the general shorthand of describing church attendance in 1851 as about 50% and in 1990 as about 10% is that comparable figures are repeatedly found in very detailed local studies. For example, Margaret Stelfox of the Department of Religious Studies, University of Lancaster, who has been collecting data on the churches in Kendal, gave figures of 48% (not including Sunday scholars) for 1851 and 9.4% (including Sunday scholars) for 1998 at the 1998 'Religion Beyond Church and Chapel' consultation at the University of Lancaster.
39. C. Kirk Hadaway, Penny Long Marler, and Mark Chaves, 'What the Polls don't Show: A Closer Look at US Church Attendance', *American Sociological Review*, 58 (1993), 741–52.

40. These and other data from the Nordic wing of international Religious and Moral Pluralism Project were presented at the 14th Nordic Conference on Sociology of Religion in Helsinki, August 1998.
41. Robin Gill, C. Kirk Hadaway, and Penny Long Marler, 'Is Religious Belief Declining in Britain?', *Journal for the Scientific Study of Religion*, 37 (1998), 507–16.
42. Brierley, *Religious Trends*, table 2.5.1.
43. Ibid. table 4.8.1.
44. Phillip Rose (ed.), *Social Trends 23* (London: Her Majesty's Stationery Office, 1993), table 11.7.
45. Barrie Gunter and Rachel Viney, *Seeing is Believing: Religion and Television in the 1990s* (London: John Libbey/Independent Television Commission, 1994), 53.
46. Stark and Iannaccone, 'Supply-Side Interpretation', 234.
47. James Obelkevitch, 'Religion', in F. M. L. Thompson (ed.), *The Cambridge Social History of Britain 1750–1950*, iii. *Social Agencies and Institutions* (Cambridge: Cambridge University Press, 1990), 311.
48. Gill, *Empty Church*, 46.
49. Obelkevitch, 'Religion', 315–16.
50. James Obelkevitch, *Religion and Rural Society: South Lindsay 1825–1875* (Oxford: Oxford University Press, 1976), 157.
51. Steve Bruce, 'Pluralism and Religious Vitality', in Steve Bruce (ed.), *Religion and Modernization: Sociologists and Historians Debate the Secularization Thesis* (Oxford: Oxford University Press, 1992), 187.
52. See n. 67.
53. Ieuan Gwynedd Jones, *Mid-Victorian Wales* (Cardiff: University of Wales Press, 1992), 15.
54. Obelkevitch, *Religion and Rural Society*; Stephen Yeo, *Religion and Voluntary Organizations in Crisis* (London: Croom Helm, 1976); Jeffrey Cox, *The English Churches in a Secular Society: Lambeth 1870–1930* (Oxford: Oxford University Press, 1982); and S. J. D. Green, *Religion in the Age of Decline: Organization and Experience in Industrial Yorkshire 1870–1920* (Cambridge: Cambridge University Press, 1996). It is worth noting the presence of the phrase 'secular society' in the title of Cox's book. In the first and last chapters he enthusiastically (but, as I hope I have made clear in Chapter 1 of this book, mistakenly) criticizes the secularization thesis for postulating inevitable decline. The bulk of his book describes perfectly the very process the secularization thesis tries to comprehend and offers explanations entirely compatible with it.
55. G. E. Mingay, *Rural Life in Victorian England* (London: Heinemann, 1976), 147.
56. Ibid.
57. Franklin Hamlin Littell, *From State Church to Pluralism: A Protestant Interpretation of Religion in American History* (Chicago: Aldine, 1962), 5.
58. Martin E. Marty, *Righteous Empire: The Protestant Experience in America* (New York: Dial Press, 1970).

59. Naomi Turner, *Sinews of Sectarian Warfare? State Aid in New South Wales 1836–1862* (Canberra: Australian National University Press, 1972).
60. Crockett, 'Secularising Geography?', 144–5.
61. Bruce, 'Pluralism'.
62. Rodney Stark, Roger Finke, and Laurence Iannaccone, 'Pluralism and Piety: England and Wales 1851', *Journal for the Scientific Study of Religion*, 34 (1995), 440.
63. Crockett, 'Secularising Geography?', 277.
64. Stark, Finke, and Iannaccone, 'Pluralism and Piety', 441.
65. Robert Tudor Jones, 'Religion, Nationality and State in Wales, 1840–90', in Donal A. Kerr (ed.), *Religion, States and Ethnic Groups* (Aldershot: Dartmouth, 1992), 261.
66. Stark, Finke, and Iannaccone, 'Pluralism and Piety', 442–3.
67. Roger Finke, in 'An Unsecular America', in Steve Bruce (ed.), *Religion and Modernization: Sociologists and Historians Debate the Secularization Thesis* (Oxford: Oxford University Press, 1992), 160. Despite this concession, he proceeds to use a method of statistical description that overlooks internal diversity and, in their contrasts between state-supported churches and freely competing sects, he and his colleagues continue to treat national churches as monoliths.
68. Crockett, 'Secularising Geography?', 209.
69. Ibid. 259
70. Alan D. Gilbert, *Religion and Society in Industrial England: Church, Chapel and Social Change 1740–1914* (London: Longman, 1976), 99.
71. Jones, *Mid-Victorian Wales*, 16.
72. Brierley, *Religious Trends*, table 2.12.3.
73. Jones, *Mid-Victorian Wales*, 130.
74. For good general histories of religion in Scotland, see J. H. S. Burleigh, *A Church History of Scotland* (Oxford: Oxford University Press, 1973), and Gordon Donaldson, *Scotland: Church and Nation through 16 Centuries* (London: SCM Press, 1960).
75. Andrew L. Drummond and James Bulloch, *The Scottish Church 1688–1843* (Edinburgh: St Andrew Press, 1973), 118.
76. This does not, of course, undermine one of the other supply-side claims: that competition forces clergy to be responsive to the demands of actual or potential congregants and hence that diversity will continue to be beneficial past the threshold at which all likely variants of the dominant tradition are catered for.
77. The Aberdeen church membership and church attendance data were compiled by Paul Chmiel and I am grateful for his assistance in preparing this section.
78. Paul Chmiel, 'Pluralism and Religious Vitality in Aberdeen, 1851–1991', unpublished M.Phil. thesis, University of Aberdeen, 1999.
79. A. Allan MacLaren, *Religion and Social Class: The Disruption Years in Aberdeen* (London: Routledge & Kegan Paul, 1974).
80. Ibid. 109.
81. On Presbyterian discipline, see Stewart J. Brown, 'The Decline and Fall of Kirk-Session Discipline in Presbyterian Scotland c.1830–1930', unpublished paper, 1991.
82. But they can be found in Chmiel, 'Pluralism and Religious Vitality'.

Chapter 4. Pluralism and Religion: Europe

1. A major attempt to test the supply-side theory with data on sixteen countries from the WVS concluded that it did not work: 'in general, culture and modernization were more important than the religious market structure' (Johan Verweij, Peter Ester, and Rein Nauta, 'Secularization as an Economic and Cultural Phenomenon: A Cross-National Analysis', *Journal for the Scientific Study of Religion*, 36 (1997), 309). Even though this result supports my case, I remain sceptical about the value of such work. All the quite proper concerns about the wording of survey questions, the meaning given to them by respondents, and the meaning of their responses are magnified tenfold when researchers try to use a common instrument across cultures. Does asking the 'same' question in Italy and Finland mean using the closest translation of the words or trying to capture best the sense? Furthermore, there are so many compromises involved in coding and aggregating the data, and the correlations normally found in such studies are so weak, that resulting statistical relationships seem likely to be spurious.

    Another source of uncertainty, commonly overlooked in cross-national comparisons, is the movement of people between units. Consider my comparison of levels of religious vitality in the two parts of Germany. I do not mention that almost half a million people moved from East to West; that will have raised the relative proportion of Lutherans in the FRG. Does that dull FRG church attendance (because until recently Catholics were generally more observant) or raise it (because some of the migrants will have been convinced evangelicals)?

    Apart from concluding that we must be very cautious about our inferences from statistical analysis, I would recommend that we accept the conclusions of societal level statistical comparisons only when they accord with what we learn from the generality of other sources. This does mean that we will sometimes be fooled by a mistaken consensus and miss the small gem of hidden truth, but I cannot believe that the iconoclastic sociologist is right terribly often.

2. Yves, Lambert, 'Un paysage religeux en profonde évolution', in H. Riffault (ed.), *Les Valuers des français* (Paris: PUF, 1994), 123–62. See also Lambert, 'Vers une ère post-chrétienne?', in *Futuribles 220*, special issue on 'L'évolution des valuers des Européans' (July–Aug. 1995), 85–111. We might note that France in the 1990s had a large Muslim population (around 4 million), the first generation of which at least is considerably more religiously observant than the native French.

3. Anne Van Meerbeeck, 'The Importance of a Religious Service at Birth: The Persistent Demand for Baptism in Flanders', *Social Compass*, 42 (1995), 47.

4. Paul Dekker and Peter Ester, 'Depillarization, Deconfessionalization and Deinstitutionalization: Empirical Trends in Dutch Society 1958–1992', *Review of Religious Research*, 37 (1996), 335.

5. J. W. Becker and R. Vink, *Secularatie in Nederland, 1966–91: De Verandering vasn Opvattingen en Enkele Gedragingen* (Rijswijk: Sociaal en Cultureel Planbureau, 1994).

6. Rodney Stark and William Sims Bainbridge, *The Future of Religion: Seculariza-*

tion, Revival and Cult Formation (Berkeley and Los Angeles: University of California Press, 1985), 495.

7. Roy Wallis, 'Figuring Out Cult Receptivity', *Journal for the Scientific Study of Religion,* 25 (1986), 494–503.

8. The historical detail of this section is drawn from Leslie S. Hunter, *Scandinavian Churches: A Picture of the Development and Life of the Churches of Denmark, Finland, Iceland, Norway and Sweden* (London: Faber & Faber, 1965); John T. Flint, 'The Secularization of Norwegian Society', *Comparative Studies in Society and History,* 6 (1964), 325–44; Frederick Hale, 'The Development of Religious Freedom in Norway', *Journal of Church and State,* 23 (1981), 47–68; R. F. Thomasson, 'The Religious Situation in Sweden', *Social Compass,* 15 (1968), 491–8; the various articles on 'Religion in the Nordic Countries' in *Social Compass,* 35 (1988); and the respective country entries in Hans Mol (ed.), *Western Religion* (The Hague: Mouton, 1972).

9. Einar-Arne Drivenes, 'Religion, Church and Ethnic Minorities in Norway, 1850–1940', in Donal A. Kerr (ed.), *Religion, States and Ethnic Groups* (Aldershot: Dartmouth, 1992), 205–28.

10. Paavo Seppanen, 'Finland', in Mol (ed.), *Western Religion,* 157.

11. Berndt Gustafsson, 'Sweden', in Mol (ed.), *Western Religion,* 480.

12. Harri Heino, Kari Salonen, and Jaakko Rusama, *Response to Recession: The Evangelical Lutheran Church of Finland in the Years 1992–1995* (Tampere: The Research Institute of the Evangelical Lutheran Church of Finland, 1997), 25. See also Jouko Sihvo, 'Religion and Secularization in Finland', *Social Compass,* 35 (1988), 67–90.

13. Ole Riis, 'Trends in Danish Religion', *Social Compass,* 35 (1988), 48.

14. Heino, Salonen, and Rusama, *Response to Recession,* shows that 2% of Lutherans withdrew during the deep recession years brought about by, among other things, the collapse of the Soviet economy. This only serves to highlight how few left previously. Whether this marks the start of a general revaluation of church membership that will bring it into line with the low levels of claimed religious beliefs remains to be seen.

15. Rodney Stark and Laurence Iannaccone, 'A Supply-Side Interpretation of the "Secularization" of Europe', *Journal for the Scientific Study of Religion,* 33 (1994), 237.

16. Ibid.

17. Rodney Stark, 'German and German–American Religiousness', *Journal for the Scientific Study of Religion,* 36 (1997), 185.

18. G. E. Mingay, *Rural Life in Victorian England* (London: Heinemann, 1976), 150.

19. Ronald Inglehart, Miguel Basanez, and Alejandro Moreno, *Human Values and Beliefs: A Cross-Cultural Sourcebook* (Ann Arbor: University of Michigan Press, 1998).

20. Peter Brierley, *World Churches Handbook: Based on the Operation World Database by Patrick Johnston* (London: Christian Research Association, 1997).

21. Much of the detail in this section comes from John Hiden and Patrick Salmon, *The Baltic Nations and Europe* (London: Longman, 1994), and from the respective country entries in Joel Krieger (ed.), *The Oxford Companion to the Politics of the World* (Oxford: Oxford University Press, 1993).

22. Hank Johnston, 'Religio-Nationalist Subcultures under the Communists: Comparisons from the Baltics, Transcaucasia and Ukraine', *Sociology of Religion,* 54 (1993), 237–55.

23. Hiden and Salmon, *The Baltic Nations and Europe,* 18.

24. Alfred Senn, 'Lithuania: Rights and Responsibilities of Independence', in Ian Bremner and Ray Taras (eds.), *New Nations, New Politics: Building the Post-Soviet Nations* (Cambridge: Cambridge University Press, 1997), 354.

25. Nils Muizneks, 'Latvia: Restoring a State, Rebuilding a Nation', in Ian Bremner and Ray Taras (eds.), *New Nations, New Politics: Building the Post-Soviet Nations* (Cambridge: Cambridge University Press, 1997), 381.

26. Barbara Strassberg, 'Changes in Religious Culture in Post-World War II Poland', *Review of Religious Research,* 48 (1988), 342–54.

27. Zdzislawa Walascek, 'An Open Issue of Legitimacy: The State and Church in Poland', *Annals of the American Academy of Political and Social Science,* 483 (1986), 133.

28. Christel Lane, *Christian Religion in the Soviet Union: A Sociological Study* (London: George Allen & Unwin, 1978), 192–3.

29. For a book-length treatment of conservative Protestant politics, see Steve Bruce, *Conservative Protestant Politics* (Oxford: Oxford University Press, 1998).

30. V. C. Chrypinski, 'Czechoslovakia', in Stuart Mews (ed.), *Religion in Politics: A World Guide* (London: Longman, 1989), 53.

31. Erika Kadlecová, 'Czechoslovakia', in Mol (ed.), *Western Religion,* 118.

32. Philip Walters, *World Christianity: Eastern Europe* (Monrovia, Calif.: MARC, 1988), 181; Niels Nielsen, *Revolutions in Eastern Europe* (Maryknoll, NY: Orbis Books, 1991), 94.

33. Nielsen, *Revolutions,* 93.

34. Walters, *World Christianity,* 178.

35. Chrypinksi, 'Czechoslovakia', 53.

36. Kadlecová, 'Czechoslovakia', 121. Although the data are slightly more dubious than most, in that the first survey covered all the Czech lands while the second covered only North Moravia (the most industrialized part of Czechoslovakia), Kadlecová compares various indices of religious belief and behaviour in 1946 and 1963 that show clear and large decline. For example, 'regular' churchgoing fell from 64 to 34%.

37. Edward Lucas, 'The Church has a Better Chance than Ever', *Independent,* 21 Apr. 1990. A very well-informed observer of eastern Europe in 1994 wrote: 'The first survey conducted for half a century . . . suggested low religious observance rates [in the Czech Republic] ranging from less than 1 per cent in Litoměřice to 8 per cent in Olosouc. In Slovakia, by contrast, there are signs that Christianity remains a mass phenomenon' (Jonathan Luxmoore, 'Eastern Europe 1994: A Review

of Religious Life in Bulgaria, Romania, Hungary, Slovakia, the Czech Republic and Slovakia', *Religion, State and Society,* 23 (1995), 218).

38. Walters, *World Christianity,* 178.
39. Cited in Mary L. Gaultier, 'Church Attendance, Religious Belief in Post-Communist Societies', *Journal for the Scientific Study of Religion,* 36 (1997), 289–96.
40. Jack D. Shand, 'The Decline of Traditional Christian Beliefs in Germany', *Sociology of Religion,* 59 (1998),
41. Calculated on 1980 religious community data, the Herfindahl Index for the FRG was 0.52 and for the GDR 0.23.
42. This line of reasoning is supported by the observation of Walters (*World Christianity,* 217) that the Catholic Church, which remained much more detached from the state, declined less severely.
43. V. C. Chrypinski, 'German Democratic Republic', in Mews (ed.), *Religion in Politics,* 81.
44. Walters, *World Christianity,* 210.
45. Quoted in Nielsen, *Revolutions,* 54.
46. Ibid. 57.
47. Figure from my own analysis of the WVS dataset. I am grateful to the ICPSR, University of Michigan, and the ESRC Data Archive, University of Essex, for making the data available, and to Paula Surridge, University of Aberdeen, for her assistance in accessing the data.
48. Paulina Almerich, 'Spain', in Mol (ed.), *Western Religion,* 470–1.
49. Original analysis of WVS data.
50. Rudolf Andorka, 'Recent Changes in Social Structure, Human Relations, and Values in Hungary', *Social Compass,* 42 (1995), 14. It is worth noting that Andorka both doubts his earlier more optimistic forecasts of religious revival and specifically rejects the claim that new religious movements are having any major impact on the country's religious profile. See also Miklós Tomka, 'Secularization or Anomy? Interpreting Religious Change in Communist Societies', *Social Compass,* 38 (1991), 93–102, and 'The Changing Social Role of Religion in Eastern and Central Europe: Religion's Revival and its Contradictions', *Social Compass,* 42 (1995), 17–26.
51. Johnston, 'Religio-Nationalist Subcultures', 250.
52. Lane, *Christian Religion in the Soviet Union,* 47.
53. Preliminary reports from Penny Long Marler on her 1998 study of actual as against claimed church attendance suggests that the actual decline will have been greater, which would be consistent with the reports of my acquaintances within the Irish Church that there are now unprecedented problems with clergy recruitment and fund-raising.
54. Hugh McLeod, 'Secular Cities? Berlin, London and New York in the Later Nineteenth and Early Twentieth Centuries', in Steve Bruce (ed.), *Religion and Modernization: Sociologists and Historians Debate the Secularization Thesis* (Oxford: Oxford University Press, 1992), 84.

55. Ronald Inglehart, *Modernization and Postmodernization: Cultural, Economic and Political Change in 43 Societies* (Princeton: Princeton University Press, 1997).
56. David Martin, *A General Theory of Secularization* (Oxford: Basil Blackwell, 1978), 101.
57. Ibid. 105.
58. Stark and his colleagues are right that religion can provide promises of a better future. They are only wrong to think that such promises can be linked to individual action through the mechanism of the autonomous individual maximizing rather than through the strength of social bonds or that this one observation about what some people sometimes do with religion can provide the basis for a complete theory of religion.

Chapter 5. Rational Choice: The Basic Errors

1. R. Stephen Warner, 'Work in Progress toward a New Paradigm for the Sociological Study of Religion in the United States', *American Journal of Sociology*, 98 (1993), 1044–93.
2. Émile Durkheim, *Suicide* (London: Routledge & Kegan Paul, 1970).
3. Rodney Stark, 'German and German–American Religiousness', *Journal for the Scientific Study of Religion*, 36 (1997), 185.
4. Douglas Davies, Caroline Pack, Susanne Seymour, Christopher Short, Charles Watkins, and Michael Winter, *Parish Life and Rural Religion: Rural Church Project Vol. III* (Cirencester and Nottingham: Royal Agricultural College and University of Nottingham, 1990).
5. Gary L. Tidwell, *Anatomy of a Fraud: Inside the Finances of the PTL Ministries* (New York: John Wiley & Sons, 1993).
6. I have not pursued this point because, in the end, whether an explanation is better or worse than its rivals depends on its internal cohesion and its fit with the evidence, not on the motives of its proponents. However, I think it is not coincidence that the rational choice model finds less support among European social scientists, who have some acquaintance with social democracy, than among their US counterparts.
7. Laurence Iannaccone, 'Sacrifice and Stigma: Reducing Free-Riding in Cults, Communes and Other Collectives', *Journal of Political Economy*, 100 (1992), 271–92, and 'Why Strict Churches are Strong', *American Journal of Sociology*, 99 (1994), 1180–1211.
8. P. Diesing, *Reason in Society* (Westport, Coun.: Greenwood Press, 1973), 22.
9. Ibid. 45.
10. Iannaccone, 'Why Strict Churches are Strong', 1181.
11. The point, of course, is that charismatic leaders are relatively free from the inhibitions of tradition and ecclesiastical structure. Indeed, they may deliberately change their teachings radically in order to test the strength of their charismatic

bond with followers. A good example is the erratic Moses David, the founder of the Children of God (later the Family of Love or just The Family). However, his drastic changes of direction were not consciously conceived as responses to unpopularity. See Roy Wallis, 'Charisma: Commitment and Control in a New Religious Movement', in Roy Wallis (ed.), *Millennialism and Charisma* (Belfast: The Queen's University of Belfast, 1982), 73–140.

12. *Religion Watch*, 14 (Nov. 1998), 3.
13. Jon Elster, 'Introduction', in Jon Elster (ed.), *Rational Choice* (Oxford: Basil Blackwell, 1986), 17.
14. Diesing, *Reason in Society*, 63.
15. Talcott Parsons, 'Motivations in Economic Analysis', in his *Essays in Sociological Theory* (New York: Free Press, 1954), 52.
16. Reginald Bibby, *Fragmented Gods* (Toronto: Stoddard, 1987).
17. Peter L. Berger, *The Heretical Imperative: Contemporary Possibilities of Religious Affirmation* (London: Collins, 1980).

Chapter 6. Conservative Religion

1. These data are from Reginald Bibby, *Unknown Gods: The Ongoing Story of Religion in Canada* (Toronto: Stoddard, 1993).
2. These figures were calculated from the original data in the various publications of Peter Brierley listed in the bibliography and from data in Robert Currie and Alan D. Gilbert, 'Religion', in A. H. Halsey (ed.), *Trends in British Society since 1900* (London: Macmillan, 1972), 407–50, and Robert Currie, Alan D. Gilbert, and Lee Horsley, *Churches and Churchgoers: Patterns of Church Growth in the British Isles since 1700* (Oxford: Oxford University Press, 1977).
3. For a history of the 'house church', see Andrew Walker, *Restoring the Kingdom: The Radical Christianity of the House Church Movement* (Guildford: Eagle, 1998).
4. A couple of methodological observations: Brierley's figures for the Witnesses are estimates; they refuse to supply him with their own data. The Mormon data come from the Mormon Church. In the light of the healthy cynicism that the work of Hadaway and Marler has introduced to the study of indices of church affiliation, it is worth adding that I and others with whom I have discussed the problem see little evidence around Britain of the sort of growth implied in these data. However, Brierley does not doubt their basic contours. Perhaps it is time for someone to attempt an independent validation of the figures for the Mormons and the Witnesses. There is also some doubt about the trajectory of growth of the Elim Pentecostal Church and the Assemblies of God. Currie and Gilbert ('Religion') give the Elim 45,000 congregants in 286 congregations. Brierley (*UK Christian Handbook Religious Trends 1998/99 No. 1* (London: Christian Research Association, 1997)) gives them 30,750 members in 354 congregations for 1980. There is a similar disparity for the Assemblies of God. Currie and Gilbert give them 80,000

congregants in 543 congregations in 1962. Brierley gives them 35,000 in 571 congregations in 1980. Brierley believes that Currie and Gilbert are actually listing attendance figures, whereas he lists members, and Pentecostal churches often have more attenders than members. Fortunately we can be confident on the figures for congregations and we can also be sure that these two churches have shown considerable growth, which is all that is needed for my purposes here.

5. Some of the original figures used for these calculations were collected directly from the churches. Others came from Currie and Gilbert, 'Religion', and from John Highet, *The Scottish Churches* (London: Skeffington, 1960). The most recent figures came from Brierley, *Religious Trends*.

6. Penny Long Marler and C. Kirk Hadaway, 'Church Attendance and Membership in Four Nations: A Comparative, Historical Study of "Gaps", Discrepancies and Changes', Final Narrative Report to the Lily Foundation, Aug. 1997, 13.

7. J. D. Bollen, *Protestants and Social Reform in New South Wales 1890–1910* (Melbourne: Melbourne University Press, 1971), appendix. Other data in this section come from Philip Hughes, *Religion in Australia: Facts and Figures* (Kew, Victoria: Christian Research Association, 1997).

8. Two comprehensive sources are Dean R. Hoge and David A. Roozen (eds.), *Understanding Church Growth and Decline: 1950–78* (New York: Pilgrim Press, 1979), and Wade Clark Roof and William McKinney, *American Mainline Religion: Its Changing Shape and Future* (New Brunswick: Rutgers University Press, 1987).

9. The Hadaway and Marler research on the gap between what people say about their church attendance and what they actually do raises the possibility that the conservative–liberal difference may be greater or not so great as it appears, if one group is more prone to misrepresent its behaviour than the other.

10. John Sawkins, 'Church Affiliation Statistics: Counting Methodist Sheep', paper given at Soundings conference, Stirling, 14 Mar. 1998.

11. Reginald Bibby and Martin Brinkerhoff, 'The Circulation of the Saints: A Study of People who Join Conservative Churches', *Journal for the Scientific Study of Religion*, 12 (1973), 273–85; 'Circulation of the Saints Revisited: A Longitudinal Look at Conservative Church Growth', *Journal for the Scientific Study of Religion*, 22 (1983), 253–62.

12. Bibby, *Unknown Gods*, 45.

13. Robin D. Perrin, Paul Kennedy, and Donald E. Miller, 'Examining the Sources of Conservative Church Growth', *Journal for the Scientific Study of Religion*, 36 (1997), 71–80.

14. Almost a third reported no conversions at all in the previous two years (Peter Brierley, Graham Bown, Boyd Myers, Harold Rowdon, and Neil Summerton, *The Christian Brethren as the Nineties Began* (Carlisle: Paternoster Press, 1993)).

15. Rodney Stark and William Sims Bainbridge, *The Future of Religion: Secularization, Revival and Cult Formation* (Berkeley and Los Angeles: University of California Press, 1985), 316–20.

16. Dean Kelley, *Why the Conservative Churches are Growing* (New York: Harper & Row, 1972); 'Why the Conservative Churches are Still Growing', *Journal for the Scientific Study of Religion*, 17 (1978), 129–37.

17. Dean R. Hoge, 'A Test of Theories of Denominational Growth and Decline' in Hoge and Roozen (eds.), *Understanding Church Growth*, 179.
18. Rosabeth M. Kanter, *Commitment and Community: Communes and Utopias in Sociological Perspective* (Cambridge, Mass.: Harvard University Press, 1972).
19. Laurence Iannaccone, 'Sacrifice and Stigma: Reducing Free-Riding in Cults, Communes and Other Collectives', *Journal of Political Economy*, 100 (1992), 272. Worse for Iannaccone's approach, the more sectarian movements always had very high turnover. 'Many of the NRMs that triggered opposition experienced steep declines in membership by 1980, following a few years of rapid growth, when affiliation rates tailed off while disaffiliation rates remained robust' (David Bromley, 'The Social Construction of Contested Exit Roles', in Bromley (ed.), *The Politics of Religious Apostasy* (Westport, Conn.: Praeger, 1998), 39). See Eileen Barker, 'Defection from the Unification Church: Some Strategies and Distinctions', in David Bromley (ed.), *Falling from the Faith* (Newbury Park, Calif.: Sage, 1988), 166–84.
20. Iannaccone, 'Sacrifice and Stigma', 272.
21. Laurence Iannaccone, 'Why Strict Churches are Strong', *American Journal of Sociology*, 99 (1994), 1183. Iannaccone exaggerates the 'costs' of strict religion. He lists such sacrifices as giving up alcohol and coffee without noticing that very many people, for widely differing reasons, also give up such things, which means that the deviation of the sectarian is not only slight but may pass unnoticed and thus be unable to perform one of the roles (stigmatizing the sectarian) that Iannaccone attributes to it.
22. Iannaccone, 'Sacrifice and Stigma', 280. For incisive criticism of the 'free rider' notion, see Gerald Marwell, 'We Still Don't Know if Strict Churches are Strong, Much Less Why: Comment on Iannaccone', *American Journal of Sociology*, 101 (1996), 1097–1108.
23. Joseph B. Tamney and Stephen D. Johnson, 'A Research Note on the Free-Rider Issue', *Journal for the Scientific Study of Religion*, 36 (1997), 104–8.
24. For Iannaccone there is only the church (liberal) and the sect (strict). The denomination and the cult are fudges developed by sociologists to disguise the inadequacy of their conceptualization. This puts him at odds with Stark, who in earlier incarnations distinguished churches (religious bodies at ease with society), sects (schismatic religions in high tension with surrounding society), and cults (high-tension religious innovations) (Stark and Bainbridge, *The Future of Religion*, 21–37). Both formulations seem markedly less useful than the Wallis model introduced in Chapter 1.
25. For example, the Mormons only set off from New England because of the hostility they encountered. They settled briefly in Nauvoo, Illinois, but moved on again after Joseph Smith and his brother were murdered in jail by a lynch-mob. It was in order to find space for their distinctive culture that the Mormons, led by Brigham Young, headed for the Rockies and the Great Salt Lake.
26. I have elaborated the contrasting structures of broadcasting in the UK and USA in Steve Bruce, *Pray TV* (London: Routledge, 1990), 48–53, and *The Rise and Fall*

of the New Christian Right (Oxford: Oxford University Press, 1988), 68–76. See also Kenneth M. Wolfe, *The Churches and the British Broadcasting Corporation 1922–1956: The Politics of Broadcast Religion* (London: SCM Press, 1984), and Andrew Quicke and Juliet Quicke, *Hidden Agendas: The Politics of Religious Broadcasting in Britain 1987–1991* (Virginia Beach, Va.: Dominion Kings Grant Publications, 1992).

27. Balmer offers a rich description of one such summer camp in the Adirondacks that he describes as 'a sanctuary for fundamentalist parents to send their children, a place where strict parental rules would be enforced, where some sort of religious commitment would be exacted' (Randall Balmer, *Mine Eyes Have Seen the Glory: A Journey into the Evangelical Subculture in America* (Oxford: Oxford University Press, 1989), 95).

28. Edward Deming Andrews, *The People Called Shakers: A Search for the Perfect Society* (New York: Dover, 1963).

29. Norman Adams, *Goodbye, Beloved Brethren* (Aberdeen: Impulse Books, 1972).

30. James Davidson Hunter, *Evangelicalism: The Coming Generation* (Chicago: University of Chicago Press, 1987), 59.

31. Hunter also observes a considerable change in evangelicals' notions of God and the purpose of religion. Increasingly they see God as a psychotherapist and the primary purpose of their faith as personal contentment and satisfaction. The 'this-worldly' orientation is taken even further in that strand of conservative Protestantism known as the 'health and wealth' gospel. In the nineteenth century evangelicals had hoped that, by working diligently in their calling, they might prosper (or not, that was a matter for divine providence); at the end of the twentieth century televangelists now preach that simple faith (and a donation to the Lord's servant!) is all that is required to be showered with God's blessings. This suggests that even the more conservative strands of US Protestantism are being influenced by the same social forces that have produced the New Age.

32. Elizabeth Isichei, *Victorian Quakers* (Oxford: Oxford University Press, 1970).

33. Eileen Barker, 'Standing at the Crossroads: The Politics of Marginality in "Subversive Organizations"', in Bromley (ed.), *The Politics of Religious Apostasy*, 75–93.

34. Most of these observations were first made by the American theologian and historian H. Richard Niebuhr, *The Social Sources of Denominationalism* (New York: Meridian, 1962).

35. Donald A. Rooksby, *The Man in Leather Breeches: The Quakers in North-West England* (Colwyn Bay: Donald A. Rooksby).

36. Robert Michels, *Political Parties: A Sociological Study of the Oligarchic Tendencies of Modern Democracy* (New York: Free Press, 1962).

37. Michael R. Watts, *The Dissenters, i. From the Reformation to the French Revolution* (Oxford: Oxford University Press, 1978), 386.

38. Bryan Wilson, 'How Sects Evolve: Issues and Inferences', in Wilson, *The Social Dimensions of Sectarianism: Sects and New Religious Movements in Contemporary Society* (Oxford: Oxford University Press, 1990), and 'The Persistence of Sects', *Diskus*, 1 (1993), 1–12.

39. Malcolm Bull and Keith Lockhart, *Seeking a Sanctuary: Seventh-Day Adventism and the American Dream* (New York: Harper & Row, 1989).
40. Bruce, *The Rise and Fall of the New Christian Right*, and *Conservative Protestant Politics* (Oxford: Oxford University Press, 1998), ch. 5.

Chapter 7. Liberal Religion

1. Paul Heelas, *The New Age Movement: The Celebration of the Self and the Sacralization of Modernity* (Oxford: Basil Blackwell, 1996).
2. David V. Barrett, *Sects, 'Cults' and Alternative Religions: A World Survey and Sourcebook* (London: Blandford, 1996), 239–41.
3. In 1920 religious titles were 6.8% of all books published in the UK, and 3.3% of those were 'occult'. The respective figures for 1980 were 3.6 and 15.0 (Peter Brierley, *A Century of British Christianity: Historical Statistics 1900–1985 with Projections to 2000* (Research Monograph 14; London: MARC Europe, 1989)).
4. Reginald Bibby, *Unknown Gods: The Ongoing Story of Religion in Canada* (Toronto: Stoddard, 1993), 50–3.
5. Dr Collins made this point at the 1998 University of Lancaster Consultation on 'Religion beyond Church and Chapel'.
6. Jon P. Bloch, 'Individualism and Community in Alternative Spiritual "Magic"', *Journal for the Scientific Study of Religion*, 37 (1998), 293.
7. Ibid. 295.
8. This aspect of the secularization of mainline Protestantism, and the later similar changes in the evangelical churches, are discussed at length in Steve Bruce, *Religion in the Modern World: From Cathedrals to Cults* (Oxford: Oxford University Press, 1996), ch. 6.
9. Wade Clark Roof, 'God is in the Details: Reflections on Religion's Public Presence in the United States in the mid-1990s', *Sociology of Religion*, 57 (1996), 153.
10. One partial exception, which I have not explored, is the secular application of empowerment 'training' in 'human resource' management. See Heelas, *The New Age Movement*.
11. Bloch, 'Individualism and Community', 295.
12. Ibid. 297.
13. I am grateful to David Martin for reminding me of this at the Lancaster Symposium.
14. Émile Durkheim, *The Elementary Forms of the Religious Life* (London: George Allen & Unwin, 1971), 42.
15. Bloch, 'Individualism and Community', 287.
16. Ibid. 287, 291.
17. Ibid. 288.
18. William Shaw, *Spying in Guru Land: Inside Britain's Cults* (London: Fourth Estate, 1994), 19–70.

19. Barrett, *Sects, 'Cults', and Alternative Religions*, 249.
20. Jeremy Slocombe, 'Last Thoughts', *One Earth: The Findhorn Foundation and Community Magazine*, 14 (Summer 1994), 19.
21. Eileen Caddy and Liza Hollingshead, *Flight into Freedom: The Autobiography of the Co-Founder of the Findhorn Community* (Longmead, Dorset: Element, 1988).
22. Judith L. Boice, *At One With All Life: A Personal Journey in Gaian Communities* (Forres: Findhorn Press, 1989), 21.
23. Ibid. 21.
24. Ibid. 203.
25. Ibid. 65.
26. Ibid. 78.
27. Ibid. 108.
28. Quoted in Georg Feuerstein, 'Holy Madness: The Dangerous and Disillusioning Example of Da Free John', *What is Enlightenment* (Spring–Summer 1996), 14–15.
29. On the Children of God, see Deborah Davis, *The Children of God: The Inside Story* (Grand Rapids, Mlich.: Zondervan, 1984); Roy Wallis, *The Elementary Forms of the New Religious Life* (London: Routledge & Kegan Paul, 1984). On Rajneeshism, see Lewis F. Carter, *Charisma and Control in Rajneeshpuram: The Role of Shared Values in the Creation of a Community* (Cambridge: Cambridge University Press, 1990).
30. Bibby, *Unknown Gods*, 108. For US data, see Laurence Iannaccone, Daniel V. A. Olson, and Rodney Stark, 'Religious Resources and Church Growth', *Social Forces*, 74 (1995), 705–31.
31. John N. Wolffe (ed.), *Evangelical Faith and Public Zeal: Evangelicals and Society in Britain 1780–1980* (London: SPCK, 1995).
32. Heelas, *The New Age Movement*, 203.
33. Bloch, 'Individualism and Community', 289.
34. Tanya M. Luhrmann, *Persuasions of the Witch's Craft: Ritual Magic in Contemporary England* (Oxford: Basil Blackwell, 1989).
35. Roy Wallis, *The Rebirth of the Gods? Reflections on the New Religions in the West* (Belfast: The Queen's University of Belfast, 1978), 4. Had Wallis, as others have done, defined sects by 'tension with the wider society', then this point would be tautological. That sect and cult mapped onto world-rejecting and world-affirming would be largely a matter of definition. However, while one part of the Wallis typology of ideological organizations is concerned with societal reactions to the religion (and hence is close to the above tautology), the other element—the epistemological foundation—is quite separate—which allows me to draw attention to the lack of movements that are both 'cultic' and 'world-rejecting' to make a causal claim.
36. David Martin, *Pacifism: An Historical and Sociological Study* (London: Routledge & Kegan Paul, 1965), 194–5.
37. Ibid.
38. J. Gordon Melton, Jerome Clark, and Aidan A. Kelly, *New Age Almanac* (New York: Visible Ink, 1991), 40.

39. Barrett, *Sects, 'Cults' and Alternative Religions*, 212–13.
40. A good example is John Milbank, *Theology and Social Theory: Beyond Secular Reason* (Oxford: Basil Blackwell, 1990).
41. Ronald Inglehart, *Modernization and Postmodernization: Cultural, Economic and Political Change in 43 Societies* (Princeton: Princeton University Press, 1997), 285.
42. Bibby, *Unknown Gods*, 146–7.
43. *Daily Record*, 8 Jan. 1999. The pornography millionaire Larry Flynn was so offended by what he saw as the hypocrisy of leading Republicans attacking Clinton's morals that he offered very large rewards for anyone providing solid evidence of wrongdoing by Republican Congressmen and Senators. Such evidence was quickly forthcoming.

APPENDIX

TABLE A3.1. *Church membership, Britain, 1800, 1850, and 1900*

Church	1800	1850	1900
Episcopalian	*577,000*	*1,390,000*	*2,089,189*
Church of England		1,300,000	1,902,000
Church of Wales		70,000	141,008
Episcopalian Church of Scotland		20,000	46,181
Presbyterian	*313,000*	*528,070*	*1,245,412*
Church of Scotland		252,000	661,629
Free Church of Scotland		127,000	4,008
United Presbyterian Church of Scotland		126,070	—
United Free Church of Scotland		—	492,964
Original Seceders		5,000	3,700
Free Presbyterian Church of Scotland		—	6,000
Reformed Presbyterian Church of Scotland		6,000	1,040
Presbyterian Church of England		12,000	76,071
Methodist	*211,000*	*513,105*	*770,406*
Wesleyan Methodist Conference		334,458	410,384
New Connexion		17,656	31,782
Bible Christians		13,758	27,572
Primitive Methodists		102,222	186,466
Wesleyan Methodist Association		21,192	—
United Methodists		—	72,085
Methodists in Wales		19,720	33,926
Methodists in Scotland		4,099	8,191
Other Nonconformists	—	*360,877*	*955,841*
General Baptist New Connexion		18,277	—
Baptist Union		—	239,144
Baptists in Wales		35,000	106,566
Baptists in Scotland		5,000	16,899
Congregationalists, England		165,000	257,435
Congregationalists, Wales		60,000	147,513
Congregationalists, Scotland		25,000	30,170
Presbyterian Church of Wales		52,600	158,114

TABLE A3.1. (*Continued*)

Church	1800	1850	1900
Roman Catholics	*103,200*	*770,000*	*1,221,600*
England and Wales		630,000	940,200
Scotland		140,000	281,400
Others	—	*53,545*	*42,959*
Churches of Christ		2,000	11,789
Mormons		30,747	4,183
Moravians		3,000	3,500
New Church		2,798	6,334
Quakers		15,000	17,153
Total church membership	1,204,200	3,615,597	6,325,407
Total population aged 15 and over	6,769,000	13,314,000	24,678,000
Church members as % of adult population	17.8	27.2	25.6

Notes

[1] Episcopalian figures for 1850 and 1900 are for Easter Day communicants—a total that is around half of the 'members' as defined by the electoral rolls.

[2] Abrupt changes and missing figures reflect schisms and unions.

[3] To make RC statistics comparable to those of Protestant churches, one needs to use some formula to reduce it to those who are in some sense active in their faith. We know that the proportion attending Mass has steadily declined. In these figures, the following proportions have been used: 1800—80%, 1850—70%, 1900—60%, 1990—33%. This last figure is based on reliable figures for total baptized population and Mass attendance (Peter Brierley and Val Hiscock, *UK Christian Handbook 1994/95 Edition* (London: Christian Research Association, 1993)). The others are backwards extrapolations.

Source: The primary source for the above is Robert Currie, Alan D. Gilbert, and Lee Horsley, *Churches and Churchgoers: Patterns of Church Growth in the British Isles since 1700* (Oxford: Oxford University Press, 1977). The 1800 figures have been given only for major blocks because, as the notes to *Churches and Churchgoers* (table 2.3) make clear, these data were compiled from a very large number of best guesses based on such practices as extrapolating from the number of clergymen.

TABLE A3.2. *Church membership, Britain, 1990*

Episcopalian	*1,706,499*
Church of England	1,540,000
Church of Wales	108,200
Episcopalian Church of Scotland	58,299
Presbyterian	*1,005,416*
United Reformed Church	119,868
Presbyterian Church of Wales	61,616
Church of Scotland	786,787
Free Church of Scotland	20,000
United Free Church of Scotland	8,075
Free Presbyterian Church of Scotland	6,070
Associate Presbyterian Church	3,000
Methodist	*432,350*
Methodist Church in Great Britain	424,500
Wesleyan Reform Union	2,996
Other Methodists	4,854
Baptists	*223,037*
Baptist Union	149,2622
Baptist Union of Wales	26,763
Baptists in Scotland	16,212
Grace Baptist Assembly	10,000
Strict Baptists	6,500
Other Baptists	14,300
Independents	*325,527*
Brethren	81,185
Fell. of Ind. Evangelical Churches	33,000
Churches of Christ	4,500
Evan. Fell. of Congregational Churches	6,200
Congregational Federation	9,275
Union of Welsh Independents	53,027
Congregational Union of Scotland	18,340
New Churches ('House Churches')	80,000
Other non-denominational churches	40,000
Lucheran	*13,300*
Non-Trinitarian Churches	*412,049*
Latter-Day Saints	149,000
Jehovah's Witnesses	116,612
New Church	75,000
Spirtualists	48,837
Christian Science	11,000
Unitarian and Free Christian	8,500
Others	3,000

TABLE A3.2. (*Continued*)

Roman Catholics	*1,671,068*
England and Wales	1,387,435
Scotland	283,633
Orthodox	*265,686*
Pentecostal	*158,695*
Apostolic Church	6,100
Oneness Apostolic Churches	11,969
Assemblies of God	48,000
Elim Pentecostal Church	36,081
Afro-Caribbean Churches	45,086
Other Pentecostals	11,459
Others	*97,630*
Seventh Day Adventist	17,739
Moravians	2,579
Quakers	18,084
Salvation Army	59,228
Total church membership	6,311,257
Total population aged 15 and over	41,951,370
Church members as % of adult population	15

Notes

[1] Catholic figures are for average weekly Mass attendance.

[2] As I am concerned only with the relative popularity of the Christian churches, I have removed from the total adult population used to create the church-membership proportion an allowance for those Britons who, by virtue of belonging to a non-Christian religion, are not likely to be recruited to the Christian churches. Hence the total adult population of just over 45 million is reduced to just under 42 million. Making a similar adjustment Brierley comes to a church-membership figure of 14.3%.

Source: Brierley and Hiscock, *UK Christian Handbook 1994/95 Edition*, various figures.

TABLE A3.3. *Church membership, Britain, 1900–1990*

Year	Protestant (m.)	Catholic (m.)	All Christian		
			Total in millions	Ratio	% of adult population
1900	5.4	2.0	7.4	100	30
1930	7.1	2.8	9.9	133	29
1950	6.1	3.5	9.6	129	25
1970	5.2	2.7	7.9	107	19
1990	3.4	2.2	5.6	76	14

Source: Peter Brierley, *A Century of British Christianity: Historical Statistics 1900–1985 with Projections to 2000* (Research Monograph 14; London: MARC Europe, 1989).

TABLE A3.4. Church membership, Aberdeen, 1851–1991

Year	Presbyterian	Other Protestant	Brethren	Catholic	Non-Christian	Total	Total adult population (000s)	% of adult population in church membership
1851	19,796	571	—	1,000	—	21,367	47	45
1861	24,575	541	—	1,027	—	26,143	49	53
1871	33,756	238	—	1,226	—	35,220	58	60
1881	38,563	270	154	1,462	100	40,549	67	60
1891	41,354	712	234	1,006	105	43,411	84	51
1901	46,065	889	458	1,338	140	48,890	101	49
1911	50,101	985	493	1,654	201	53,434	109	49
1921	54,982	881	562	2,285	200	58,910	110	54
1931	57,215	1,072	584	2,600	140	61,611	121	51
1941	61,840	1,673	629	4,366	115	68,623	131	53
1951	59,051	2,684	650	6,133	112	68,630	140	49
1961	59,597	3,818	781	4,820	169	69,185	140	49
1971	49,070	2,252	961	4,454	178	56,915	142	40
1981	44,316	1,932	934	4,008	746	51,936	163	32
1991	35,897	2,430	837	6,174	3,546	48,884	181	27

Notes
[1] The 1991 Catholic figure includes 70 Eastern Orthodox.
[2] The large rise in non-Christian totals for 1981 and 1991 is entirely due to immigration and does not reflect growth of new religious movements.
Source: These data were collected by Paul Chmiel.

TABLE A3.5. *Church attendance, Aberdeen, 1851–1995*

Year	Attendance	% of adult population
1851	28,423	60
1878	24,704	37
1891	26,785	32
1901	27,293	27
1980	21,130	13
1984	19,820	12
1995	19,790	11

Source: Paul Chmiel, 'Pluralism and Religious Vitality in Aberdeen, 1851–1991', unpublished M. Phil. thesis, University of Aberdeen, 1999.

TABLE A3.6. *Changes in Presbyterian church membership, Aberdeen, 1851–1991*

Year	Adult Population (% gain)	Church of Scotland		Free Church		United Presbyterian		United Free Church	
		Members (000s)	% change	Members (000s)	% change	Members (000s)	% change	Members (000s)	% change
1851		5		12		3			
1861	4	9	+80	13	+8	3	0		
1871	18	16	+77	14	+8	3	0		
1881	14	20	+25	13	−7	3	0		
1891	25	23	+15	13	0	3	0		
1901	20	28	+22	—		—		18	+13
1911	8	30	+7	—		—		20	+11
1921	1	32	+7	—		—		23	+15
1931	10	57	+78	—		—		—	—
1941	8	61	+7	—		—		—	—
1951	7	58	+5	—		—		—	—
1961	0	59	+2	—		—		—	—
1971	1	49	−17	—		—		—	—
1981	15	44	−10	—		—		—	—
1991	11	36	−18	—		—		—	—

Source: Calculated from original data supplied by Paul Chmiel.

TABLE A4.1. *Church attendance, Nordic countries, 1890–1997*

Year	Percentage of population attending Lutheran churches on an average Sunday			
	Denmark	Norway	Sweden	Finland
1890			17.0	
1927	11.0		5.6	
1931	8.3			
1935	8.0			
1938	8.0			*3.4*
1939	7.2			
1943	6.5			
1947	6.3			
1951	5.9			
1952–8			2.9	
1955	5.4			
1956		2.7		
1957				2.8
1958		2.9		2.8 *3.1*
1959	4.9			
1960				2.8
1961–6			2.7	
1963	4.7			
1967	4.2			2.5
1970			2.2	2.3
1976		2.0	2.0	2.1 [2.8]
1978		2.5		2.3 *2.5*
1980			2.0 [2.5]	2.3 [3.0]
1984	2.5			2.0
1985/6			[2.4]	1.9 [2.6]
1987			2.1	
1990	1.4		[2.3]	
1992		2.4		
1993		2.4		
1994		2.4		[2.0]
1995		2.5		
1996		2.4		
1997		2.4		

Notes and Sources

[1] The general source is Göran Gustafsson, 'Religious Change in the Five Scandinavian Countries, 1930–1980', *Comparative Social Research*, 10 (1987), 145–81.

[2] Denmark data come from the following: for 1927 and 1967, Jørgen Thorgaard, 'Denmark', in Hans Mol (ed.), *Western Religion* (The Hague: Mouton, 1972), 135–41; for 1960, L. S. Hunter, *Scandinavian Churches: A Picture of the Development and Life of the Churches of Denmark,*

Finland, Iceland, Norway and Sweden (London: Faber & Faber, 1965). The other data from 1927 to 1967 come from the work of Per Salomonsen, included in Agnete Brink, Michael Schelde, and Erik Bredmose Simonsen, *Sekulariseringen i Danmark* (Aarhus ANIS, 1984), 402–22. These figures are derived from clergy returns and do not include Copenhagen, which almost certainly means the later numbers are an overestimate for Denmark as a whole. The 1990 estimate comes from Søren Rouland-Nørgaard, 'Et Signalement af Kirken i Danmark', *Gør Danerne Kristne* (SALT, 1992), 23–72. Hans Ruan Iversen and Anders P. Thyssen (*Kirke og Folk i Danmark* (Aarhus: ANIS, 1986), 324–9), for four parishes in south Jutland (thus not including Copenhagen) estimate 11% in 1927 and 2.5% in 1984.

[3] Swedish data come from Göran Gustafsson, *Tro, Samfund och Samhälle: Sociologiska Perspektiv* (Örebro: Bokförlaget Libris, 1997), table 21.

[4] Norway data come from the following: for 1958, 1978, and 1992–7 data were supplied by Per Tangaard, Adviser, Church of Norway National Council; for 1976, F. Hale, 'Development of Religious Freedom in Norway', *Journal of Church and State*, 23 (1981), 47–68; for 1956, Edward D. Vogt, 'Norway', in Mol (ed.), *Western Religion*, 393.

[5] Finnish data come from two sources. The primary figures for 1957–86 come from Harri Heino, the Director of the Lutheran Research Institute (in Peter Brierley (ed.), *Finnish Christian Handbook Part 1: Churches* (London: MARC Europe, 1988), table 22). The figures for 1938, 1958, and 1978 (shown in italics) come from Susan Sundback, 'Finland', in Göran Gustafsson (ed.), *Religiös Förändring i Norden 1930–80* (Malmö: Liber, 1985), 92. Further data can be found in Jouko Sihvo, 'Religion and Secularization in Finland', *Social Compass*, 35 (1988), 67–90; and Paavo Seppanen, 'Finland', in Mol (ed.), *Western Religion*.

[6] The Swedish data describe attendance only at the main Sunday services, which is reliable for 1927 when there were few other services but less so for more recent dates because there has been a proliferation of other services during the week. Gustafsson says that, when taking all services into account, the 1987 figure would be 3.1%.

[7] The pre-1980 figures for Sweden show the proportion of the whole population attending Lutheran services, which underestimates total attendances by omitting Free Church and Catholic Church attendances. The figures in square brackets for that year and subsequently are for the proportion of Lutherans attending Lutheran services. Sihvo's Finnish data, also displayed in square brackets, show a similar adjustment required. For Sweden, Gustafsson has calculated attendances at all services as a percentage of Lutherans and arrives at the following figures: 1980—5.2; 1985—5.3; 1990—4.5; 1992—4.3; 1994—4.3.

[8] It is interesting to note that both Heino (in Brierley, *Finnish Christian Handbook*, table 24) and Gustafsson (private communication) report a considerable increase in the popularity of communion. Heino shows number of communions served declining steadily from 816,753 in 1918 to a low of 482,831 in 1941 and then rising to 1,852, 791 in 1986, with the sharpest rises in the late 1960s and 1970s but adds: 'The increase means that people are going more frequently, not that more people are going, as the latter percentage has not changed significantly over the last thirty years.' For Sweden, Gustafsson reports that between 1970 and 1995 the number of communions served more than doubled. This would appear to be a consequence of two things: one a story about supply, the other a story about demand. In the 1930s and 1940s a 'high church' movement set about consciously trying to raise the status of communion and the frequency with which it was offered. The 'demand' part of the story is one we also see in Britain. As the churches have declined, casual attenders have fallen away and the population has become increasingly polarized into church people and the rest. The small part of the population that remains attached to the churches once churchgoing is no longer the norm contains those who are serious in their faith and who are interested in additional opportunities to show their commitment.

Table A4.2. *Church attendance, Nordic countries, 1947–1996*

Year	Percentage of population attending church 'at least monthly'			
	Denmark	Norway	Sweden	Finland
1947	27			
1957	21	18		
1964	8			
1970	(13)			
1975	6			
1979	(9)			
1981	(11)	14	13	11
1987	3 (12)	14	13	12
1990	(11)	13	10	11
1993	5 (6)			
1996	9	9	8	13

Notes

[1] These data are derived from opinion polls and refer to the general population and to any form of religious worship.

[2] The Danish figures in parentheses seem to form one sequence that is markedly higher than the others and the discrepancies remind us how dependent such figures are on the wording of questions and sampling frames used.

Sources: The 1981 and 1990 data come from my own analysis of the WVS dataset. Except for that for Denmark, the 1987 figures come from Gustaffsson, 'Religious Change in the Five Scandinavian Countries, 1930–1980', in Thorleif Pettersson and Ole Riis (eds.), *Scandinavian Values: Religion and Morality in the Nordic Countries* (Uppsala: Acta Universitatis Upsalcenics, 1994), 47. The remaining Danish data come from Jesper Johansen and Ole Riis, *Danskernes syn på kirke og religion igennem 50 år. 1944–94 En religionssociologisk dataoversigt.* (Aarhus: Aarhus Universitet, 1995) and Ole Riis, 'Religion and Secularization in Denmark', *Social Compass*, 35 (1988), 49. The 1957 Norwegian figure comes from S. Rokkan and H. Valen, 'Regional Contrasts in Norwegian Politics', in E. Allardt and Y. Littunen (eds.), *Cleavages, Ideologies and Party systems* (Helsinki: Westermarck Society, 1964).

Table A4.3. *Church attendance, Nordic countries, 1947–1996*

Year	Percentage of population 'never' attending church			
	Denmark	Norway	Sweden	Finland
1947	12			
1957	8			
1964	31			
1970	28			
1975	45			
1981	45	20 or 37	36	1
1982	36			
1985		43		
1987	37			
1990	44	40	48	15
1993	25			
1996	34	33	32	19

Note: The full Danish data partly explain the erratic results after 1964. Over the period, 'From time to time' declines steadily: 1964—25, 1975—22, 1987—19, 1993—17%. 'Not a member' rises steadily: 1964—4, 1975—6, 1987—9, 1993—12%. Taking those who are not members and those who never attend together, we get the following: 1964—35, 1975—51, 1987—46, 1993—37%.

Sources: As for Table A4.2, plus, for Norway, data for 1981 and 1985 supplied by Per Tangaard from Norske Gallup Institutt studies.

Table A4.4. *Religious communities, Nordic countries, 1960–1990* (000s)

Church membership	1960	1970	1980	1990
Denmark				
Anglican	6	6	6	6
Baptist	14	13	12	11
Catholic	28	28	28	29
Lutheran	4,357	4,670	4,716	4,610
Methodist	6	5	3	3
Orthodox	0.2	0.2	0.3	0.4
Pentecostal	10	10	10	13
Presbyterian	2	2	1	1
Other	18	17	18	18
Non-Trinitarian	20	28	29	36
TOTAL	4,461	4,779	4,823	4,727

TABLE A4.4. (*Continued*)

Church membership	1960	1970	1980	1990
Norway				
Anglican	2	2	2	2
Baptist	14	13	13	12
Catholic	5	10	12	29
Lutheran	3,382	3,573	3,693	3,804
Methodist	18	18	18	15
Orthodox	0.1	0.4	2	2
Pentecostal	63	61	60	64
Other	75	87	93	104
Non-Trinitarian	10	14	17	19
TOTAL	3,569	3,778	3,910	4,051
Sweden				
Anglican	3	3	3	3
Baptist	80	76	68	71
Catholic	26	59	97	140
Lutheran	6,747	7,256	7,481	7,382
Methodist	25	15	8	8
Orthodox	22	43	61	99
Pentecostal	127	170	181	180
Other	372	342	283	269
Non-Trinitarian	27	32	43	53
TOTAL	7,429	7,996	8,165	8,203
Finland				
Anglican	0.3	0.3	0.2	0.2
Baptist	5	3	3	3
Catholic	3	3	3	4
Lutheran	4,092	4,244	4,325	4,414
Methodist	3	3	2	2
Orthodox	73	56	55	54
Pentecostal	62	62	74	88
Other	27	31	37	39
Non-Trinitarian	16	18	27	35
TOTAL	4,281	4,420	4,496	4,639

Source: Peter Brierley, *World Churches Handbook: Based on the Operation World Database by Patrick Johnstone* (London: Christian Research Association, 1997).

TABLE A4.5. *Religious diversity, Nordic countries, 1960 and 1990*

Country	1960		1990	
	Herfindahl Index	No. of options	Herfindahl Index	No. of options
Sweden	0.17	25	0.19	36
Norway	0.10	18	0.13	19
Finland	0.09	20	0.09	18
Denmark	0.05	16	0.05	15

Note: The Herfindahl Index of diversity was calculated using the community data presented in Table A4.5. It would have been interesting to try it with figures for 'active members', but, because of the nature of religion in the Nordic countries, such data are not readily available. The figures for 'members' given in the *World Churches Handbook* seem extremely unreliable. The proportion of Lutheran 'community' counted as members is as follows: Denmark—20%; Finland—18%; Sweden—39%, Norway—74%. And there seems no obvious justification for supposing that Norwegian nominal Lutherans are three times as likely to be actual members as Finnish Lutherans.

As we can see, the Herfindahl Index values hardly change. There is some slight increase for Sweden and Norway but no change for Finland and Denmark. We see equally little change if we count the number of different religions on offer.

What is clear from more detailed inspection of the figures compressed in Table A4.5 is that 'diversity' in the Nordic countries has very little to do with supply-side notions of choices and a great deal to do with ethnic identification. For example, Sweden has six Lutheran churches. Two of them represent competing religious preferences: the main church and the evangelical alternative. The other four are the Estonian, Finish, Hungarian, and Latvian churches. In 1960 there were only three Orthodox communities: Finnish, Greek, and Estonian. By 1990 migration had brought Ethiopian, Macedonian, Romanian, Russian, Serbian, and Syrian Orthodox churches.

TABLE A4.6. *Church communities and membership, Czech Republic and Slovakia, 1995*

Church	Czech Republic			Slovakia		
	Community (000s)	%	Members (000s)	Community (000s)	%	Members (000s)
Roman Catholic	5,534	53	4,041	3,683	69	2,688
Hussite Catholic	247	2	173	20	—	14
Old Catholics	2	—	2	—	—	—
Uniate Catholic	126	1	90	67	1	48
Evangelical Czech Brethren	255	3	156	—	—	—
Orthodox	72	1	39	39	1	21
Lutheran	49	1	35	322	6	225
Seventh Day Adventists	15	—	8	—	—	—
Evangelical Free Church	10	—	5	—	—	—
Pentecostal	10	—	6	2	—	1
Methodist	6	—	3	—	—	—
Baptist	6	—	2	—	—	—
Reformed Christian Church	—	—	—	144	3	97
Slovak Calvinist Church	—	—	—	20	—	14
Other Trinitarian	18	—	10	10	—	5
Non-Trinitarian	6	—	4	3	—	2
None	3,940	38	—	1,043	20	
Total population	10,296	99	45	5,353	100	58
Herfindahl Index of diversity			0.19			0.24

Source: Brierley, *World Churches Handbook*.

Table A6.1. *Religious community identification, Australia, 1901, 1933, 1961, and 1991*

Community	1901 (000s)	1933 (000s)	1961 (000s)	1991 (000s)	% change 1901–91
Anglican	1,498	2,565	3,669	4,019	+168
Baptist	89	106	150	280	+215
Brethren	9	10	15	23	+155
Catholic	858	1,302	2,620	4,607	+437
Churches of Christ	24	63	96	78	+225
Congregational	74	65	74	6	−78
Jehovah's Witnesses	*	*	*	79	*
Latter-Day Saints	1	3	*	38	+3,700
Lutheran	75	61	160	251	+235
Methodist	504	684	1,076	*	*
Oriental Christian	*	*	*	23	*
Orthodox	*	28	160	475	*
Other Protestant	21	73	99	26	+14
Pentecostal	*	*	*	151	*
Presbyterian/Reformed	426	713	977	732	+72
Quaker	1	1	*	2	+100
Salvation Army	31	31	51	72	+132
Seventh Day Adventists	3	14	32	48	+1,500
Unitarian	3	1	*	1	−66
Uniting	*	*	*	388	*
Other Christian	8	8	101	172	+2,075
Total Christian	3,626	5,728	9,274	12,466	+443
Total Non-Christian	53	28	69	445	+739
No religion	7	12	38	2,176	
Not stated/Inadequately described/Other	119	1,710	2,293	5,701	
Total population	3,773	6,630	10,508	16,850	+347

Note: * marks those values either absent, less than 1,000, or infinity.

Source: Hilary M. Carey, Believing in Australia: A Cultured History of Religious (St Leonards, NSW: Allen & Unwin, 1996), 198–209.

TABLE A6.2. *Church attendance, Australia, 1991*

Church	Average Sunday attendance as % of those claiming identity in census
Anglican	5
Presbyterian	5
Uniting Church	12
Lutheran	20
Baptist	37
Salvation Army	39
Churches of Christ	56
Seventh Day Adventist	77
Pentecostal	>100

Source: Philip Hughes, *Religion in Australia: Facts and Figures* (Kew, Victoria: Christian Research Association, 1997).

TABLE A6.3. *Church attendance, Australia, 1950–1991* (%)

Year	Percentage of community attending church at least monthly				
	Catholic	Other Christian	Uniting/ Methodist/ Presbyterian	Anglican	Total
1950	76	*	43	34	44
1960	69	56	44	31	41
1967	61	58	30	19	34
1970	61	52	32	22	36
1972	54	47	28	18	30
1975	53	46	25	17	29
1978	57	39	*	18	28
1980	45	44	25	16	25
1984	44	42	22	14	24
1991	*	*	18	8	*

Note: * = data missing.

Sources: Figures for 1950–84 come from a large number of surveys collected by Peter Kaldor, *Who Goes Where? Who Doesn't Care?* (Homebush, NSW: Lancer, 1987); figures for 1991 are from Hughes, *Religion in Australia: Facts and Figures.*

TABLE A6.4. *Social mores of young evangelicals, USA, 1951, 1961–3, and 1982* (%)

The following are 'morally wrong all the time'	1951	1961–3	1982
Studying on Sunday	13	2	0
Playing pool	26	4	0
Playing cards	77	33	0
Social dancing (tango, waltz, etc.)	91	61	0
Folk dancing	59	31	0
Attending 'Hollywood-type' movies	46	14	0
Attending 'R'-rated movies	—	—	7
Smoking cigarettes	93	70	51
Drinking alcohol	98	78	17
Smoking marijuana	99	—	70
Casual petting	—	48	23
Heavy petting	—	81	45
Premarital sexual intercourse	—	94	89
Extramarital sexual intercourse	—	98	97

Source: James D. Hunter, *Evangelicalism: The Coming Generation* (Chicago: University of Chicago Press, 1987), 59.

BIBLIOGRAPHY

Adams, Norman, *Goodbye, Beloved Brethren* (Aberdeen: Impulse Books, 1972).

Aitken, Don, *Stability and Change in Australian Politics* (Canberra: Australian National University Press, 1977).

Almerich, Paulina, 'Spain', in Hans Mol (ed.), *Western Religion* (The Hague: Mouton, 1972), 459–77.

Andorka, Rudolf, 'Recent Changes in Social Structure, Human Relations and Values in Hungary', *Social Compass*, 42 (1995), 9–16.

Andrews, Edward Deming, *The People Called Shakers: A Search for the Perfect Society* (New York: Dover, 1963).

Bailey, Edward, 'The Implicit Religion of Contemporary Society: An Orientation and a Plea for its Study', *Religion*, 13 (1983), 69–83.

Bainbridge, William Sims, *Satan's Power: A Deviant Psychotherapy Cult* (Berkeley and Los Angeles: University of California Press, 1978).

—— and Jackson, D. H., 'The Rise and Decline of Transcendental Meditation', in Bryan Wilson (ed.), *The Social Impact of New Religious Movements* (New York: Rose of Sharon Press, 1981), 135–58.

—— and Stark, Rodney, 'Cult Formation: Three Compatible Models', *Sociological Analysis*, 40 (1979), 283–97.

Balmer, Randall, *Mine Eyes Have Seen the Glory: A Journey into the Evangelical Subculture in America* (Oxford: Oxford University Press, 1989).

Barker, Eileen, 'Who'd be a Moonie', in Bryan Wilson (ed.), *The Social Impact of New Religious Movements* (New York: Rose of Sharon Press, 1981), 59–96.

—— 'Defection from the Unification Church: Some Strategies and Distinctions', in David Bromley (ed.), *Falling from the Faith* (Newbury Park, Calif.: Sage, 1988), 166–84.

—— 'Standing at the Crossroads: The Politics of Marginality in "Subversive Organizations"', in David Bromley (ed.), *The Politics of Religious Apostasy* (Westport, Conn.: Praeger, 1998), 75–93.

Barrett, David V., *Sects, 'Cults' and Alternative Religions: A World Survey and Sourcebook* (London: Blandford, 1996).

Bates, Vernon L., 'Rhetorical Pluralism and Secularization in the New Christian Right: The Oregon Citizens Alliance', *Review of Religious Research*, 37 (1995), 46–64.

Becker, Gary, 'The Economic Approach to Human Behavior', in Jon Elster (ed.), *Rational Choice* (Oxford: Basil Blackwell, 1985), 108–22.

Becker, J. W., and Vink, R., *Secularatie in Nederland, 1966–91: De Verandering vasn Opvattingen en Enkele Gedragingen* (Rijswijk: Sociaal en Cultureel Planbureau, 1994).

Berger, Peter L., *The Social Reality of Religion* (London: Faber & Faber, 1969).

BERGER, PETER L. (cont.), *The Heretical Imperative: Contemporary Possibilities of Religious Affirmation* (London: Collins, 1980).

——BERGER, BRIGITTE, and KELLNER, HANSFRIED, *The Homeless Mind* (Harmondsworth: Penguin, 1974).

BETTEY, J. H., *Church and Community: The Parish Church in English Life* (Bradford-on-Avon: Moonraker Press, 1979).

BEYER, PETER, 'Religious Vitality in Canada', *Journal for the Scientific Study of Religion*, 36 (1997), 272–88.

BIBBY, REGINALD, 'Why the Conservative Churches are Really Growing: Kelley Revisited', *Journal for the Scientific Study of Religion*, 17 (1978), 129–37.

——*Fragmented Gods* (Toronto: Stoddard, 1987).

——*Unknown Gods: The Ongoing Story of Religion in Canada* (Toronto: Stoddard, 1993).

——'Going, Going, Gone: The Impact of Geographical Mobility on Religious Involvement', *Review of Religious Research*, 38 (1997), 289–307.

BIBBY, REGINALD, and BRINKERHOFF, MARTIN, 'The Circulation of the Saints: A Study of People who Join Conservative Churches', *Journal for the Scientific Study of Religion*, 12 (1973), 273–85.

————'Circulation of the Saints Revisited: A Longitudinal Look at Conservative Church Growth', *Journal for the Scientific Study of Religion*, 22 (1983), 253–62.

——and WEAVER, HAROLD R., 'Cult Consumption in Canada: A Further Critique of Stark and Bainbridge', *Sociological Analysis*, 46 (185), 445–60.

BISSET, PETER, 'Size and Growth', in Peter Brierley and Fergus Macdonald (eds.), *Prospects for Scotland: From a Census of the Churches in 1984* (London: MARC Europe, 1985), 17–25.

BLAU, JUDITH R., LAND, KENNETH C., and RUDDING, KENT, 'The Expansion of Religious Affiliation: An Explanation of the Growth in Church Participation in the United States, 1850–1930', *Social Science Research*, 21 (1991), 329–52.

————'Ethnocultural Cleavages and the Growth of Church Membership in the United States, 1860–1930', *Sociological Forum*, 8 (1993), 609–37.

BLOCH, JON P., 'Alternative Spirituality and Environmentalism', *Review of Religious Research*, 40 (1998), 55–74.

——'Individualism and Community in Alternative Spiritual "Magic"', *Journal for the Scientific Study of Religion*, 37 (1998), 286–302.

BOCIURKIW, BOHDAN R., *Eastern Europe: Religion and Nationalism* (Boulder, Colo.: Westview, 1985).

BOICE, JUDITH L., *At One With All Life: A Personal Journey in Gaian Communities* (Forres: Findhorn Press, 1989).

BOLLEN, J. D., *Protestants and Social Reform in New South Wales 1890–1910* (Melbourne: Melbourne University Press, 1971).

BORDEAUX, MICHAEL, *The Role of Religion in the Fall of Soviet Communism* (London: Centre for Policy Studies, 1992).

BREAULT, KEVIN D., 'New Evidence on Religious Pluralism, Urbanism, and Religious Participation', *American Sociological Review*, 54 (1989), 1048–53.

—— 'A Re-Examination of the Relationship between Religious Diversity and Religious Adherents: Reply to Finke and Stark', *American Sociological Review*, 54 (1989), 1056–9.

BRIERLEY, PETER, *UK Protestant Missions Handbook*, ii. *Home* (London: Evangelical Alliance/Bible Society, 1978).

—— (ed.), *Finnish Christian Handbook Part 1: Churches* (London: MARC Europe, 1988).

—— *A Century of British Christianity: Historical Statistics 1900–1985 with Projections to 2000* (Research Monograph 14; London: MARC Europe, 1989).

—— *Prospects for the Nineties: Trends and Tables from the English Church Census* (London: MARC Europe, 1991).

—— *World Churches Handbook: Based on the Operation World Database by Patrick Johnston* (London: Christian Research Association, 1997).

—— *UK Christian Handbook Religious Trends 1998/99 No. 1* (London: Christian Research Association, 1997).

—— and EVANS, BYRON, *Prospects for Wales: Report of the 1982 Census of the Churches* (London: MARC Europe, 1983).

—— and HISCOCK, VAL, *UK Christian Handbook 1994/95 Edition* (London: Christian Research Association, 1993).

—— and MACDONALD, FERGUS (eds.), *Prospects for Scotland: From a Census of the Churches in 1984* (London: MARC Europe, 1985).

—— —— (eds.), *Prospects for Scotland 2000: From a Census of the Churches in 1994* (Edinburgh and London: National Bible Society of Scotland and Christian Research Association, 1995).

—— BROWN, GRAHAM, MYERS, BOYD, ROWDON, Harold, and SUMMERTON, NEIL, *The Christian Brethren as the Nineties Began* (Carlisle: Paternoster Press, 1993).

BRINK, AGNETE, SCHELDE, MICHAEL, and SIMONSEN, ERIK BREDMOSE, *Sekulariseringen i Danmark* (Aarhus: ANIS, 1984).

BROMLEY, DAVID, 'The Social Construction of Contested Exit Roles', in Bromley (ed.), *The Politics of Religious Apostasy* (Westport, Conn.: Praeger, 1998), 19–48.

BROWN, ANDREW, 'Birth Celebration without Religion Offered', *Independent*, 23 July 1994.

BROWN, CALLUM, *The Social History of Religion in Scotland since 1730* (London: Methuen, 1987).

—— 'The Costs of Pew-Renting: Church Management, Church-Going and Social Class in Nineteenth-Century Glasgow', *Journal of Ecclesiastical History*, 38 (1987), 347–61.

—— 'A Revisionist Approach to Religious Change', in Steve Bruce (ed.), *Religion and Modernization: Sociologists and Historians Debate the Secularization Thesis* (Oxford: Oxford University Press, 1992), 31–58.

—— *The People in the Pews: Religion and Society in Scotland since 1780* (Glasgow: Economic and Social History Society of Scotland, 1993).

BROWN, STEWART J., 'The Decline and Fall of Kirk-Session Discipline in Presbyterian Scotland *c.*1830–1930', unpublished paper, 1991.

BRUCE, STEVE, 'A Sociological Account of Liberal Protestantism', *Religious Studies*, 20 (1984), 401–15.

—— 'Authority and Fission: The Protestants' Divisions', *British Journal of Sociology*, 36 (1985), 592–603.

—— *The Rise and Fall of the New Christian Right* (Oxford: Oxford University Press, 1988).

—— *A House Divided: Protestantism, Schism and Secularization* (London: Routledge, 1990).

—— *Pray TV* (London: Routledge, 1990).

—— 'Pluralism and Religious Vitality', in Steve Bruce (ed.), *Religion and Moderniza-tion: Sociologists and Historians Debate the Secularization Thesis* (Oxford: Oxford University Press, 1992), 170–94.

—— 'Religion and Rational Choice: A Critique of Economic Explanations of Religious Behavior', *Sociology of Religion*, 54 (1993), 193–205.

—— 'The Truth about Religion in Britain', *Journal for the Scientific Study of Religion*, 34 (1995), 417–30.

—— 'A Novel Reading of Nineteenth Century Wales: A Reply to Stark, Finke and Iannaccone', *Journal for the Scientific Study of Religion*, 34 (1995), 520–2.

—— *Religion in Modern Britain* (Oxford: Oxford University Press, 1995).

—— *Religion in the Modern World: From Cathedrals to Cults* (Oxford: Oxford University Press, 1996).

—— *Conservative Protestant Politics* (Oxford: Oxford University Press, 1998).

BULL, MALCOLM, and LOCKHART, KEITH, *Seeking a Sanctuary: Seventh-Day Adventism and the American Dream* (New York: Harper & Row, 1989).

BURLEIGH, J. H. S., *A Church History of Scotland* (Oxford: Oxford University Press, 1973).

CADDY, EILEEN, and HOLLINGSHEAD, LIZA, *Flight into Freedom: The Autobiography of the Co-Founder of the Findhorn Community* (Longmead, Dorset: Element, 1988).

CAMPBELL, ROBERT A., and CURTIS, JAMES E., 'Religious Involvement across Societies: Analyses for Alternative Measures in National Surveys', *Journal for the Scientific Study of Religion*, 33 (1994), 215–29.

CAPLOW, THEODORE, 'Contrasting Trends in European and American Religion', *Sociological Analysis*, 46 (1985), 101–8.

CAREY, HILARY, *Believing in Australia: A Cultural History of Religions* (St Leonards, NSW: Allen & Unwin, 1996).

CARTER, LEWIS F., *Charisma and Control in Rajneeshpuram: The Role of Shared Values in the Creation of a Community* (Cambridge: Cambridge University Press, 1990).

CHAVES, MARK, 'On the Rational Choice Approach to Religion', *Journal for the Scientific Study of Religion*, 34 (1995), 98–104.

—— and CANN, DAVID E., 'Regulation, Pluralism and Religious Market Structure', *Rationality and Society*, 4 (1992), 272–90.

CHMIEL, PAUL, 'Pluralism and Religious Vitality in Aberdeen, 1851–1991', unpublished M.Phil. thesis, University of Aberdeen, 1999.

CHRISTIANO, KEVIN J., *Religious Diversity and Social Change: American Cities, 1890–1906* (New York: Cambridge University Press, 1987).

CHRYPINSKI, V. C., 'Czechoslovakia', in Stuart Mews (ed.), *Religion in Politics: A World Guide* (London: Longman, 1989), 53–8.

——'German Democratic Republic', in Stuart Mews (ed.), *Religion in Politics: A World Guide* (London: Longman, 1989), 80–3.

COHN, NORMAN, *The Pursuit of the Millennium* (St Albans: Paladin, 1970).

COLLINSON, PETER, *The Religion of Protestants: The Church in English Society 1559–1625* (Oxford: Oxford University Press, 1982).

COX, JEFFREY, *The English Churches in a Secular Society: Lambeth, 1870–1930* (Oxford: Oxford University Press, 1982).

CRESSY, DAVID, 'Purification, Thanksgiving and the Churching of Women in Post-Reformation England', *Past and Present*, 141 (1993), 106–46.

CROCKETT, ALASDAIR, 'A Secularising Geography? Patterns and Processes of Religious Change in England and Wales, 1676–1851', unpublished Ph.D. thesis, University of Leicester, 1998.

CURRIE, ROBERT, and GILBERT, ALAN D., 'Religion', in A. H. Halsey (ed.), *Trends in British Society since 1900* (London: Macmillan, 1972), 407–50.

——————and HORSLEY, LEE, *Churches and Churchgoers: Patterns of Church Growth in the British Isles since 1700* (Oxford: Oxford University Press, 1977).

DAVIES, DOUGLAS, PACK, CAROLINE, SEYMOUR, SUSANNE, SHORT, CHRISTOPHER, WATKINS, CHARLES, and WINTER, MICHAEL, *Parish Life and Rural Religion: Rural Church Project Vol. III* and *The Views of Rural Parishioners: Rural Church Project Vol. IV* (Cirencester and Nottingham: Royal Agricultural College and University of Nottingham, 1990).

DAVIS, DEBORAH, *The Children of God: The Inside Story* (Grand Rapids, Mich.: Zondervan, 1984).

DEKKER, PAUL, and ESTER, PETER, 'Depillarization, Deconfessionalization and De-ideologization: Empirical Trends in Dutch Society 1958–1992', *Review of Religious Research*, 37 (1996), 325–41.

DE TOQUEVILLE, ALEXIS, *Democracy in America* (New York: Vintage, 1969).

——*Travels to England and Ireland* (New Brunswick: Transaction, 1988).

DIESING, P., *Reason in Society* (Westport, Conn.: Greenwood Press, 1973).

DONALDSON, GORDON, *Scotland: Church and Nation through 16 Centuries* (London: SCM Press, 1960).

DRIVENES, EINAR-ARNE, 'Religion, Church and Ethnic Minorities in Norway, 1850–1940', in Donal A. Kerr (ed.), *Religion, States and Ethnic Groups* (Aldershot: Dartmouth, 1992), 205–28.

DRUMMOND, ANDREW L., and BULLOCH, JAMES, *The Scottish Church 1688–1843* (Edinburgh: St Andrew Press, 1973).

DURKHEIM, ÉMILE, *The Division of Labor in Society* (New York: Free Press, 1964).

——*Suicide* (London: Routledge & Kegan Paul, 1970).

——*The Elementary Forms of the Religious Life* (London: George Allen & Unwin, 1971).

ELLISON, CHRISTOPHER G., 'Rational Choice Explanations of Individual Religious Behaviour: Notes on the Problem of Social Embeddedness', *Journal for the Scientific Study of Religion*, 34 (1995), 89–97.

ELSTER, JON, *Rational Choice* (Oxford: Basil Blackwell, 1986).

FEUERSTEIN, GEORG, 'Holy Madness: The Dangerous and Disillusioning Example of Da Free John', *What is Enlightenment?* (Spring–Summer 1996), 14–15.

FINKE, ROGER, 'How the Upstart Sects Won America: 1776–1850', *Journal for the Scientific Study of Religion*, 28 (1989), 27–44.

—— 'Demographies of Religious Participation: An Ecological Approach, 1850–1980', *Journal for the Scientific Study of Religion*, 28 (1989), 45–88.

—— 'Religious De-Regulation: Origins and Consequences', *Journal of Church and State*, 32 (1990), 609–26.

—— 'An Unsecular America', in Steve Bruce (ed.), *Religion and Modernization: Sociologists and Historians Debate the Secularization Thesis* (Oxford: Oxford University Press, 1992), 145–69.

—— and IANNACCONE, LAURENCE, 'Supply-Side Explanations for Religious Change', *Annals of the American Academy of Political and Social Science*, 527 (1993), 27–39.

—— and STARK, RODNEY, 'Religious Economies and Sacred Canopies: Religious Mobilization in American Cities, 1906', *American Sociological Review*, 53 (1988), 41–9.

—— —— 'Evaluating the Evidence: Religious Economies and Sacred Canopies', *American Sociological Review*, 54 (1988), 1054–6.

—— —— *The Churching of America, 1776–1990: Winners and Losers in our Religious Economy* (New Brunswick: Rutgers University Press, 1992).

—— —— 'Religious Choice and Competition', *American Sociological Review*, 63 (1998), 761–6.

—— GUEST, A. M., and STARK, R., 'Mobilizing Local Religious Markets: Religious Pluralism in the Empire State, 1855 to 1865', *American Sociological Review*, 61 (1996), 203–18.

FLINT, JOHN T., 'The Secularization of Norwegian Society', *Comparative Studies in Society and History*, 6 (1964), 325–44.

GALLUP, GEORGE H., Jr., *The Gallup International Public Opinion Polls; Great Britain 1937–1975* (New York: Random House, 1976).

—— *Religion in America 50 years: 1935–1985* (Princeton: Gallup, 1985).

—— and JONES, SARAH, *101 Questions and Answers: Religion in America* (Princeton: Princeton Religious Research Centre, 1989).

GAULTIER, MARY L., 'Church Attendance, Religious Belief in Post-Communist Societies', *Journal for the Scientific Study of Religion*, 36 (1997), 289–96.

GAUSTAD, EDWIN S., *Historical Atlas of Religion in America* (New York: Harper & Row, 1962).

GELLNER, ERNEST, *Nations and Nationalism* (Oxford: Basil Blackwell, 1983).

—— *Plough, Sword and Book: The Structure of Human History* (London: Paladin, 1991).

——'From Kinship to Ethnicity', in his *Encounters with Nationalism* (Oxford: Basil Blackwell, 1994), 34–46.

——'Nations, States and Religions', in Richard English and Charles Townsend (eds.), *The State: Historical and Political Dimensions* (London: Routledge, 1998), 240–66.

GERARD, DAVID, 'Religious Attitudes and Values', in Mark Abrams, David Gerard, and Noel Timms (eds.), *Values and Social Change in Britain* (London: Macmillan, 1985), 50–92.

GILBERT, ALAN D., *Religion and Society in Industrial England: Church, Chapel and Social Change 1740–1914* (London: Longman, 1976).

GILL, ROBIN, 'Secularization and Census Data', in Steve Bruce (ed.), *Religion and Modernization: Sociologists and Historians Debate the Secularization Thesis* (Oxford: Oxford University Press, 1992), 90–117.

——*The Myth of the Empty Church* (London: SPCK, 1993).

——HADAWAY, C. KIRK, and MARLER, PENNY LONG, 'Is Religious Belief Declining in Britain', *Journal for the Scientific Study of Religion*, 37 (1998), 507–16.

GIRNIUS, KETUTIS K., 'Nationalism and the Catholic Church in Lithuania', in Pedro Ramet (ed.), *Religion and Nationalism in Soviet and East European Politics* (Durham: Duke University Press, 1984), 82–103.

GREEN, S. J. D., *Religion in the Age of Decline: Organization and Experience in Industrial Yorkshire 1870–1230* (Cambridge: Cambridge University Press, 1996).

GREER, PAUL, 'The Aquarian Confusion: Conflicting Theologies of the New Age', *Journal of Contemporary Religion*, 10 (1995), 151–66.

GREGORY, DIANA, *A Social Survey of the Presbyterian Church of Wales: The Churches* (Cardiff: Open University in Wales, 1997).

GUNTER, BARRIE, and VINEY, RACHEL, *Seeing is Believing: Religion and Television in the 1990s* (London: John Libbey/Independent Television Commission, 1994).

GUSTAFSSON, BERNDT, 'Sweden', in Hans Mol (ed.), *Western Religion* (The Hague: Mouton, 1972), 479–511.

GUSTAFSSON, GÖRAN (ed.), *Religiös Förändring i Norden 1930–80* (Malmö: Liber, 1985).

——'Religious Change in the Five Scandinavian Countries, 1930–1980', *Comparative Social Research*, 10 (1987), 145–81. An expanded version appears in Thorleif Pettersson and Ole Riis (eds.), *Scandinavian Values: Religion and Morality in the Nordic Countries* (Uppsala: Acta Universitatis Upsaliensis, 1994), 11–57.

——*Tro, Samfund och Samhälle: Sociologiska Perspektiv* (Örebro: Bokförlaget Libris, 1997).

HADAWAY, C. KIRK, and MARLER, PENNY LONG, 'All in the Family: Religious Mobility in America', *Review of Religious Research*, 35 (1993), 97–116.

————and CHAVES, MARK, 'What the Polls don't Show: A Closer Look at US Church Attendance', *American Sociological Review*, 58 (1993), 741–52.

HALE, FREDERICK, 'The Development of Religious Freedom in Norway', *Journal of Church and State*, 23 (1981), 47–68.

HAMBERG, EVA, and PETTERSSON, THORLIEF, 'The Religious Market: Denominational

Competition and Religious Participation in Contemporary Sweden', *Journal for the Scientific Study of Religion,* 33 (1994), 205–26.

HAMILTON, BERNARD, *Religion in the Medieval West* (London: Edward Arnold, 1986).

HARPER-BILL, CHRISTOPHER, *The Pre-Reformation Church in England 1400–1530* (London: Longman, 1996).

HASTINGS, ADRIAN, *The Construction of Nationhood: Ethnicity, Religion and Nationalism* (Cambridge: Cambridge University Press, 1997).

HEELAS, PAUL, *The New Age Movement: The Celebration of the Self and the Sacralization of Modernity* (Oxford: Basil Blackwell, 1996).

HEINO, HARRI, 'Religion in Finland', in Peter Brierley (ed.), *Finnish Christian Handbook Part 1: Churches* (London: MARC Europe, 1988), 9–11.

——SALONEN, KARI, and RUSAMA, JAAKKO, *Response to Recession: The Evangelical Lutheran Church of Finland in the Years 1992–1995* (Tampere: The Research Institute of the Evangelical Lutheran Church of Finland, 1997).

HERBERG, WILL, *Protestant–Catholic–Jew: An Essay in American Religious Sociology* (Chicago: University of Chicago Press, 1983).

HIDEN, JOHN, and SALMON, PATRICK, *The Baltic Nations and Europe* (London: Longman, 1994).

HIGHET, JOHN, *The Scottish Churches* (London: Skeffington, 1960).

HILL, ROSALIND, 'From the Conquest to the Black Death', in Sheridan Gilley and W. J. Sheils (eds.), *A History of Religion in Britain: Practice and Belief from Pre-Roman Times to the Present* (Oxford: Basil Blackwell, 1994), 45–60.

HOGE, DEAN R., and ROOZEN, DAVID A. (eds.), *Understanding Church Growth and Decline: 1950–78* (New York: Pilgrim Press, 1979).

HUGHES, PHILIP, *Religion in Australia: Fact and Figures* (Kew, Victoria: Christian Research Association, 1997).

——'Clergy: A Major Part of the Church's Workforce', *Pointers: Bulletin of the Christian Research Association,* 8 (Mar. 1998), 1–5.

HUNTER, JAMES DAVIDSON, *Evangelicalism: The Coming Generation* (Chicago: University of Chicago Press, 1987).

HUNTER, LESLIE S., *Scandinavian Churches: A Picture of the Development and Life of the Churches of Denmark, Finland, Iceland, Norway and Sweden* (London: Faber & Faber, 1965).

IANNACCONE, LAURENCE, 'A Formal Model of Church and Sect', *American Journal of Sociology,* 94 (1988), S241–S68.

——'Religious Practice: A Human Capital Approach', *Journal for the Scientific Study of Religion,* 29 (1990), 297–314.

——'The Consequences of Religious Market Structure', *Rationality and Society,* 3 (1991), 156–77.

——'Sacrifice and Stigma: Reducing Free-Riding in Cults, Communes and Other Collectives', *Journal of Political Economy,* 100 (1992), 271–92.

——'Why Strict Churches are Strong', *American Journal of Sociology,* 99 (1994), 1180–1211.

——'Second Thoughts: A Response to Chaves, Demerath and Ellison', *Journal for the Scientific Study of Religion,* 34 (1995), 113–20.

——'Strictness and Strength Revisited—Reply', *American Journal of Sociology*, 101 (1996), 1103–8.

——OLSON, DANIEL V. A., and STARK, RODNEY, 'Religious Resources and Church Growth', *Social Forces*, 74 (1995), 705–31.

INGLEHART, RONALD, *Culture Shift in Advanced Industrial Society* (Princeton: Princeton University Press, 1990).

——*Modernization and Postmodernization: Cultural, Economic and Political Change in 43 Societies* (Princeton: Princeton University Press, 1997).

——BASANEZ, MIGUEL, and MORENO, ALEJANDRO, *Human Values and Beliefs: A Cross-Cultural Sourcebook* (Ann Arbor: University of Michigan Press, 1998).

INGLIS, K. S., 'Patterns of Religious Worship in 1851', *Journal of Ecclesiastical History*, 11 (1960), 74–87.

ISICHEI, ELIZABETH, *Victorian Quakers* (Oxford: Oxford University Press, 1970).

IVERSEN, HANS RUAN, and THYSSEN, ANDERS P., *Kirke og Folk i Danmark* (Aarhus: ANIS, 1986).

JOHANSEN, JESPER, and RIIS, OLE, *Danskernes syn på kirke og religion igennem 50 år. 1944–94 En religionssociologisk dataoversigt* (Aarhus: Aarhus Universitet, 1995).

JOHNSON, BENTON, 'A Critical Appraisal of the Church–Sect Typology', *American Sociological Review*, 22 (1957), 88–92.

JOHNSTON, HANK, 'Religio-Nationalist Subcultures under the Communists: Comparisons from the Baltics, Transcaucasia and Ukraine', *Sociology of Religion*, 54 (1993), 237–55.

JONES, IEUAN GWYNEDD, *Mid-Victorian Wales* (Cardiff: University of Wales Press, 1992).

JONES, ROBERT TUDOR, 'Religion, Nationality and State in Wales, 1840–90', in Donal A. Kerr (ed.), *Religion, States and Ethnic Groups* (Aldershot: Dartmouth, 1992), 261–76.

KADLECOVÁ, ERIKA, 'Czechoslovakia', in Hans Mol (ed.), *Western Religion* (The Hague: Mouton, 1972), 117–34.

KALDOR, PETER, *Who Goes Where? Who Doesn't Care?* (Homebush, NSW: Lancer, 1987).

KAMEN, HENRY, *The Rise of Toleration* (London: Weidenfeld & Nicolson, 1967).

KANTER, ROSABETH, M., *Commitment and Community: Communes and Utopias in Sociological Respective* (Cambridge, Mass.: Harvard University Press, 1972).

KEEN, MAURICE, *English Society in the Later Middle Ages* (Harmondsworth: Penguin, 1990).

KELLEY, DEAN, *Why the Conservative Churches are Growing* (New York: Harper & Row, 1972).

——'Why the Conservative Churches are Still Growing', *Journal for the Scientific Study of Religion*, 17 (1978), 129–37.

KRIEGER, JOEL (ed.), *The Oxford Companion to the Politics of the World* (Oxford: Oxford University Press, 1993).

LAKATOS, IMRE, 'Falsification and the Methodology of Scientific Research Programmes', in Imre Lakatos and Alan Musgrave (eds.), *Criticism and the Growth of Knowledge* (Cambridge: Cambridge University Press, 1970), 91–5.

LAERMANS, RUDI, 'From Truth to Values: A Sociological Analysis of the Public Discourse of Catholic Organizations in Flanders', *Social Compass*, 42 (1995), 69–77.

LAMBERT, YVES, 'Un paysage religeux en profonde évolution', in H. Riffault (ed.), *Les Valuers des français* (Paris: PUF, 1994), 123–62.

—— 'Vers une ère post-chrétienne?', in *Futuribles 220*, special issue on 'L'Évolution des valuers des Européans' (July–Aug. 1995), 85–111.

LAND, KENNETH C., DEANE, GLENN, and BLAU, JUDITH R., 'Religious Pluralism and Church Membership', *American Sociological Review*, 56 (1991), 237–49.

LANE, CHRISTEL, *Christian Religion in the Soviet Union: A Sociological Study* (London: George Allen & Unwin, 1978).

LASLETT, PETER, *The World We Have Lost* (London: Methuen, 1983).

LITTELL, FRANKLIN HAMLIN, *From State Church to Pluralism: A Protestant Interpretation of Religion in American History* (Chicago: Aldine, 1962).

LOFLAND, JOHN, and STARK, RODNEY, 'Becoming a World-Saver: A Theory of Conversion to a Deviant Perspective', *American Sociological Review*, 30 (1965), 862–75.

LUCAS, EDWARD, 'The Church has a Better Chance than Ever', *Independent*, 21 Apr. 1990.

LUHRMANN, TANYA M., *Persuasions of the Witch's Craft: Ritual Magic in Contemporary England* (Oxford: Basil Blackwell, 1989).

LUXMOORE, JONATHAN, 'Eastern Europe 1994: A Review of Religious Life in Bulgaria, Romania, Hungary, Slovakia, the Czech Republic and Slovakia', *Religion, State and Society*, 23 (1995), 213–18.

MACLAREN, A. ALLAN, *Religion and Social Class: The Disruption Years in Aberdeen* (London: Routledge & Kegan Paul, 1974).

MCLEOD, HUGH, 'Secular Cities? Berlin, London and New York in the Later Nineteenth and Early Twentieth Centuries', in Steve Bruce (ed.), *Religion and Modernization: Sociologists and Historians Debate the Secularization Thesis* (Oxford: Oxford University Press, 1992), 59–89.

MARLER, PENNY LONG, and HADAWAY, C. KIRK, 'Church Attendance and Membership in Four Nations: A Comparative, Historical Study of "Gaps", Discrepancies and Change', Final Narrative Report to the Lily Foundation, Aug. 1997.

MARTIN, DAVID, *Pacifism: An Historical and Sociological Study* (London: Routledge & Kegan Paul, 1965).

—— *The Religious and the Secular* (Oxford: Basil Blackwell, 1969).

—— *A General Theory of Secularization* (Oxford: Basil Blackwell, 1978).

—— *The Dilemmas of Contemporary Religion* (Oxford: Basil Blackwell, 1978).

—— 'A Definition of Cult: Terms and Approaches', in Joseph Fichter (ed.), *Alternatives to American Mainline Churches* (Barrytown: Unification Theological Seminary, 1983), 27–42.

MARTY, MARTIN E., *Righteous Empire: The Protestant Experience in America* (New York: Dial Press, 1970).

MARWELL, GERALD, 'We Still Don't Know if Strict Churches are Strong, Much Less Why: Comment on Iannaccone', *American Journal of Sociology*, 101 (1996), 1097–1108.

MELTON, J. GORDON, CLARK, JEROME, and KELLY, AIDAN A., *New Age Almanac* (New York: Visible Ink, 1991).

MERTON, ROBERT K., *Science, Technology and Society in the 17th Century* (New York: Fettig, 1970).

MICHELS, ROBERT, *Political Parties: A Sociological Study of the Oligarchic Tendencies of Modern Democracy* (New York: Free Press, 1962).

MILBANK, JOHN, *Theology and Social Theory: Beyond Secular Reason* (Oxford: Basil Blackwell, 1990).

MINGAY, G. E., *Rural Life in Victorian England* (London: Heinemann, 1976).

MOL, HANS (ed.), *Western Religion* (The Hague: Mouton, 1972).

MUIZNEKS, NILS, 'Latvia: Restoring a State, Rebuilding a Nation', in Ian Bremner and Ray Taras (eds), *New States, New Politics: Building the Post-Soviet Nations* (Cambridge: Cambridge University Press, 1997), 376–404.

NIEBUHR, H. RICHARD, *The Social Sources of Denominationalism* (New York: Meridian, 1962).

NIELSEN, NIELS, *Revolutions in Eastern Europe* (Maryknoll, NY: Orbis Books, 1991).

OBELKEVITCH, JAMES, *Religion and Rural Society: South Lindsay 1825–1875* (Oxford: Oxford University Press, 1976).

—— 'Religion', in F. M. L. Thompson (ed.), *The Cambridge Social History of Britain 1750–1950*, iii. *Social Agencies and Institutions* (Cambridge: Cambridge University Press, 1990), 311–56.

OFSHE, RICHARD, 'The Social Development of the Synanon Cult', *Sociological Analysis*, 41 (1980), 109–27.

OLSON, DANIEL V. A., 'Religious Pluralism in Contemporary US Counties', *American Sociological Review*, 63 (1998), 757–61.

—— 'Religious Pluralism and US Church Membership: A Reassessment', *Sociology of Religion*, forthcoming.

—— and HADAWAY, KIRK C., 'Religious Pluralism and Affiliation among Canadian Counties and Cities', *Journal for the Scientific Study of Religion*, forthcoming.

PARSONS, TALCOTT, 'Motivations in Economic Analysis', in his *Essays in Sociological Theory* (New York: Free Press, 1954), 50–68.

PERRIN, ROBIN D., KENNEDY, PAUL, and MILLER, DONALD E., 'Examining the Sources of Conservative Church Growth', *Journal for the Scientific Study of Religion*, 36 (1997), 71–80.

PETTERSSON, THORLEIF, 'Swedish Church Statistics', *Social Compass*, 35 (1988), 67–90.

—— and RIIS, OLE (eds.), *Scandinavian Values: Religion and Morality in the Nordic Countries* (Uppsala: Acta Universitatis Upsaliensis, 1994).

POPPER, KARL, *The Logic of Scientific Discovery* (London: Hutchinson, 1959).

—— *Conjectures and Refutations* (New York: Basic Books, 1962).

QUICKE, ANDREW, and QUICKE, JULIET, *Hidden Agendas: The Politics of Religious Broadcasting in Britain 1987–1991* (Virginia Beach, Va.: Dominion Kings Grant Publications, 1992).

RAUN, TOVIO, 'Estonia: Independence Redefined', in Ian Bremner and Ray Taras (eds.),

New States, New Politics: Building the Post-Soviet Nations (Cambridge: Cambridge University Press, 1997), 405–35.

RIIS, OLE, 'Trends in Danish Religion', *Social Compass*, 35 (1988), 67–90.

ROBERTSON, ROLAND, *The Sociological Interpretation of Religion* (Oxford: Basil Blackwell, 1970).

ROKKAN, S., and VALEN, H., 'Regional Contrasts in Norwegian Politics', in E. Allardt and Y. Littunen (eds.), *Cleavages, Ideologies and Party Systems* (Helsinki: Westermarck Society, 1964).

ROOF, WADE CLARK, 'God is in the Details: Reflections on Religion's Public Presence in the United States in the Mid-1990s', *Sociology of Religion*, 57 (1996), 149–62.

—— and McKINNEY, WILLIAM, *American Mainline Religion: Its Changing Shape and Future* (New Brunswick: Rutgers University Press, 1987).

ROOKSBY, DONALD A., *The Man in Leather Breeches: The Quakers in North-West England* (Colwyn Bay: Donald A. Rooksby).

ROSE, PHILLIP (ed.), *Social Trends 23* (London: Her Majesty's Stationery Office, 1993).

ROULAND-NØRGAARD, SØREN, 'Et Signalement af Kirken i Danmark', *Gør Danerne Kristne* (SALT, 1992), 23–72.

SAWKINS, JOHN, 'Church Affiliation Statistics: Counting Methodist Sheep', paper given at Soundings conference, Stirling, 14 Mar. 1998.

SENN, ALFRED, 'Lithuania: Rights and Responsibilities of Independence', in Ian Bremner and Ray Taras (eds.), *New States, New Politics: Building the Post-Soviet Nations* (Cambridge: Cambridge University Press, 1997), 353–75.

SEPPANEN, PAAVO, 'Finland', in Hans Mol (ed.), *Western Religion* (The Hague: Mouton, 1972), 143–73.

SHAND, JACK D., 'The Decline of Traditional Christian Beliefs in Germany', *Sociology of Religion*, 59 (1998), 179–84.

SHAW, WILLIAM, *Spying in Guru Land: Inside Britain's Cults* (London: Fourth Estate, 1994).

SIHVO, JOUKO, 'Religion and Secularization in Finland', *Social Compass*, 35 (1988), 67–90.

SLOCOMBE, JEREMY, 'Last Thoughts', *One Earth: The Findhorn Foundation and Community Magazine*, 14 (Summer 1994), 19.

SPUFFORD, MARGARET, 'Can we Count the "Godly" and the "Conformable" in the Seventeenth Century?', *Journal of Ecclesiastical History*, 36 (1985), 428–38.

STARK, RODNEY, 'Must All Religions be Supernatural?', in Bryan Wilson (ed.), *The Social Impact of New Religious Movements* (New York: Rose of Sharon Press, 1981), 159–77.

—— 'German and German–American Religiousness', *Journal for the Scientific Study of Religion*, 36 (1997), 182–93.

—— and BAINBRIDGE, WILLIAM SIMS, 'Toward a Theory of Religion: Religious Commitment', *Journal for the Scientific Study of Religion*, 19 (1980), 114–28.

—————— *The Future of Religion: Secularization, Revival and Cult Formation* (Berkeley and Los Angeles: University of California Press, 1985).

—————— *A Theory of Religion* (New York: Peter Lang, 1987).

——and IANNACCONE, LAURENCE, 'A Supply-Side Interpretation of the "Secularization" of Europe', *Journal for the Scientific Study of Religion*, 33 (1994), 230–52.

——————'Truth and the Status of Religion in Britain Today: A Reply to Bruce', *Journal for the Scientific Study of Religion*, 34 (1995), 516–19.

——————'Recent Religious Declines in Quebec, Poland and the Netherlands: A Theory Vindicated', *Journal for the Scientific Study of Religion*, 35 (1996), 265–71.

——and McCANN, JAMES C., 'Market Forces and Catholic Commitment: Exploring the New Paradigm', *Journal for the Scientific Study of Religion*, 33 (1994), 111–24.

——FINKE, ROGER, and IANNACCONE, LAURENCE, 'Pluralism and Piety: England and Wales 1851', *Journal for the Scientific Study of Religion*, 34 (1995), 431–44.

STRASSBERG, BARBARA, 'Changes in Religious Culture in Post-World War II Poland', *Review of Religious Research*, 48 (1988), 342–54.

SUNDBACK, SUSAN, 'Finland', in Göran Gustafsson (ed.), *Religiös Förändring i Norden 1930–80* (Malmö: Liber, 1985).

SVENNEVIG, MICHAEL, HALDANE, IAN, SPEIRS, SHARON, and GUNTER, BARRIE, *Godwatching: Viewers, Religion and Television* (London: John Libbey/Independent Broadcasting Authority, 1989).

TATLOW, TISSINGTON, *The Story of the Student Christian Movement* (London: SCM Press, 1933).

TAMNEY, JOSEPH B., and JOHNSON, STEPHEN D., 'A Research Note on the Free-Rider Issue', *Journal for the Scientific Study of Religion*, 36 (1997), 104–8.

THOMAS, KEITH, *Religion and the Decline of Magic* (Harmondsworth: Penguin, 1973).

THOMASSON, R. F., 'The Religious Situation in Sweden', *Social Compass*, 15 (1968), 491–8.

THORGAARD, JØRGEN, 'Denmark', in Hans Mol (ed.), *Western Religion* (The Hague: Mouton, 1972), 135–41.

TIDWELL, GARY L., *Anatomy of a Fraud: Inside the Finances of the PTL Ministries* (New York: John Wiley & Sons, 1993).

TOMKA, MIKLÓS, 'Secularization or Anomy? Interpreting Religious Change in Communist Societies', *Social Compass*, 38 (1991), 93–102.

——'The Changing Social Role of Religion in Eastern and Central Europe: Religion's Revival and its Contradictions', *Social Compass*, 42 (1995), 17–26.

——'Coping with Persecution: Religious Change in Communism and in Post-Communist Reconstruction in Central Europe', *International Sociology*, 13 (1998), 229–48.

TROELTSCH, ERNEST, *The Social Teaching of the Christian Churches* (Chicago: University of Chicago Press, 1976).

TURNER, NAOMI, *Sinews of Sectarian Warfare: State Aid in New South Wales 1836–1862* (Canberra: Australian National University Press, 1972).

VAN MEERBECK, ANNE, 'The Importance of a Religious Service at Birth: The Persistent Demand for Baptism in Flanders, *Social Compass*, 42 (1995), 47–58.

VERWEIJ, JOHAN, ESTER, PETER, and NAUTA, REIN, 'Secularization as an Economic and

Cultural Pheneomeon: A Cross-National Analysis', *Journal for the Scientific Study of Religion*, 36 (1997), 309–24.

VOGT, EDWARD D., 'Norway', in Hans Mol (ed.), *Western Religion* (The Hague: Mouton, 1972), 381–401.

WALASCEK, ZDZISLAWA, 'An Open Issue of Legitimacy: The State and Church in Poland', *Annals of the American Academy of Political and Social Science*, 483 (1986), 118–34.

WALKER, ANDREW, *Restoring the Kingdom: The Radical Christianity of the House Church Movement* (Guildford: Eagle, 1998).

WALLIS, ROY, 'Ideology, Authority and the Development of Cultic Movements', *Social Research*, 14 (1974), 299–327.

—— *The Road to Total Freedom: A Sociological Analysis of Scientology* (London: Heinemann, 1976).

—— *The Rebirth of the Gods? Reflections on the New Religions in the West* (Belfast: The Queen's University of Belfast, 1978).

—— *Salvation and Protest: Studies of Social and Religious Movements* (London: Frances Pinter, 1979).

—— 'Charisma: Commitment and Control in a New Religious Movement', in Roy Wallis (ed.), *Millennialism and Charisma* (Belfast: The Queen's University of Belfast, 1982), 73–140.

—— *The Elementary Forms of the New Religious Life* (London: Routledge & Kegan Paul, 1984).

—— 'Figuring Out Cult Receptivity', *Journal for the Scientific Study of Religion*, 25 (1986), 494–503.

—— and BRUCE, STEVE, *Sociological Theory, Religion and Collective Action* (Belfast: The Queen's University of Belfast, 1986).

WALTERS, PHILIP, 'The Russian Orthodox Church and the Soviet States', *Annals of the American Academy of Political and Social Science*, 483 (1986), 135–45.

—— *World Christianity: Eastern Europe* (Monrovia, Calif.: MARC, 1988).

WARNER, R. STEPHEN, 'Work in Progress toward a New Paradigm for the Sociological Study of Religion in the United States', *American Journal of Sociology*, 98 (1993), 1044–93.

WATTS, MICHAEL R., *The Dissenters*, i. *From the Reformation to the French Revolution* (Oxford: Oxford University Press, 1978).

WATTS, SHELDON, *A Social History of Western Europe 1450–1720* (London: Hutchinson, 1984).

WEBER, MAX, *The Protestant Ethic and the Spirit of Capitalism* (London: George Allen & Unwin, 1976).

WHITING, ROBERT, *The Blind Devotion of the People: Popular Religion in the English Reformation* (Cambridge: Cambridge University Press, 1989).

WILSON, BRYAN, 'An Analysis of Sect Development', *American Sociological Review*, 24 (1959), 3–15.

—— 'Religion and the Churches in Contemporary America', in William G. McLoughlin and Robert N. Bellah (eds.), *Religion in America* (Boston: Houghton Mifflin, 1968), 73–110.

—— 'The Secularization Debate', *Encounter*, 45 (1975), 77–83.

—— *Religion in Sociological Perspective* (Oxford: Oxford University Press, 1982).

—— 'Morality in the Evolution of the Modern Social System', *British Journal of Sociology*, 36 (185), 315–32.

—— 'How Sects Evolve: Issues and Inferences', in Wilson, *The Social Dimensions of Sectarianism: Sects and New Religious Movements in Contemporary Society* (Oxford: Oxford University Press, 1990).

—— 'The Persistence of Sects', *Diskus*, 1 (1993), 1–12.

WITHRINGTON, DONALD J., 'The 1851 Census of Religious Worship and Education: With a Note on Church Accommodation in Mid-19th Century Scotland', *Records of the Scottish Church History Society*, 18 (1974), 133–48.

WOLFE, KENNETH M., *The Churches and the British Broadcasting Corporation 1922–1956: The Politics of Broadcast Religion* (London: SCM Press, 1984).

WOLFE, JOHN N., and PICKFORD, M., *The Church of Scotland: An Economic Survey* (London: Geoffrey Chapman, 1980).

WOLFFE, JOHN (ed.), *Evangelical Faith and Public Zeal: Evangelicals and Society in Britain 1780–1980* (London: SPCK, 1995).

YAMANE, DAVID, 'Secularization on Trial: In Defense of a Neosecularization Paradigm', *Journal for the Scientific Study of Religion*, 37 (1997), 109–22.

YEO, STEPHEN, *Religion and Voluntary Organizations in Crisis* (London: Croom Helm, 1976).

INDEX